HARVEY MUDD COLLEGE

Harvey Mudd College

The First Twenty Years

JOSEPH B. PLATT

Fithian Press

SANTA BARBARA • 1994

Design and typography by Jim Cook

Published by Fithian Press
Post Office Box 1525
Santa Barbara, California 93120

LIBRARY OF CONGRESS CATALOGING-IN-PUBLICATION DATA

Platt, Joseph B., 1915–
Harvey Mudd College: the first twenty years / Joseph B. Platt.
p.   cm.
Includes index.
ISBN 1-56474-097-8
ISBN 1-56474-100-1 (pbk.)
1. Harvey Mudd College. I. Title
T171.H35P53 1994   94-7452
CIP

I dedicate this book to my wife, Jean Ferguson Platt,
in warm gratitude for the many freshman dinners she served in our home,
the faculty teas she arranged, and the trustees she welcomed during the twenty years
I report here. Furthermore, it was and is a joy to live and work with Jeanie.

Table of Contents

FOREWORD   9

Chapter 1:   How I Got Involved in Harvey Mudd College   15

Chapter 2:   The Idea of the College   21

Chapter 3:   The Founding Trustees   25

Chapter 4:   The Campus—The First Decade   38

Chapter 5:   The Faculty and Staff   58

Chapter 6:   Our Students—The Early Classes   67

Chapter 7:   Money   83

Chapter 8:   Saddle Rock!   100

Chapter 9:   The First Ten Years—A Summing Up   120

Chapter 10:   Going Up in Size—Impact/72   145

Chapter 11:   Our Second Decade—An Overview   161

Chapter 12:   Trustees of the Second Decade   168

Chapter 13:   Faculty and Staff of the Second Decade   179

Chapter 14:   Students of the Second Decade—1966-76   194

Chapter 15:   Educational Innovation   208

Chapter 16:   An Evaluation   229

APPENDIX   239

INDEX   253

SOME of my good friends who have read drafts of this book have criticized me on two counts: I have said little of my own early history, and I have downplayed my own role in the events I report.

The first omission is readily rectified. I am Joseph B. Platt, born in Portland, Oregon. My family moved to Rochester, New York, during my father's service in the First World War. I grew up in Rochester, and attended the University of Rochester, graduating in 1937 with honors in physics. I completed the work for my doctorate in physics at Cornell University in 1941, returning to the University of Rochester as an instructor in physics. Cornell granted me my doctorate in 1942. I taught at Rochester and helped develop war-related optical devices until July 1943, when I joined the M.I.T. Radiation Laboratory to work on airborne radars. Much of 1944 I spent in the European theater, a civilian assigned to work with the Ninth Bomber Command, U.S. Army Air Corps. In the summer of 1945 I was in the Philippines with a similar assignment. In October 1945, I met Jean Ferguson Rusk, and we were married the following February; thus began what are now nearly five full and happy decades together. The University of Rochester reappointed me in late 1945 as assistant professor; in addition to teaching I was responsible for a portion of the design of a synchrocyclotron, the first to be built outside Berkeley. In 1949 Kenneth Pitzer, then director of research for the Atomic Energy Commission, invited me to spend two years in his division as head of its physics and mathematics branch, and I did so. Returning to the University of Rochester in 1951, I remained as associate and then full professor until 1956, when I became president of Harvey Mudd College. During these five years, in addition to my teaching, my students and I found the first evidence for "man-made mesonic

Joseph B. Platt

atoms"—the synchrocyclotron produced mesons, and when negative mesons are stopped in matter they briefly form a type of atom.

My "non-professional" activities have included about eleven months as a merchant seaman, before and during my college years; varsity swimming at Rochester and later some coaching for the Cornell swimming team; and membership in and advisor to more local, regional, national, and international committees than we need list here.

I do not believe I have downplayed my own role at Harvey Mudd College. One of the joys of that responsibility was that trustees, faculty, staff, and students were all involved, and I was another member of the team. However, my colleague of eight years, and friend of thirty-three years, President Eugene Hotchkiss of Lake Forest College, does not quite agree. Here is his statement:

> The early history of Harvey Mudd College is as much the story of an individual as it is of the years of a precocious institution. Dr. Joseph B. Platt served as midwife and parent to the college as it experienced the pleasures and pains of the rapid growth he describes so charmingly in this history of the college's first two decades. The college of today, recognized nationally as a "producer" of future engineering and science Ph.D. graduates, owes its intellectual wealth and its prominence, more than any other, to this remarkable leader.

> The pages that follow describe how the college came to be, as progeny of the distinctive Claremont Plan. Yet, it is obvious that a successful institution is shaped not just by those individuals serving as trustees, faculty, staff, and students (whom the author credits) but primarily by its leader. Surely, this is particularly so with a new, fledgling institution. Harvey Mudd's leader for its first two decades was Joe Platt, a youthful, highly respected teacher and physicist when he arrived in Claremont from the University of Rochester in 1956.

> Joe recruited his first faculty not with promises of prestige, advancement and ample salary (as do most college presidents), but with his persuasive enthusiasm and by sharing his excitement in a great educational venture to be undertaken. Those who signed on in the early years found his courage contagious. With his leadership, they dared to build a new and different curriculum; to set demanding standards for themselves and their students; and to foster scientific inquiry in an atmosphere of academic freedom. With his leadership, they recruited remarkable students, also adventurers, who dared to enroll in an unknown college. In a short time, again with his leadership, the excitement of this new college spread to those corporations and foundation leaders whose support would ensure the college's future.

Over coffee in the faculty lounge, or at Sunday night suppers for freshmen at the president's house, or in conference rooms and hallways, the community looked to its president for solace in difficult times, humor in better times, and guidance at all times. Whether from the loneliness of the president's office or the warmth of his home, whether rested from a beach weekend or fatigued by "red-eye flights" to and from Washington, D.C., whether balancing the budget with his trusty slide rule or singing old songs about Nobel physicists while accompanying himself on his guitar, he exuded confidence and hope to all around as quietly and determinedly as he spun the fabric of this new college.

The story of Harvey Mudd College is in no small way the story of its first president, Joseph B. Platt, his wife, Jean Ferguson Platt, and their daughters Ann and Beth. All shared their lives as they shared his faith in the future of the college.

[Gene Hotchkiss]

ACKNOWLEDGMENTS

Hank Riggs, early in his presidency of Harvey Mudd College, asked me to write this book. Cliff Miller, chairman of the Board of Trustees, gave me valuable suggestions about the organization and the style of the narrative. Both Hank and Cliff have followed the progress of the book and encouraged me. Harvey Mudd College appointed Dana Ditwiler, a doctoral candidate in history, as my research assistant, and she turned out to be an excellent locator of forgotten documents as well as a first-rate editor and astute critic. (Dana had previously served as research assistant to Leonard Levy, professor of history at Claremont Graduate School. Leonard holds the Pulitzer Prize in history, and I don't. I'm grateful for the standards he taught Dana.)

The information drawn upon for this book came from a variety of sources. The minutes of the Board of Trustees of Harvey Mudd College were made available to me by former board secretary George McKelvey, who also provided minutes of board committees; the minutes of the officers of the Associated Students of Harvey Mudd College, made available by current ASHMC officers; George Wickes's excellent early diary of the college, along with many other records kept by the Special Collections Department of the Honnold Library, including financial records, student publications, and college catalogues; the minutes of the Harvey Mudd College faculty meetings, made available by Dean of Faculty Sam Tanenbaum; alumni records made available by the Alumni Office; financial and fundraising records made available by the Development Office; archival records made available by the President's Office; as well as file cabinets, baskets, and cardboard boxes of my own memorabilia. I also occasionally used my memory, checking against more trustworthy sources when possible. Photographs were located by Rachel Gomez of the College Relations Office.

Once Dana and I had assembled the material for a chapter, I wrote a draft version, and we then circulated the draft to others who remembered the events reported in the draft. Back came additions and corrections. We redrafted and recirculated until we believed we had reported the facts accurately. Accordingly we have had a great deal of help from many people, and I warmly appreciate this support. I take full responsibility for any remaining errors of fact or of interpretation.

Two of my former colleagues on the Harvey Mudd faculty have been particularly helpful. They are Bill Davenport and Dave Sanders, both professors emeriti of English. Whatever economy of phrase or facility of expression this book may possess is very probably owed to them. Each has also assisted me in sorting out significant portions of the early history of the college.

Both Henry Mudd and Norman Sprague knew of the hope of the college before I did. Indeed, the Mudd family had all known and loved the man for whom the college was named; I arrived after Harvey S. Mudd was gone. Henry lived long enough to read and comment on my first three chapters. Norman has read and reviewed most of this book. We have had substantial help from other trustees of our first two decades, and their family members. Ray and Pat Kusche, son-in-law and daughter of our founding trustee Raymond Hill, remembered the initial planning of the campus that Ray had done at the request of the board. Vicki and Bill Coberly read portions of the early chapters prior to Vicki's death. Marian Garrett, Lee Atwood, and Bob Hastings—all associated with the board before we had admitted students—have read and commented on the early chapters. Ken Pitzer, a trustee through our formative academic years and the person who nominated me for the presidency, has been generous with his records and his encouragment. As we began to build the college in the early 1960s, we were greatly helped by George Gose, Ernie Loebbecke, and Clair Peck, each of whom has helped review portions of the book. Later, as we grew to the 360 students we then thought would be our "full size," Alec Hixon and his wife, Adelaide, were essential to our progress, and they have reviewed portions covering those years. To each of these, my thanks.

My colleagues on the Harvey Mudd faculty have contributed much. Graydon Bell, our first appointment in physics, has read every draft chapter. I have had help as well from my fellow physicists Tom Helliwell, Bob Wolf, and Jack Waggoner. Bob Borrelli, Court Coleman, John Greever, Melvin Henriksen, Alden Pixley, the late Stavros Busenberg, and Alvin White have helped, not only in recalling the development of our programs in mathematics, but in remembering much of the rest of the life of the college. In chemistry, I have been advised by Mits Kubota, Phil

Myhre, Bill Sly, Jerry Van Hecke (who is also an alumnus advisor), and Dotty Campbell, who has been part of HMC and its programs in chemistry since she first helped her late husband Art develop both. The Harvey Mudd College curriculum differs from those of other technical institutes especially in engineering and in the humanities and social sciences. Accordingly I particularly thank our engineers of those first two decades: Jack Alford, Mack Gilkeson, John Molinder, Jim Monson, Rich Phillips, Don Remer, Sedat Serdengecti, Harry Williams, and Tom Woodson. They *know* how our engineering program developed.

In the humanities and social sciences, in addition to Bill Davenport and Dave Sanders, I have been advised by George Wickes (now of the University of Oregon), Bill Allen (currently dean of James Madison College, Michigan State University), Tad Beckman (also a chemistry advisor), Dick Olson (also an alumnus advisor), J'nan Sellery, and especially by Ted Waldman. Bill Arce and John Zinda have refreshed my memory on our athletics and physical education programs. Iris Critchell has seen to it that our remarkable aeronautical program has been fairly reported. Octávio Bubión and Linda Dell'Osso have helped me trace the early days of the Upward Bound and MESA programs.

My administrative colleagues have also helped: Spif Little, George McKelvey, and Emery Walker, who were with me when the college opened its doors; Mike Kearney, who helped us raise money to grow the college; Gene Hotchkiss, our first and only dean of the college (at the time of this writing just retiring from over two decades as president of Lake Forest College); Dean of Faculty Sam Tanenbaum, a warm friend and an able evaluator; Bill Gann, sometime dean of students at HMC; and Jean Walton, who was dean of students at Pomona College; our former chaplains, Bob Rankin and Pete Reckard; and Dave Ridgeway, who was with us during the early history of the CHEM Study.

A number of my presidential colleagues have also read portions of the drafts, and given me the benefit of their comments: First and foremost, George C. S. Benson, founding president of Claremont McKenna College, the man who first told me of Harvey Mudd College, and an early HMC trustee; David Alexander, president emeritus of Pomona College; Howard Brooks, president emeritus of Scripps College and my close associate at Claremont University Center; John Atherton, founding president of Pitzer College, and his successor, Bob Atwell (now president of the American Council on Education); and Louis Benezet, president emeritus of Claremont Graduate School and University Center.

In addition to the help I have had from alumni Dick Olson '62 and Jerry Van Hecke '61, many other alumni have shared stories with me, some appearing in this book and others reflected in the descriptions of student and alumni life. In particular, I thank Joe Barrera '62, Jack Appleman '68, and Jim Johnson '71.

I am grateful to Jack Schuster of the Claremont Graduate School and Alexander (Sandy) Astin of UCLA, both scholars of higher education, for their comments on portions of the manuscripts. I thank each of them.

I thank my wife, Jean Platt, who remembers all these times and was often the first person to review each chapter.

Finally, I acknowledge with gratitude the generous support of the John Randolph Haynes & Dora Haynes Foundation, which made possible the publication of this book. This help is particularly meaningful to me, since Francis H. Lindley, a member of the Committee on Future Colleges of the Board of Fellows of Claremont University Center, was one of the small group who recommended the founding of Harvey Mudd College. Mr. Lindley also was associated with the Haynes Foundation for many years. He and his wife knew of Harvey Mudd College before I did, and both of them welcomed the Platts to Claremont. His son, F. Haynes Lindley, Jr., a current member of the Board of Fellows, is now president of the foundation. I warmly appreciate this interest and encouragement from two generations of Lindleys.

CHAPTER I

How I Got Involved
in Harvey Mudd College

IN mid-February of 1956 I came home about sunset on a crisp winter's day. I was at that time professor of physics at the University of Rochester in upstate New York. My wife, Jean, greeted me with the day's news: Our baby could now crawl a bit, and the faculty wives were agreed about who was expected to entertain whom at the conference on high energy physics to be held two weeks hence. And a Mr. George Benson was trying to reach me by telephone. He had left his number.

Mr. Benson's call was from California, where it was still mid-afternoon, so I returned it. He was president of Claremont Men's College in Claremont, California, one of four private colleges located there. A new college was being founded, and its trustees had asked Mr. Benson to develop a list of candidates for its presidency. Some unidentified nominator had proposed my name. Might Mr. Benson visit me in Rochester next week to discuss the matter?

Why not? A new college would be a real adventure.

I had in fact once invented a college. Six years earlier, in 1950, I had been on leave from the University of Rochester, working for the Atomic Energy Commission in Washington, D.C. A good friend and neighbor, Dick Coiner, an Air Force colonel assigned at that time to the AEC, had stimulated the inventing. Jean and I had invited him for dinner while his wife was vacationing at her parents' home in Texas. After dinner Dick had asked me how I would design a college for engineers and scientists if I were free to start afresh. We spent a pleasant two hours conjuring up a college for about four hundred students, with a faculty of forty, strong in the natural sciences. With the increasing responsibility to use technology for the benefit of all of society, our students would need a sound background as well in the humanities and social sciences. There were some new ideas on teaching the engineering sciences that would need looking into. Dick said that some of his wife's friends in Texas were not indigent, and would I write up a prospectus for such a college?

I did, and I had even saved a copy for myself, which I can no longer find; it probably got purged from my abandoned files at the University of Rochester several decades ago. I do remember that I had sketched out, in addition to the faculty, curriculum, and staff, a rough estimate of the necessary buildings and equipment and had guessed that it might take $20 million in 1950 dollars to give the college a good start—about $10 million in plant and equipment, and $10 million in endowment.

Mr. Benson had Sunday breakfast with us a week after our telephone conversation. Jean and I learned that the Claremont Colleges were a planned group of independent private colleges, intended to preserve the intimacy of each college while providing the group with the advantages of a sizeable library and enough depth to support graduate study. The group included Pomona and Scripps Colleges, of which we had heard (without knowing they were associated), but we learned of Claremont Men's College and the offerings of Claremont College for the first time.

It was time to found the next college, and the immediate impetus was the death of Mr. Harvey S. Mudd. Mr. Mudd, a distinguished mining engineer, had been involved with the Claremont Colleges since the Group Plan had been initiated in the 1920s; he had served as board chairman of Claremont College, which founded new colleges, and had helped to organize the founding of Scripps College and Claremont Men's College. He had been involved in the planning for the next college and had explored the possibility of support with some prospective donors. Mr. Mudd died shortly after Easter 1955. His colleagues on the boards of the existing colleges had felt that the next college should be named for him and had asked Mr. Mudd's wife and children for their permission. The family had agreed to the naming and was willing to consider being among the supporters. Accordingly, a board of trustees had been appointed, land for a campus was largely acquired, and the State of California had chartered Harvey Mudd College. Friends of Mr. Mudd's among the trustees of other colleges had made pledges which might total nearly a million dollars, and while the family had as yet made no firm commitment, they had been generous before, in the million-dollar range.

Mr. Benson suggested that we think it over and that if we did not withdraw my name he would include it on the list for board consideration. The board would no doubt invite the top several candidates to the Los Angeles area for interviews and hoped to appoint a president by early May, to take office as soon as possible thereafter. We agreed to think it over.

A week later the Department of Physics at the University of Rochester was playing host to about one hundred physicists from around the world, come to discuss the most recent developments in high energy physics. Among our guests was Dr. Robert F. Bacher, an old friend, then chairman of the Division of Physics, Mathematics and Astronomy at the California Institute of Technology. I asked him why one would found a new private college of engineering, with high standards, fifteen miles from Caltech. He told me that Caltech had had 1,500 applications for admission that year for 180 freshman openings and that within the top third they could have picked any group and found it well-qualified. He told me that the Claremont Colleges had an excellent academic reputation. He knew and thoroughly respected the Mudd name. In summary, he said, "Come on in—the water's fine." He also promised any help he could properly give.

Nevertheless, I found myself with second thoughts. My research program at Rochester was going well. I had doctoral candidates who would have to find new thesis supervisors. I was enjoying my teaching, and we had just put an addition on our house. There was a substantial gap between the $2 million that might be in sight and the $20 million that would be needed. A new college would clearly be a great adventure, but so is jumping off a bridge. With limited funds in hand, it was hardly fair to a new college to accept a round-trip flight to California if I were not interested in the presidency.

On the other hand, Jean and I had regularly found that opportunities around the corner were usually quite worth exploring. When I returned to Rochester after World War II, intending to teach and do research, I became involved in designing and building a big particle accelerator—a synchrocyclotron—which took all my research time and more for two years, but which worked. Then I was invited to Washington to recommend research in physics and mathematics to the Atomic Energy Commission, a bureaucratic step which my research colleagues had told me would be the death of my research career. I got an unusual overview of what everyone else was doing in research and returned to the University of Rochester ready and eager to build a new research program, which I did. Who knew what lay beyond this next possible fork in the road?

In mid-March I was invited to Claremont, and I went. I arrived in what I have since come to call recruiting weather—when one leaves dirty snow in the East to discover clear sunshine in California and in Claremont an unsullied view of Mounts San Gorgonio and Old Baldy. My host was Robert J. Bernard, who bore the unusual title of managing director of Claremont College. He told me the story of the Claremont Colleges as he showed them to me. He had been assistant to Mr. Blaisdell, president of Pomona College in the 1920s, when Mr. Blaisdell had proposed what became the Group Plan. Mr. Bernard clearly believed these colleges had an unlimited future. Later, during interviews with each

Kenneth S. Pitzer

1. Kenneth S. Pitzer, then Dean of the College of Chemistry at the Berkeley campus of the University of California, was later president of Rice University and then of Stanford University. A distinguished chemist, he was no

of the college presidents, I asked Wilson Lyon, president of Pomona College, what the managing director did. "Bob?" said President Lyon. "He's Mr. Claremont Colleges." And Bob was.

I was much impressed with the trustees of the newly organized Harvey Mudd College. One group—William Clary, Garner Beckett, Ford Twaits, Rudolph J. Wig, Van Renssalaer G. Wilbur, Robert J. Bernard, and George Benson—had long been associated with the Claremont Colleges and knew what such a venture required. Others were members or close associates of the Mudd family: Mrs. Harvey S. Mudd, her son Henry T. Mudd, her daughter Caryll and son-in-law Norman F. Sprague, M.D., and close friends and associates Alfred Thomas, Robert P. Hastings, and LeRoy Garrett, also a group with substantial trustee experience; and Raymond Hill, an internationally recognized civil engineer, who had grown up on the campus of the Colorado School of Mines where his father was professor of civil engineering and, for a time, acting president.

Each of the trustees had clearly learned what changes were then taking place in engineering education and had thoughtful questions on the opportunities a new beginning could make possible. They were a friendly, informed, and committed group, and I concluded clearly Harvey S. Mudd must have been quite a man to have engaged their loyalty.

I shared with Bob Bernard my concern about the financing of Harvey Mudd College. He suggested that I discuss the matter with Henry Mudd. Mr. Mudd told me the family expected to help and that as far as fundraising was concerned I could usefully study the methods of George Benson, which Mr. Mudd, as a trustee of Claremont Men's College, knew well. President Benson, while walking the CMC campus with me later, told me how his college had been funded. "We started this college with $80,000 in pledges," he stated. I looked around, and there was clearly a college: buildings, students, and a faculty of major university stature.

I called my wife that evening and reported, "Jeanie, this is the closest thing we'll ever see to that Texas college."

On April 26, 1956, back in Rochester, a letter came from Robert J. Bernard. Acting as secretary to the new Board of Trustees, he wrote to offer me the presidency of Harvey Mudd College. I accepted.

That's how we became involved in Harvey Mudd College.

A month or so later I learned that Kenneth S. Pitzer had nominated me for the presidency. I had known Ken when he was director of research of the Atomic Energy Commission and I was his branch chief for physics and mathematics.[1] Ken has done Harvey Mudd College and the Platts many favors. I am particularly grateful it was he who proposed my name.

I now know that the founding of a privately supported college doesn't happen every week. Founding a privately supported college of engineering and science doesn't even happen every year. There are 3,300 accredited universities and colleges in the United States, of which most were founded between 1840 and 1940. Of these 3,300, perhaps 700 are privately supported. In this century only twelve new private institutions have been founded that have accredited baccalaureate engineering programs. Of these, only three have over 50 percent of the student body enrolled in degree programs in engineering or the natural sciences: Northrop University, Western New England College, and Harvey Mudd College. Northrop University began as a portion of Northrop Aircraft Company, and Western New England College began as a branch campus of Northeastern University. Both are now private and independent institutions, but began otherwise.[2] Harvey Mudd College is therefore quite unusual in the constellation of higher education in the United States.[3]

Harvey Mudd College is unique in its distinctive combination of: (1) an unspecialized engineering program emphasizing system design; (2) a commitment to the humanities and social sciences which requires all students to devote nearly a third of their time to these studies; (3) an unusual amount of undergraduate research or design experience; and (4) a student body of high academic ability. This book is devoted to reporting on the first twenty years of this experiment.

A number of elements are essential to the founding and nurturing of a college. The first is an idea: a concept which defines what the college hopes to do. The second is a group of founders who support the concept and bring it into being. The third is, of course, a campus; and a fourth is a faculty. All these are brought together to serve the fifth essential: students. The sixth is continuing financial support, without which the college will not long endure. The seventh: If the college does endure, it requires skillful academic and business direction by trustees, faculty, and administration. One chapter will be devoted to each of these major areas of the life of Harvey Mudd College; other chapters will report how they fit together.

Twenty years is a brief time in the life of a college, but it is long enough to begin to see how the idea works out. By that time some graduates are established in careers. The college has been evaluated by regional accrediting bodies, which certify that it is doing what it claims to do, and by professional accreditation groups, which certify that its graduates are adequately prepared for the professions they expect to enter. Donors, who have ample opportunity to compare private colleges, have indicated their evaluations by their support or lack of it; national foundations, in particular, regularly make comparisons among all the institutions that appeal to them for funds. Other universities and colleges compete for faculty and ideas the college has developed, giving an indication of evaluation by peer institutions. And, most important, all entering stu-

stranger to Claremont. He grew up in the area. His father, Russell K. Pitzer, was active with the Claremont Colleges over several decades: he was a founding trustee of Claremont Men's College, made the initial gift toward the founding of Harvey Mudd College, and later helped to found Pitzer College, which bears his name. Ken graduated from the California Institute of Technology, married a Pomona College alumna, and was nationally recognized as a chemist at the time he sought me out to work for the Atomic Energy Commission. The reader will find the Pitzer name recurring in this book. Ken Pitzer nominated two of us for the Harvey Mudd College presidency: Professor J. Arthur Campbell and me.

2. As of 1992, Northrup University has become Northrup-Rice Aviation Institute of Technology, offering a baccalaureate degree in Aircraft Maintenance Engineering Technology.

3. While Harvey Mudd College is, to the best of my knowledge, the first engineering college to be founded under independent private support since 1900, we were followed in 1958 by the Florida Institute of Technology of Melbourne, Florida, also privately supported.

The future site of Harvey Mudd College

dents evaluate the college by choosing it over others. All these indicators are clues to the status of the college.

Every college is also regularly self-evaluated by its own trustees, faculty, students, and graduates. The records of Harvey Mudd College contain thousands of pages of such evaluations.

Accordingly, one chapter will be devoted to my own summary of evaluations.

I make no claim to disinterest. My bias is in favor of Harvey Mudd College. I am grateful for our years here. I have had the good fortune to work with many able and great-hearted people. And I have concluded, perhaps more through faith than cold logic, that we have made a creditable beginning on an important task.

This is a first-hand account. But it has been tested against the views of many other participants in these exciting twenty years. I thank each of these good colleagues for helping me through one more assignment.

CHAPTER 2

The Idea of the College

SCHOOLS, colleges, and universities have two complementary purposes: to enable students to develop their abilities to understand the world about them and find a satisfying place in it, and to provide the society at large with the skilled and understanding leadership needed to conduct its affairs. Any particular institution begins with an idea about the need it can best meet. Thus Harvard College was founded, as one of its founders wrote in 1643, "to advance *Learning* and perpetuate it to Posterity; dreading to leave an illiterate Ministry to the Churches, when our present Ministers shall lie in the dust."[1] Over the next century other colonial colleges were founded by Anglicans, Presbyterians, Dutch Reformed, and Baptists, each desirous of a share of the intellectual leadership of posterity. The idea of broad access to higher education came later. Congress, in agreeing to make land funds available to the states that claimed the benefit, stated in the Morrill Act of 1862 that the funds were provided to each such state "to support and maintain at least one college where the leading object shall be, . . . *to teach such branches of learning as are related to the agricultural and mechanical arts,. . . . in order to promote the liberal and practical education of the industrial classes in the several pursuits and professions in life. . . .*"[2]

The idea comes first. What was the idea that led to the founding of Harvey Mudd College?

The idea grew from four sources: first, the national concern that the United States needed to expand its higher educational system to accommodate the "baby boom" that followed World War II; second, the country's need for more engineers and scientists; third, the concern within the engineering profession that new methods of teaching engineering were needed; and fourth, the Claremont Group Plan, whereby the Claremont

1. *The Founding of Harvard College*, Samuel Eliot Morison, (Cambridge, MA., 1935), p. 432.

2. Hofstadter, Richard and Wilson Smith, *American Higher Education: A Documentary History*, (University of Chicago Press, 1961), p. 568.

3. President's Committee on Education Beyond the High School. *First Interim Report to the President*. Washington, D.C., U.S Government Printing Office, 1956.

4. *A Master Plan for Higher Education in California, 1960-1975*, California State Department of Education, Sacramento, 1960.

Colleges grow by the addition of new colleges rather than by the overexpansion of existing ones.

In 1955 it was clear that the number of students seeking college admission would increase sharply; the President's Committee on Education Beyond the High School predicted the numbers could treble by 1970.[3] President Eisenhower, and many others, were concerned that despite the increase in numbers not enough students would enter the fields of engineering and science to meet the national needs. It was becoming well known that the Soviet Union and Japan, for example, were attracting much larger fractions of their young people into technical careers than was the United States. Accordingly national attention was directed to increasing the available facilities for college and university teaching and in particular to making sure that as large a fraction as possible of the expected "tidal wave of students" would have the opportunity to become engineers or scientists. In California, the state legislature, projecting nearly a tripling of post-secondary students from 1958 to 1975,[4] adopted the Master Plan for Higher Education, which defined the functions of the three publicly supported segments of higher education and established a framework for the expected major growth. However, the expansion of California's private sector of higher education remained a private responsibility. In summary, many more students were expected nationally and in California, and there was a growing sense of national need for engineers and scientists.

Engineering education was in ferment in the 1950s. The American Society for Engineering Education had commissioned a major study entitled *Goals of Engineering Education* to set guidelines for college and university teachers of engineering—indeed, for everyone involved in engineering education, including the professional societies and accreditation bodies. A preliminary portion of that study, the "Grinter Report" (written by Dean Linton E. Grinter of the University of Florida) was widely read in 1955 while still in draft circulation. Reflecting the views of practicing engineers as well as teachers, this document spelled out the most urgent issues we faced in planning a new engineering education. Here are highlights of these issues:

First, the report observed that major new scientific and technical developments of the 1930s and 1940s, including radar, solid state electronics, nuclear energy, the development of new chemical and physical materials, and the advent of electronic computers had vastly increased the physical and intellectual tools available to the engineer. They were also destroying any static nature the art and practice of engineering may once have enjoyed. One could no longer learn engineering skills and expect them to remain current; the engineer must expect to need lifelong learning.

Just as obviously, the society at large was being reshaped by new technologies such as air travel, nuclear weapons, and television, as nine-teenth-century Britain was reshaped by the steam engine or nineteenth-century North America by the railroads, but the reshaping was coming more rapidly. Accordingly, an important part of the responsibility of the engineer is to anticipate the social effects of engineering activity and to design systems and advise clients in ways likely to maximize the social utility of an engineering development. This understanding requires a breadth of education not built into many engineering curricula in fields such as political economy, psychology, and history.

Third, the engineer needs increasingly to be able to communicate verbally and in writing with his colleagues, with his superiors, and with the public at large, to be able to work with others and to persuade. Many practicing engineers find themselves with increasing management respon-sibility in each passing year. Each decade a larger fraction of senior cor-porate executives began their careers with engineering degrees.

Finally, Dean Grinter and his colleagues warned that no single solu-tion can be expected for a "proper" engineering education. Many exper-iments should be tried and assessed. One can expect more engineering specialties to appear while a more general approach to engineering is also needed. It is more true than ever that the engineer needs continual renewal through job experience, postgraduate education, and self-study.

Dr. James A. Blaisdell

I learned when I first visited the trustees of Harvey Mudd College that they were familiar with these national debates on engineering educa-tion and that several of them who were engineers had sought out mem-bers of the "Goals" committee to discuss the issues. Those trustees believed strongly in the importance of liberal education for engineers and in the need for a sound understanding of basic science and mathematics as background for engineering applications. In fact, they had known broadly educated, socially responsible engineers of great competence. Harvey S. Mudd had been such a man, and Herbert C. Hoover another. The trustee consensus was that the world needed more such engineers.

The fourth reason for a new college was the Claremont Group Plan.

The Claremont Group Plan was first proposed in 1923 by Mr. James A. Blaisdell, then president of Pomona College. "My own very deep hope," he said, "is that instead of one great, undifferentiated university, we might have a group of institutions divided into small colleges—some-what on the Oxford type—around a library and other facilities which they would use in common. In this way I should hope to preserve the inestimable *personal* values of the small college while securing the *facilities* of the great university. Such a development would be a new and wonder-ful contribution to American education."[5]

Accordingly, Claremont Colleges[6] was incorporated on September 29, 1925, charged among other things with the responsibility[7] "to estab-lish, maintain, conduct and assist financially or otherwise *other* institutions

5. Letter from James A. Blaisdell to Ellen Browning Scripps, October 3, 1923.

6. On September 26, 1967 the name of the central coordinating institution was changed to Claremont University Center, its name at the time of this writing.

7. Articles of Incorporation, Claremont Colleges, Section (e), October 1925.

8. Claremont Men's College became Claremont McKenna College in 1981.

9. Again, the central coordinating institution. Since the Claremont Group Plan is unusual in higher education, it has not been easy to settle upon a name for the central coordinating institution. (The early 1960s joke was that the Claremont Graduate School tower would carry in twinkling lights the time, temperature, and most recent institutional name.) The name should connote the graduate study and research facilities associated with a university, while carrying no hint that sister colleges were in any sense subordinate. The initial name, Claremont Colleges, was proposed by Mr. Blaisdell in analogy to the United States; in 1944 the Board of Fellows changed the name to Claremont College; in 1961 to Claremont University College; in 1962 to Claremont Graduate School and University Center; and in 1967 to Claremont University Center. The present author thinks Mr. Blaisdell was right the first time.

10. Robert J. Bernard, *An Unfinished Dream*, The Castle Press, 1982; pp 459 et seq.

11. The Committee on Future Colleges, 1954: William W. Clary, Chairman; Robert J. Bernard, Francis H. Lindley, George R. Martin, Ford J. Twaits, and Rudolph J. Wig.

of learning of any nature. . . ." Two years later Scripps College was founded. Claremont Men's College[8] was founded in 1946. In 1955, then, there were four Claremont Colleges: Pomona, Claremont University Center, Scripps, and Claremont Men's College.

There was also the clear intention to found more colleges. The Board of Fellows, the governing board of Claremont College[9], had established on November 29, 1954, a Standing Committee on Future Colleges.[10] The members of this committee[11] were fully aware of the need for more educational facilities and for more engineers and scientists. They had read and reflected upon the "Interim Report of the American Society for Engineering Education Concerning Evaluation of Engineering Education." They knew the Claremont Colleges and believed the time was right to found the next college.

In particular, a technical college would bring balance to the group. Pomona College was a general liberal arts college with strong science departments; Claremont Graduate School had no permanent faculty in the sciences; Scripps College taught predominantly the humanities and fine arts; and Claremont Men's College emphasized the broad field of political economy. Additional strength in engineering and the sciences would add opportunity for students of all the colleges. Accordingly, on October 27, 1955, this committee recommended to the Board of Fellows the founding of "a college which teaches engineering and science in a humanistic setting."

This was the idea of Harvey Mudd College.

CHAPTER 3

The Founding Trustees

T HE man who provided the impetus for Harvey Mudd College never knew of its founding. He was Harvey Seeley Mudd and the college was named in his memory. I had the good fortune to know his wife, his children and their families, and any number of Mr. Mudd's friends and associates from the many activities in which he had played a part. Here is some of what I have learned:

Harvey S. Mudd was a mining engineer, as was his father, Colonel Seeley W. Mudd,[1] and was his son, Henry Thomas Mudd. Harvey Mudd was born in 1888 in Leadville, Colorado, where his father was managing the Small Hope mine. The Mudd family moved to Los Angeles when Harvey was fifteen, and he graduated from Los Angeles High School. He attended Stanford University for two years and transferred to the Columbia University School of Mines. He served in Washington during World War I as assistant secretary of the War Minerals Committee and later with the Bureau of Mines developing the production of essential minerals. After the war he was involved in a variety of mining ventures, both with his father and alone. Harvey Mudd established a national professional reputation, served a term as president of the American Institute of Mining, Metallurgical, and Petroleum Engineers, and in 1948 was the first Californian to be awarded the Egleston Columbia University Engineering Medal.

Among the Mudds' many mining ventures was the Cyprus Mines Corporation, which located and reopened long forgotten mines on the island of Cyprus that had produced copper from prehistoric times to the fall of the Byzantine empire. These mines were rediscovered, and their value appraised, by a determined prospector named C. Godfrey Gunther, while searching the Middle East for copper mines on which the Bronze

1. I am sometimes asked if these Mudds are related to the Dr. Samuel A. Mudd of Maryland, who set the leg of Lincoln's assassin, John Wilkes Booth. A good fraction of the Mudds in the United States are indeed related. The most recent common ancestor of these Samuel Mudd and Harvey Mudd branches of the family was Thomas Mudd of Maryland, who died in 1736. Dr. Richard Dyer Mudd, a grandson of Dr. Samuel A. Mudd, has published *The Mudd Family of the United States,* (Edwards Brothers, Inc., Ann Arbor, Michigan, 1951) which details these relationships. Thomas Mudd of Maryland was the third generation of Mudds on this continent, according to this record.

2. *The Story of the Cyprus Mines Corporation,* David Lavender, The Huntington Library, 1962.

3. The portrait, a gift of Robert P. Hastings, is a copy of one painted by the late Arthur Cahill.

4. Private communication from R. J. Bernard to the author, about 1970.

5. On April 14th, at its next scheduled concert, the Los Angeles Philharmonic Orchestra dedicated the performance of Verdi's *Requiem* to his memory.

6. William W. Clary became Chairman of the Board of Fellows in the academic year 1953-54. He succeeded Harvey S. Mudd; Mr. Mudd remained a member of the Board to the end of his life.

Age had been founded. He was financed by Seeley W. Mudd and another backer. The remarkable story of this development is told in David Lavender's book, *The Story of the Cyprus Mines Corporation.*[2] Under the leadership of Seeley W. Mudd, then of Harvey S. Mudd, and finally of Henry T. Mudd, this corporation ultimately prospered and had a great deal to do with Harvey Mudd College. Earnings from Cyprus copper and other Mudd family holdings have helped to underwrite Pomona College, Claremont University Center, Claremont McKenna College, Harvey Mudd College, and much else in the public interest in the United States.

A portrait—really a cartoon—of Harvey Mudd hangs in Galileo Hall on the Harvey Mudd College campus.[3] It shows a beaming Harvey Mudd confidently juggling a miner's pick, a violin, a tomahawk, a gavel, and an academic cap. These symbolize some of the many community activities to which he gave leadership: the Los Angeles Philharmonic Orchestra, the Southwest Museum, the Claremont Colleges, and the California Institute of Technology are examples. The miner's pick symbolizes not only his profession but also his leadership in the Institute of Mining, Metallurgical, and Petroleum Engineers. The gavel symbolizes more chairmanships than we have space to list here. But what the portrait really symbolizes is a much trusted man who used his leadership to benefit the community in a great many ways. It is the image of the man whose friends have given help and support to Harvey Mudd College.

We learned in Chapter 2 that the Board of Fellows of Claremont College had established, on November 29, 1954, a Standing Committee on Future Colleges. Harvey S. Mudd had been party to the discussions that led to the appointment of that committee. He knew of and supported the plan to add an engineering and science college to the Claremont Colleges, one of the choices before the committee. Mr. Mudd, over the next few months, explored with at least one engineer of means the possibility of financial support for the new college if it were to be committed to engineering and the sciences.[4]

On April 12, 1955, Harvey S. Mudd died.[5] During the next several months members of the Board of Fellows continued to explore the need, and possible sources of support, for a new college. A number of Mr. Mudd's colleagues on and off the board expressed the hope that the next college might bear his name, and informally explored the possibility with Mrs. Mudd and her family.

On October 27, 1955, the Executive Committee of the Board of Fellows of Claremont College received the report of its Committee on Future Colleges. As we have seen, this report recommended the founding of "a college which teaches engineering and science in a humanistic setting." The chairman of the Board of Fellows, William W. Clary,[6] announced that Mr. and Mrs. Russell K. Pitzer had volunteered to pro-

Harvey S. Mudd

vide a new wing on Pitzer Hall, a building of Claremont Men's College, which the new college could use for ten years or until its enrollment had reached 200. The offer was conditional on certain other gifts being made to establish the new college.

The full Board of Fellows met on November 15, 1955, and voted to accept Mr. and Mrs. Pitzer's offer. The board also received a letter from Mrs. Harvey S. Mudd, in which she wrote: "I, too, believe that a college such as that described by Mr. Pitzer should be established in the Claremont group. In order to make possible the acceptance of Mr. Pitzer's offer, I will give $250,000 for the new college. . . . In addition to

7. Robert J. Bernard, *An Unfinished Dream, A Chronicle of the Group Plan of The Claremont Colleges,* p. 470 et seq.

Harvey S. Mudd

Mildred Mudd

the foregoing gift, if it should be decided to name the college for Harvey Seeley Mudd the members of his family intend to consider additional gifts to or for the benefit of the new college."[7]

The board voted to accept with profound gratitude the gift of Mrs. Harvey S. Mudd and to have the new college bear the honored name of Harvey S. Mudd. On Mr. Bernard's motion the board then authorized the selection of an initial Board of Trustees for Harvey Mudd College, and the incorporation of the college under California law, and committed the income of $500,000 of previously unallocated Claremont College endowment for the initial educational expenditures of the new college. Dr. James A. Blaisdell, who had originally proposed the Group Plan, was present at this meeting of the Board of Fellows as president emeritus of Claremont College. At the request of the board he led the members in asking the Lord's blessing on the new venture.

The next month was a busy one—particularly, I suspect, for Robert J. Bernard. The Articles of Incorporation were drafted by Leroy A. Garrett, counsel to Mrs. Mudd, and the initial Board of Trustees of Harvey Mudd College was recruited to become the incorporators. The articles were filed with the secretary of state of California on December 14, 1955, which established the official date of founding. (Dr. Bernard, asked by the office of the secretary of state for the proposed duration of the corporation, replied, "In perpetuity.") Plans were laid to secure a campus and to secure a president.

By December 14, 1955, Harvey Mudd College was a legal entity, with trustees, property, sister colleges, an important mission, and high hopes.

The founding trustees of Harvey Mudd College were Mrs. Harvey S. Mudd, Henry T. Mudd, Norman F. Sprague, Jr., Alfred R. Thomas, Leroy A. Garrett, R. J. Wig, William W. Clary, Robert J. Bernard, V.R.G. Wilbur, Raymond A. Hill, Garner A. Beckett, and Ford J. Twaits. Who were these people, and why were they involved in this unusual venture?

Mildred Esterbrook Mudd was the widow of Harvey Mudd and the mother of their children, Henry T. Mudd and Caryll Mudd Sprague. She was involved because she knew the Claremont Colleges had been important to "my beau" and that he favored the founding of an engineering college. She had a distinguished record of leadership in her own right. A long period of service to the Girl Scouts of America culminated in her term as national president, 1939-41; and her community activities in Los Angeles were recognized by the Gold Key Award, the highest honor conferred by the Community Chest. There were many other instances of her ability to bring a group into effective service. When we first met she seemed reserved, almost shy, but I soon learned that she was a determined lady who made herself thoroughly informed, and that she had a warm and sympathetic interest in our students, our faculty, and all of us at the college. Jean and I remember her as a thoughtful and considerate friend as well as an able board leader.

Henry T. Mudd, president and chief executive officer of the Cyprus Mines Corporation at the time of founding of the college, was no stranger to the Claremont Colleges. He had joined the advisory group for Claremont Men's College on its founding in 1946 and became a trustee on its incorporation in 1947. With his father, he had followed the fortunes of all four of the Claremont Colleges through the post-war decade closely enough to know the administrators and the trustees and many of the faculty members of our sister colleges. Professionally, he was an able mining engineer (serving during World War II as chief, Fluorspar Section, of the War Production Board) and an excellent corporate president; he led the Cyprus Mines Corporation through an extensive and profitable program of diversification into mining operations in Yukon Canada, South America, Australia, and the United States. He was known and trusted by both the Turkish and the Greek factions during strife on the island of Cyprus. He was also known and trusted by community leaders in Los Angeles, a fact which won many friends for Harvey Mudd College.

Before he died on September 10, 1990, Henry read the first draft portions of this book, including the above paragraph. He commented that the college had contributed more to him than he had to the college, and I need not praise him. I now know that he had given the bulk of his personal wealth to Harvey Mudd College prior to his death, and the college was also named a major beneficiary of his estate. I quote from the memorial resolution adopted by the Board of Trustees later that month:

Norman F. Sprague

Caryll Mudd Sprague

> Henry Mudd was a distinguished mining engineer, as were his father and his grandfather before him. He was recognized nationally by the Institute for Mining, Metallurgical and Petroleum Engineers for his contributions to the mining industry, and the success of the Cyprus Mines Corporation (which he headed for twenty-four years) served its shareholders well.
>
> He also shared with his father and grandfather a commitment to the Claremont Colleges. He was a founding trustee of Claremont McKenna College and of Harvey Mudd College, and served for more than 38 years on the Board of Fellows of Claremont University Center. His breadth of view about these colleges, and about the collective contribution they can make, increased the vision of all of us, his colleagues.
>
> Henry succeeded his mother in 1958 as Chairman of the Board of Harvey Mudd College, and served in that capacity for 23 years. He was a tireless and effective leader, recruiting trustees, interesting

donors, playing host to hundreds of functions, and generously of his time, attention, and substance. He remained a committed and informed trustee to the end of his life. Many people,
including much of the Mudd family, have helped to build the college named for his father. Of all of us, Henry did the most to bring
Harvey Mudd College to its present stature.

We are grateful for the years we have shared with him.

Dr. Norman F. Sprague, Jr. was the third member of the Mudd family on the initial board. The son of a respected Los Angeles physician, he
was the husband of Caryll Mudd Sprague. Dr. Sprague graduated at an
early age from the University of California, earned his medical degree at
Harvard and had completed his internship and residency in surgery in
time to spend five years in the Army Medical Corps as a surgeon, primarily in the Pacific theater, during World War II. He returned to private practice in Los Angeles. He combined the practice of surgery with
teaching at the UCLA Medical School and with a wide range of corporate and community service. In one of my early visits with him, he was
reluctantly concluding he was too busy to take new patients and indeed
would need to phase out of the field of medicine; he did not wish to
become an "occasional surgeon." Because I had just concluded that I
could not be both a college president and a research physicist I understood his concern.

One of Dr. Sprague's early contributions to Harvey Mudd College
was his insistence on excellent architectural standards for all our campus
buildings; another was his attention to building prudent financial reserves
for the college. He and his wife, Caryll, were active partners in the planning of the college.

Two close associates of the Mudd family were also on the initial
board. The first of these was Alfred R. Thomas, at that time executive
vice president of the Cyprus Mines Corporation. Mr. Thomas had been
educated as an engineer, and most of his professional career had been in
banking. Originally a Californian, he had been a senior vice president of
Morgan Guaranty Trust Company in New York City at the time Harvey
Mudd had persuaded him to manage the finances of the Cyprus Mines
Corporation. Accordingly, Mr. Thomas had a wide range of acquain-
tances in New York City as well as Los Angeles, which served Harvey
Mudd College well. He and his gracious wife, Elise, were cordial and
informed members of the college family.

Leroy A. Garrett, a partner in the law firm of Musick, Peeler, and
Garrett, was legal counsel to members of the Mudd family and a trusted
friend of Harvey Mudd. Roy Garrett had been much involved in the discussions leading to the decision to found Harvey Mudd College. He and
his wife, Marian, were perceptive and loyal partners in finding ways to

move the college forward. Personally generous, they also were sensitive to the hopes and the uncertainties others might have concerning the college. It was always a joy, and often highly educational, to work or to relax with the Garretts.

The next group of trustees were long-term supporters—indeed, builders—of the Claremont Colleges.

Rudolph J. Wig—known universally as "R.J."—became a trustee of Pomona College in 1929, when his daughter was a Pomona student. In 1955, at the time of founding of Harvey Mudd College, he was chairman of the Pomona Board of Trustees, a member of the Board of Fellows of Claremont College, and a member of the Committee on Future Colleges, which recommended the founding of what became Harvey Mudd College. Mr. Wig, then in his seventies, was an amazing man.[8] The third of four sons of a Hungarian immigrant father and a Yankee mother, he grew up in Chicago, earned his way through Lewis Institute (a predecessor of the Illinois Institute of Technology), graduating in 1907 as a mechanical engineer. As a student, he had done research on improving the qualities of concrete, and he found a job following graduation with the Geological Survey doing more such research. In due course he was transferred to the Bureau of Standards and later became head of its Cement Division. He had much to do with establishing standards for concrete used in such large projects as the Panama Canal. During World War I he was chief engineer of the Department of Concrete Ship Construction of the United States Shipping Board. Several concrete ships were produced, and at war's end six shipyards for the production of concrete tankers, freighters, and barges were coming on stream. After the war Mr. Wig joined a firm mining diatomaceous earth, which he had found a useful ingredient in good shipbuilding concrete. The firm brought him to California, and both he and the firm found their association profitable. This was one of several ventures in which Mr. Wig's technical knowledge, energy, and clear business mind helped corporations to prosper.

Mr. Wig was even more active throughout his life as a churchman and as a volunteer leader in community affairs. His family and his ability to help his fellow man were what he lived for. He was one of thirteen representatives of higher education appointed in 1954 to recommend to the State of California methods of dealing with the expected influx of Korean War veterans. Mr. Wig relentlessly sorted out the facts on the capacity of public and private higher education and persuaded the committee it would be faster and cheaper to make scholarships available for students to attend underused private universities and colleges than to build and staff new public institutions to handle the increase. That was the beginning of the California State Scholarship program, and indeed Governor Goodwin Knight appointed Mr. Wig to the initial Scholarship

8. Much of the biographical information on Mr. Wig is taken from Clifford M. Drury's book, *Rudolph J. Wig*, The Arthur H. Clark Company, Glendale, CA, 1968.

Commission, of which he was elected chairman. Learning that there was no organized spokesperson for the private colleges and universities of California, Mr. Wig, on his own initiative, called together representatives of these institutions. That was the beginning of the Association of Independent California Colleges and Universities, formally incorporated in 1955. He served thirty-two years as director and treasurer of Goodwill Industries, Inc. He also served as a trustee of the Pasadena Presbyterian Church, and of the Los Angeles Presbytery, and on many national committees of the General Assembly of the Presbyterian Church. He was a trustee of the San Francisco Theological Seminary. And much else.

One evening in the winter of 1958 I had agreed to speak to the West Coast meeting of the Optical Society of America. It developed that the next morning I could have an appointment with the Carnegie Corporation in New York City. Nothing to do but take the night flight; I hoped I could find two adjacent empty seats, take out an armrest, and snooze a bit. At the airport I ran into R.J., also on the same flight, also in coach section, on his way to a meeting of the National Council of United Presbyterian Men. We sat together on the flight and spent five hours discussing the developing curriculum of Harvey Mudd College. When we arrived in New York City both of us knew what subjects should be included and why. We parted in New York, each to our separate meetings. R.J. was thirty-two years older than I and considerably less sleepy. I was impressed.

William W. Clary—"Will" to his many friends—was a law partner in the Los Angeles firm of O'Melveny and Myers. He had been a senior at Pomona College (and football captain) when James Arnold Blaisdell arrived as president in 1911. Will Clary had admired Dr. Blaisdell then, and when he was invited, as a Pomona alumni representative, to join the Board of Fellows of the new central coordinating institution in 1928, he accepted. He served throughout the period that Scripps College and Claremont Men's College were founded, and had succeeded Harvey Mudd as chairman of the Board of Fellows in 1953. Will was a scholar of higher education and of the Claremont Colleges in particular.[9]

Robert J. Bernard really was "Mr. Claremont Colleges." A Phi Beta Kappa graduate of Pomona College in 1917, he had been promptly appointed assistant to President Blaisdell. This association continued for eighteen years, until Dr. Blaisdell's retirement in 1935. Mr. Bernard did much of the research upon which Mr. Blaisdell based his proposal for the Claremont Group Plan; in all, Mr. Bernard visited twenty colleges and universities in the process. He was appointed secretary of the Claremont Colleges in 1925 and filed the Articles of Incorporation with the secretary of state in Sacramento on October 14 of that year, beginning the legal history of the Claremont Colleges. He helped with the founding of Scripps College and was a prime mover in the founding of Claremont

9. He gave to the Honnold Library his extensive collection of books on Oxford University and wrote what is still the definitive statement of the "constitutional history" of The Claremont Colleges. After he retired from the practice of law, he served as acting president of Claremont University Center for much of 1963, moving with his wife Elizabeth to Claremont and committing full time to the task.

McKenna College, Harvey Mudd College, and Pitzer College. He served as managing director and then as president of Claremont University Center. A gentle and a modest man of great human warmth, he developed tremendous drive when he found a chore that needed doing for the Claremont Colleges. Many people of high ability have helped to build the Claremont Colleges, but the man who orchestrated their efforts and led the way from 1935 until his death in 1981 was Robert J. Bernard.

Van Rensselaer G. Wilbur, an independent oil producer, was also a trustee of Scripps College. He and his wife were patrons of the arts, much interested in education, and generous with the use of their home in Montecito, California. He had grown up in Albany, New York, and had attended Union College, leaving school to supervise a silver mine in Mexico. Later he became a division manager of the Mexican Central Railroad. He moved in 1915 to Los Angeles, where he managed the Golden State Woolen Mills. In 1926 he organized the Wilbur Oil Company, of which he was president when we met thirty years later. Mrs. Wilbur was a writer known for her books on historic California.

Mr. Wilbur was a generous host, but his guests learned the value of prudence. He served very dry martinis which had been chilled in a mason jar in his freezer and were hence pure ice-cold gin. They were delicious, and seemed, on first taste, innocuous. A prudent guest treated a Wilbur martini with respect.

Garner A. Beckett had been a member of the Board of Fellows of Claremont College since 1936, was a founding trustee of Claremont Men's College, and was chairman of that board at the time Harvey Mudd College was founded. He was then employed as president of the Riverside Cement Company. He had graduated in 1915 from the University of Pennsylvania as a civil engineer, having twice interrupted his college career, once for a year's work in a bank and again as a civil engineer for the New York Central Railroad. He had been in the Army Corps of Engineers in World War I and saw combat in France. He joined Riverside Cement Company in 1921 and became president in 1936. He and his wife, Lillian, were married in 1917, two months before he went overseas. Garner had a record of national and community service too extensive to list here. He, too, contributed time and thought and support to whatever he undertook, and he was a pillar of strength for Harvey Mudd College.

Ford J. Twaits was also a member of the Board of Fellows and a founding trustee of Claremont Men's College. He was a builder. The Ford J. Twaits Company had constructed buildings that composed much of the downtown Los Angeles skyline of the 1950s: the Biltmore Hotel, the Pacific Mutual buildings, and many others. Ford was born in Lansing, Michigan, and graduated in civil engineering from Michigan State University (although, as we shall see, his graduation was for a time in doubt.) After working for a few years for others, he founded his own structural engineering firm in Winnipeg, working primarily for the Canadian Northern Railway. Four years of this was enough, and he moved to Southern California "to thaw out." He was chief engineer for the Pacific Marine Construction Company of San Diego, which built one of the first of Mr. Wig's concrete ships. In 1919 he persuaded the Scofield Engineering Company of Philadelphia, parent of Pacific Marine Construction, to form a postwar general construction company, of which he became vice president and general manager. He bought the company in 1934.

Ford told me one evening the story of his senior year at Michigan State University. Michigan State had a smaller campus then. In his junior year the university had conducted a study that showed it could reduce fuel costs by heating each building from a central boiler rather than by using individual furnaces. That required the construction of steam tunnels connecting the buildings, through which the insulated steam pipes could be installed and maintained. Ford decided to begin his contracting career then, and organized a group of students who bid and won the construction contract. The job was finished and the tunnels in use when Ford was a senior. It occurred to Ford one dull evening to round up some sheep in the Ag building and run them through the tunnels into the nurses' dormitory. (He observed that if he had known how much harder it is to get sheep down iron steps than it is up, he might not have tried this prank.) The dean was not amused, and Ford was left uncertain for some time about his prospects for graduation.

The one founding trustee who was new to the Claremont Colleges was Raymond Hill. He was recruited because of his reputation as an engineer and his interest in engineering education. His father, Louis Hill, also an engineer, had been on the faculty of the Colorado School of Mines and had served for a time as acting president. Raymond had been born in Golden, Colorado, and had done much of his growing up on campus. He had his civil engineering degree from the University of Michigan and had developed a firm opinion about the proper education for an engineer. When we first met (on my interview for the presidency) he drew a circle and divided it into quadrants. One quarter of the curriculum should be committed to mathematics and the sciences, ("the language of engineering,") and one quarter to the study of engineering itself. One quarter should be committed to languages and literature, ("the tools of human expression,") and one quarter to the humanities and social sciences, which an engineer needs to understand his function in society. I am certain he could have had no such program at the University of Michigan or any other then accredited engineering institution. He had made up any shortfall through self-education, and he knew how he should have been taught. His model is a noble one.

Raymond had an international reputation as an expert on dam design and construction and had many other fields of competence. Over the years I knew him he consulted with the government of Australia on its Snowy Mountains project, with the government of Pakistan on the damming of the Indus River, and on other ventures that took him wherever else people were hoping to store large quantities of water safely. He had survived a helicopter accident that had dumped him in the icy rapids of the Jhelum River in west Pakistan, a car accident rolling off a narrow Turkish mountain road in a packed Volkswagen, and I know not how many other misadventures. He had been everywhere and done everything twice, and he had thought about all of it. And he thought effectively about Harvey Mudd College.

These were the founding trustees of Harvey Mudd College. My family and I arrived in Claremont in September, 1956, nine months and two weeks after the founding date. By that time six additional trustees had been added to the board.

J. Leland Atwood was at that time president of North American Aviation Company and a legendary figure in the aircraft industry. Lee is a quiet and a thoughtful man. His father had been a professor of Bible, an ordained minister, and for some time a college president; academic life was not new to the Atwood family. Lee took his undergraduate degree in mathematics from Hardin-Simmons College and his engineering degree from the University of Texas. He became a Junior Engineer (a Civil Service rating) at Wright Field, where he began designing airplanes, and moved from this through a number of ventures in the fledgling aircraft industry, finding himself in 1934, at age thirty, chief of advanced design with Douglas Aircraft Company. His boss, the vice president for engineering, "Dutch" Kindelberger, left Douglas for a small and struggling North American Aviation Corporation, one condition being that he could take Lee Atwood with him. By the end of the 1930s their new firm had an established reputation for military training aircraft and had developed what became the B25 bomber, a stalwart of World War II. In the early 1940s the same firm began producing the P51, a highly successful fighter aircraft. All told, North American Aviation produced 10,000 B25s, 15,000 P51s, and 27,000 other aircraft during World War II. North American people have a story, perhaps apocryphal, about the first order that came in for 1,500 P51s—the largest single aircraft order the world had then seen. "I wish," Lee Atwood is reported to have said, "they'd quit ordering these things in dribs and drabs."

I will resist the temptation[10] to tell about the space-age contributions of North American Aviation and then, after the merger, Rockwell International under Lee Atwood's leadership. I do recall my first introduction to the firm Lee headed. He had invited me to visit the plant, and I showed up at eight in the morning at his office near the Los Angeles

10. The reader who wishes this information may find it in *Lee Atwood: Dean of Aerospace,* published by Rockwell International Corporation, 1980.

airport. I spent several hours learning about airframe design, including my introduction to the use of computers to simulate flight control response. Then I drove to the Rocketdyne Division, near Canoga Park, where I saw my first large rocket on a test stand. My next drive was to Downey, to visit the Autonetics Division, where some very sophisticated design activities were being conducted in guidance and other forms of electronics. I returned to Claremont shortly before midnight, having driven 120 miles and spent twelve hours in plant visits under the best possible auspices, and still having barely scratched the surface of North American Aviation.

Hugh Clary, president of Clary Corporation, a manufacturer of office equipment, also joined the board upon election at its meeting of April 3, 1956. Hugh, brother of Will Clary, was also a Pomona College alumnus, thoroughly familiar with the Group Plan and excited about the education of engineers and scientists. He and his wife, Huldah, became well acquainted with our students, our faculty, and all connected with Harvey Mudd College over the first decade of its existence.

Philip Fogg, founder and chief executive officer of Consolidated Electrodynamics Corporation, was the third trustee elected at the April meeting. A former faculty member teaching business subjects at the California Institute of Technology, Mr. Fogg became involved with startup technical ventures. His firm was the result. Consolidated Electrodynamics developed many of the early magnetic recording devices for large mainframe computers and also many other kinds of instrumentation to produce records of readings of sensing devices.

The May meeting of the board was the one at which I was elected president and also a board member. I had been professor of physics at the University of Rochester, my undergraduate alma mater. I had earned my doctorate at Cornell University. I had had two periods of leave from teaching: I had spent three years as a staff member of the M.I.T. Radiation Laboratory, introducing radar devices into combat use in the European and Pacific theaters of World War II, and two post-war years as a staff member of the Atomic Energy Commission. Excluding these leaves I had had ten years of teaching experience after completing graduate school.

At the June meeting of the board, George C.S. Benson was elected a trustee. George Benson was the founding president of Claremont Men's College and, as described earlier, had persuaded me to become a candidate for the Harvey Mudd College presidency. He was a Pomona College alumnus, and his uncle had been the founder of Pomona.[11] Later George would be involved in the founding of Pitzer College. I mentioned earlier the key role of Robert J. Bernard in bringing the Claremont Colleges into being. I have had the good fortune to know all three of the administrators primarily involved in creating this collegiate group: James Arnold Blaisdell, Robert J. Bernard, and George C.S. Benson. Others of us have

11. Professor Morton Beckner, in a series of five articles published in *Pomona Today* (Fall 1987, *et seq.*) concludes that of those involved in the founding of Pomona College, Charles Sumner was the indispensable figure.

been modestly helpful from time to time, but these three and the able trustees who shared their vision are those who made it happen.

President Benson, a political scientist, pointed out that it was a mistake to have a substantial number of trustees whose primary loyalty was to another institution, but, if the board wished, he would be happy to serve for a time. The board so wished, and I am grateful.

In the midsummer meeting of 1956 the board elected Robert P. Hastings, a partner in the law firm of Paul & Hastings.[12] Bob, the son of a much beloved Los Angeles doctor, was a Yale alumnus and a Harvard Law School graduate; he had served much of World War II as a naval officer in the Pacific theater. He returned to Los Angeles and established his legal practice here. He and his late wife, "Suzy," became staunch members of the college family and warm friends.

12. The firm is now (1990) Paul, Hastings, Janofsky and Walker.

These were the trustees who were serving at the time the Platts arrived in September of 1956. I will introduce specific trustees to the reader as they shape the college in subsequent years, but I have two reasons for introducing the founding trustees as a group. First, they were people of courage as well as of ability and standing; it took courage to assume responsibility for the first privately supported engineering college to be founded in half a century. Second, each was a person of great goodwill and understanding. Jean and our two daughters and I were a transplanted faculty family relatively innocent of wealth or status, and by any standards with which we were familiar, these people possessed both. We viewed working with the board with some apprehension, but we soon learned that we were among friends. Mrs. Mudd went out of her way to see that we were comfortably housed and satisfied with schooling for our girls; we were entertained in her home a number of times. She visited us many times in Claremont, beginning the first month we were in residence. Jean and I have in fact been guests in the homes of all these initial trustees, and they in ours. Victoria and Henry Mudd more often than not included the four Platts in their family gatherings at Christmas, and we were many times guests at their ranch, "Saddle Rock." We and our daughters weekended with Caryll and Norman Sprague and daughters at their ranch (where our Beth learned to ride a horse). We spent happy mini-vacations with the Garretts at the beach and in the desert and with the Hastings at Lake Arrowhead.

The graciousness of the trustees continued throughout the history of Harvey Mudd College, welcoming the faculty, staff, and trustees that joined us later. But in the founding years we were also bound together by our shared belief in Harvey Mudd College. The excitement and the adventure, not to mention the risks inherent in creating a new college, fostered a close, almost conspiratorial bond between the trustees, faculty, staff, and students. We are still a young institution and some of that thrill remains.

CHAPTER 4

The Campus—The First Decade

Harvey Mudd College required a campus. One of the first acts of the newly formed Board of Trustees was to acquire the necessary land. Fortunately, sister colleges in Claremont owned vacant land held for academic use, and one of the possible uses was the establishment of a new college. Accordingly, Pomona College, Scripps College, and Claremont College sold Harvey Mudd College some sixteen acres of contiguous land, and the Harvey Mudd board negotiated with several private homeowners to sell land and buildings jutting into what could become the campus. By midsummer of 1956, some nine months after the college was chartered, it owned eighteen acres of land, situated between Foothill Boulevard and Ninth Street, bounded on the east by Mills Avenue, and on the west by Amherst Avenue. There were several small houses and lawns facing either Foothill Boulevard or Amherst Avenue, but the campus consisted primarily of rocks and chaparral. A prominent feature of the campus was a gully, perhaps four feet deep and eight feet wide, which had been carved through the prospective campus in forty-eight hours during the great flood of 1938.[1] When I first saw the area in March, 1956, I was assured that since the construction of the San Antonio dam, following that disaster, no such flood was again possible.

When I returned to Claremont in August of 1956, I was surprised to learn that we were planning a different campus. The Building and Grounds Committee of the Board of Trustees, under the chairmanship of Raymond Hill, had prudently brought in the firm of Quinton Engineers, Inc., to present the board with master planning options for the campus. The initial campus was less than ideal because the laboratories our students would be using were on the opposite side of the Scripps College campus from the dormitories in which they would be housed and

1. An excellent account of the 1938 flood is given in *Pomona Today,* (Winter, 1988) by the late Professor John H. Kemble.

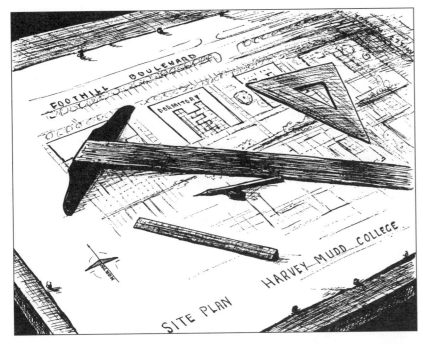

Christmas 1956: The first presidential greeting card from Harvey Mudd College. (The actual campus today bears very little resemblance to the site plan sketched here.)

because the vehicular traffic between colleges would need to use Foothill Boulevard, a busy thoroughfare, for access to Harvey Mudd College. These problems could be resolved if Harvey Mudd College were to exchange about half its acreage for an equivalent area then used for the athletic fields of Scripps College. The result would be to transform the Scripps campus from oblong to more nearly square, and to convert the Harvey Mudd campus from a long north-south axis to a long east-west axis; our dormitories and the present and proposed laboratories would be accessible without crossing the Scripps campus, and a newly created extension of Twelfth Street between campuses would give internal vehicular access.

Scripps College was quite willing to negotiate such an exchange, as long as their students were provided with equivalent playing fields, and Harvey Mudd College would replace the swimming pool it would gain in the trade. The Scripps College Board of Trustees designated its chairman, Irving C. Walker, a distinguished lawyer, as its representative, and the Harvey Mudd College board designated Robert P. Hastings. The negotiations were timely and amicable.[2] Land would be exchanged square foot for square foot, and the new portion of Twelfth Street separating the campuses would be curved to make the trade even. The building of the road would be the responsibility of Harvey Mudd College, as would the replacement of the portions of the Scripps College wall we inherited as the campus boundaries changed. We agreed to replace the swimming pool and to do the necessary grading and initial planting for new playing fields.

The remaining portion of the negotiations came later and did not

2. Robert P. Hastings writes: "If my memory serves me correctly this land exchange was indeed negotiated between Irving Walker and me. As I recollect, Irving asked me to make a rough draft of an agreement which I sent to him. Upon his receiving it he telephoned me that he would not have time to review it as he was leaving the next day for Europe, but since he and I had a complete oral understanding, it would make no difference and that, time being of the essence, Harvey Mudd College could act upon the assumption that it did indeed have title to the properties being exchanged to it by Scripps.

"As I remember, the critical time problem was that Harvey Mudd College had to enter into a construction agreement for a certain facility on the Scripps property, which I do not recall now (author's note: the swimming pool) before Irving returned from Europe.

"I cannot, at this time, be positive as to my recollection and unfortunately I do not have my Harvey Mudd College files for the year 1956. If my facts are indeed correct, here is another instance to prove the close cooperation and trust among The Claremont Colleges." (Private communication to J. B. Platt, March 25, 1991.)

Pitzer Hall North on Claremont Men's College campus—home to Harvey Mudd College's faculty, administration, and classes during the school's early years.

3. Dr. and Mrs. George E. Baxter were warm friends of The Claremont Colleges, and interested in furthering the Group Plan. Dr. Baxter, a retired physician, was a member of the Board of Fellows of Claremont College. It was the Baxters' hope to make possible common laboratories for Scripps and Claremont Men's College; they were doubly pleased to find they were helping to found the next college.

involve payment or construction. A feature of the Scripps campus area we would acquire was a double row of liquidambar (sweet gum) trees, framing (in clear weather) a magnificent view of Mount Baldy, as seen from certain Scripps College dormitories. I had solemnly to swear to Scripps alumnae representatives that we would not desecrate that grove nor offend a single elf therein. That row of liquidambars has been a beloved feature of the Harvey Mudd campus since, and neither alumnae nor alumni, of either college, would permit it to be tampered with now. I recall only one intercollegiate issue concerning the trees. Ernest Jaqua, the founding president of Scripps College, kept an eye on the area after his retirement to Claremont, and once suggested to me that the top of the northernmost tree in one column needed trimming. We trimmed it.

When the Platt family moved to Claremont in early September, 1956, the exchange was agreed upon in principle, and the details were rapidly being worked out. We had a street to build and walls on another campus to construct, but we still had our full share of rocks and chaparral, plus a swimming pool, some elegant liquidambars, and a number of other trees well worth keeping. Other than the bathhouse for the swimming pool, there were no college buildings.

The Harvey Mudd College trustees had determined it would require a year to appoint a faculty, recruit students, build any necessary buildings, and plan for subsequent years. Instruction would begin in September, 1957.

We were helped tremendously by being founded as one of the Claremont Colleges. Many of the facilities we would need were in place, and were available to us with no capital cost. The Honnold Library, then housing nearly a million volumes, was "our" library, shared with our sister colleges. We had a business office, a security force, a chaplaincy, and perhaps a dozen other shared services. I remember calculating that it would have required about $7 million in capital cost for Harvey Mudd College to provide equivalent facilities for itself. We did share in the operating costs for these services, generally on a per capita basis, so that our costs were small when our student body was small. (George Benson commented wryly that, in terms of dues, we had joined an expensive club.) We would need laboratory space as soon as we opened our doors. Fortunately, Claremont College had built Baxter Science Building to provide laboratory instruction for Scripps College and Claremont Men's College and we were welcome to share in its use.[3]

We were also helped tremendously by Claremont Men's College. Mr. and Mrs. Russell K. Pitzer had pledged Pitzer Hall North to CMC with the understanding that Harvey Mudd College could use it for ten years if needed. I had seen the plans. The building would provide all the classroom and office space we would require for a number of years, plus some laboratory space. Also CMC would be happy to feed our students in their dining facility, Collins Hall. CMC owned a nearby residence which could be rearranged to provide a president's home. We were welcome to share in the CMC admission office, and our students could be accommodated in the CMC physical education program, at that time combined with Pomona College. In short, along with moral support and many other services, CMC volunteered to provide most of our campus needs over our opening years.

OUR DORMITORIES

One need remained that our sister colleges could not provide. Harvey Mudd College would need its own dormitory when it opened its doors in 1957.

Building a dormitory was a major step for the new college for two reasons. First, if we were to have a dormitory ready when the first students arrived in September, 1957, we needed to decide how many students it should house, where it should stand, what we could afford to pay, and then find an architect and builder for a task that could easily take fifteen months. We had twelve months at most, in August, 1956, for the entire process. A second consideration, less urgent but more important, was that we build the right dormitory—that it fit the long-term plans for the full-sized college, that it be placed in the correct location with respect to the classrooms, dining facilities, laboratories, and offices to rise on our campus, and that the architectural style be one that we would be pleased to live with for a century or two.

Fortunately, the Building and Grounds Committee[4] of our Board of Trustees had begun to clarify these issues even before August, 1956. The study made by Quinton Engineers not only served as the basis for our property exchange with Scripps College, but it suggested that our laboratories should be on the western end of our campus, the dormitories on the east, with dining facilities near the dormitories and classrooms and offices near the laboratories. I had proposed to the board at its meeting in May of 1956 (the first following my appointment) that we plan in terms of a full-sized student body of some 350 students, essentially all of whom would live on campus. We could in due course accommodate such a student body in four dormitories each housing eighty-six students, and need only build as many as needed to accommodate earlier and smaller student bodies. Accordingly, one dormitory for eighty-six students was needed when we opened our doors.

Selecting an architect was a most important decision. Living on a well designed campus, functional and possessed of it own beauty, is part of the education of any student so fortunate. Such a campus requires first-rate architectural planning. Dr. Sprague, in particular, insisted that the college secure an excellent architect. The committee considered the possibility of an international architectural competition. There were two

4. As of June, 1956, the Building and Grounds Committee consisted of Raymond A. Hill, Chairman, Garner A. Beckett, Robert J. Bernard, Mrs. Harvey S. Mudd, Dr. Norman F. Sprague, Jr., and Ford J. Twaits.

Campus architect, Edward Durell Stone

problems: The time schedule did not permit the months that would be required for the competition, and noted architectural firms might not be interested in competing for the design of one small dormitory, with other buildings to follow on indefinite scheduling and financing.

Ford Twaits and Garner Beckett, who knew the construction industry in Southern California thoroughly, came up with a solution which has served Harvey Mudd College well. Both knew and respected Earl Heitschmidt, a Los Angeles architect of ability and imagination who also had a record, as an institutional architect, of wasting no money whatsoever. He really knew how to give clients value for their money. He collaborated, from time to time, with his M.I.T. classmate and good friend Edward Durell Stone, then internationally famous for designing the United States' Embassy in New Delhi, India, the Stanford Medical Center, and dozens of other notable architectural treasures. Stone and Heitschmidt had most recently collaborated on the design of the United States exhibit at the Brussels World's Fair. Would Earl Heitschmidt be interested in our campus, and would he invite his friend Ed Stone to collaborate with him?

Earl Heitschmidt would and did. On August 1, 1956, Dr. Sprague recommended on behalf of the Building and Grounds Committee, and the board authorized, a contract with the team of Stone and Heitschmidt. The two architects (and their firms) designed not only the first dormitory but nearly all the buildings constructed at Harvey Mudd College during our first twenty years. Much of the conceptual design, including the external architectural style and the disposition of space, is clearly in the Stone tradition. The architectural detail, and much of the engineering design, is primarily Heitschmidt, although the two knew and understood each other so thoroughly that I cannot clearly separate who did what.

Accordingly, at the October 18 meeting of the Board of Trustees, Dr. Sprague was able to report that our (as yet unauthorized) architects had proposed a possible master plan for the campus; the board agreed that the plan had merit and authorized the architectural contract with the firms of Edward Stone and of Earl Heitschmidt. Mrs. Mudd reported that she, as board chairman, had transmitted a letter to the Scripps College trustees proposing an exchange of properties, that the Scripps board had responded with agreement in principle, and that the two boards needed a joint committee to work out the terms of the transfer. The Harvey Mudd College board voted our portion of such a committee. Robert J. Bernard reported that one piece of private property remained on the proposed Harvey Mudd campus, and that he had been unable to secure it within the price authorized by the board. The board voted a modest increase in authorization.

In short, the college was well on its way toward constructing its present campus. While I had been kept informed of the developments of the prior five months, I had been in Claremont as president for six weeks. I was impressed; here was a board whose members got things done.

Three weeks later, following more activity by the Building and Grounds Committee and the joint committee of the two boards, I was able to report that the details of the campus property exchange were nearing mutual agreement; that the City of Claremont was sympathetic to the plan and would consider abandoning Amherst Avenue, the road we would no longer need, if we would complete the new road between campuses adequately; and that the conceptual design of the first dormitory was in hand. It was our hope that construction could begin in January.

The conceptual design of the dormitory had been considerably advanced at a meeting of the Building and Grounds Committee a week earlier, which I had attended. The architects presented a basic design and an external rendering for the building: a two-story, U-shaped building formed around an open courtyard; a basic living unit of a room for two students, opening out-of-doors, with adjacent rooms sharing a common bath; and a large lounge, plus storage rooms and a laundry. It was a well thought out, livable, and economical design. The rendering of the exterior carried a number of features of the United States Embassy in New Delhi—a pierced curtain wall completely around the building, hanging planters, and a reflecting pool with fountain in the courtyard. Ford Twaits looked at Garner Beckett. "Looks like a hot sheet Las Vegas motel," Garner observed. Out went the hanging planters, the reflecting pool, and all of the curtain wall except that which defined the courtyard. The result was a simple and attractive building that has served our students well.

At the December meeting of the Harvey Mudd College board, Mr. Hill reported that it would take at least another six weeks to complete detailed plans for the dormitory, hold a bid competition, and select a contractor. He also reported that Ford J. Twaits had volunteered to construct the building on a cost-plus-fixed-fee basis, with guaranteed maximum and to begin ordering necessary materials before detailed plans were in hand. The board voted to accept this helpful offer, noting that this action was not to be taken as a precedent with respect to competitive bidding. The board also allocated a portion of the gifts from Mrs. Mudd to cover the costs of construction.

The board met on April 10, 1957, on the Claremont Men's College campus. Prior to the board meeting most of its members had attended a ceremony on the Harvey Mudd College campus, a portion of which had been graded. The dormitory was under construction. The Ford J. Twaits Company was using a new technique known as "lift slab" in which the steel supporting columns for the second floor and roof were first put in place, then the base concrete slab poured. A day later a coat of oil was washed over the slab, and another slab (to become the second floor) was

Ann Platt, age nine, and Beth Platt, age one, keep track of progress on the first building of Harvey Mudd College.

An example of the "lift slab"
technique, Mildred Mudd Hall.

poured on it. Another day, another coat of oil, and the roof slab was poured. When all three slabs were properly cured, up went the roof and the second floor into place. The walls could then be added. The building was at this unwalled state when we held the ceremony.

Mrs. Mudd laid the cornerstone for the first building on the Harvey Mudd College campus. The Rev. W. Robert Rankin, chaplain of the Claremont Colleges, presided at the dedication. By action of the Board of Trustees two decades later the building bears the name of Mildred E. Mudd.

The Ford J. Twaits Company had the dormitory ready the following September for the first entering class, despite general Southern California strikes by the plumbers and hod carriers unions, which caused a month's delay. When the freshmen arrived, Twelfth Street and a parking lot were completed (conditions the City of Claremont had required for an occupancy permit). The area around the dormitory was graded, but not planted. Some painting was still in progress, and furniture was arriving. Harvey Mudd College had the campus it then needed.

More dormitories followed, on a somewhat more relaxed schedule. Our first entering class consisted of forty-eight students, leaving a number of our dormitory rooms available the first year for a library and for faculty offices. We did not, however, have space enough for two classes, so we would need a second dormitory the following year. With the small classes we were then admitting, the two dormitories might provide enough space for three classes. A generous gift from the Seeley W. Mudd Foundation in the fall of 1957 provided funds to make possible two additional dormitories. We now had architects, a basic plan, and time for competitive bids. Accordingly, the second dormitory was (nearly) ready for use in September, 1958, and a third dormitory was occupied in September,

Mr. and Mrs. Garner donating a
sycamore sapling from their Padua
Hills property to the courtyard of
Mildred E. Mudd Hall, March
1958.

Cornerstone laying, first building (now Mildred E. Mudd Hall). From left: Carl Wittenberg, builder; Joseph B. Platt; Reverend Robert Rankin, chaplain of the Claremont Colleges; Mildred E. Mudd; and Robert J. Bernard.

1959. We had found that any excess dormitory space available could be used by students of our sister colleges, also growing in size, enabling them to house fewer students "off campus," producing income for Harvey Mudd College, and also leading to many intercollege friendships.

Mildred E. Mudd Hall at the time of the college's opening, September 1957.

THE PRESIDENT'S HOUSE

Both the college and the Platt family benefited from a small miracle in the fall of 1957.

When we arrived in September, 1956, we moved into the major portion of a good-sized house owned by Claremont Men's College. This house, which had been a substantial private residence, had been split into six apartments of varying sizes, and three of these apartments had been rented for us. Accordingly, we had the living room, study, kitchen, dining room and two bedrooms of a large private home. The assistant chaplain of the Claremont Colleges and his wife had the upstairs apartment (converted from a large bedroom) which separated our bedroom from that of our elder daughter. There was a psychology laboratory downstairs in what had been a second parlor, and another small downstairs apartment was rented by a graduate student. We shared the entrance hall with the psychology laboratory and the chaplain's apartment.

This arrangement served us well. The living room and dining room were large enough to entertain students, faculty, and parents. We and our fellow tenants were rarely in each others' way. To all immediate appearance, we were the sole occupants of a sizeable and appropriately furnished president's home.

We were visited there one Friday afternoon by Leroy Garrett, who as counsel for the college and also chairman of our Ways and Means Committee had responsibilities that brought him to Claremont. He and his wife, Marian, had been generous with the college and had established the Garrett Fund, for purposes yet to be designated. We enjoyed glasses of iced tea and discussed college matters. He observed that he had been

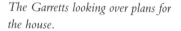

The Garretts looking over plans for the house.

concerned about our living arrangement but found the house comfortable and attractive—and, while he realized that we shared the house, we did have our own entrance. We agreed that we were well situated. As he picked up his hat in the entrance hall to leave, the door opened and in burst three undergraduate couples coming for dinner with the chaplain and his wife. Up the stairs they charged, with never a word to the three of us. Roy Garrett retrieved his hat, said, "Well!" and left.

The president's house

(The only undergraduate couple in the group that I recognized were later married. President Jack Stark and his wife, Jill, of Claremont McKenna College, showed an early talent for masterly timing.)

The next Monday morning I was informed that the Garrett Fund was to be augmented and used to build a president's house on campus and that the Building and Grounds Committee should begin the appropriate planning.

A president's house on campus was not high on my priority list at that time in the life of the college, but I was wrong. Every student to enter Harvey Mudd College during its first twenty years was invited for dinner at least once, and nearly all came. Trustees, townspeople, donors and potential donors, and visiting dignitaries came to the house. Having a gracious place for college entertaining was even more important in the early life of the college, when we had little else, than it was later. That house has returned its cost to the college manyfold in terms of gifts raised, and also it has brought to our students, faculty, and friends a sense of belonging we could not otherwise have found. Finally, three presidential families have found it a friendly and happy place to live. Roy and Marian Garrett understood these things far better than I.

The design of the president's house did not proceed without incident. The first concept came from Edward Durell Stone, who suggested a two-story home with a magnificent circular staircase. It was a dramatic design, but half the volume of the house was committed to the staircase. Roy Garrett looked at it and decided it was time to find an architect specializing in residences. Henry Eggers was selected, a Los Angeles architect with a happy combination of excellent aesthetic taste and insight into the ways space can be used in a home. We were very pleased with the house he designed.

Accordingly, in September, 1959, the Platt family moved into the new president's house, as yet unlandscaped. We had the joy, for the next seventeen years, of watching the surroundings and the college grow. We also had the joy of watching our two daughters grow into womanhood there. Our early classes remember our daughter Beth, as a kindergartner, pedaling across the campus on her toy tractor, and later classes remember our grandsons, Ann's children, on the same toy tractor. Jean's mother and father visited often and helped develop our garden. My father and stepmother, as guests, shared our excitement with our home and our college. Many other happy family memories come to mind. It is true that the president's house has served Harvey Mudd College well; it also served the Platts very well, including our cat Sassafras and our two tortoises, Dante and Explorer.

THE SCIENCE BUILDING

Thus far I have reported on the buildings we had funds to construct. We had a more challenging task with our first unfunded construction: the Science Building.

At the time Harvey Mudd College opened its doors we knew we had laboratory space available from our sister colleges that would accommodate our freshmen and sophomores. We also knew we would need laboratories of our own two years later. Since all Harvey Mudd students, whether their intended academic majors were in chemistry, engineering, mathematics, or physics, had identical laboratory programs for their first two years, we could use a few laboratories quite intensively. Harvey Mudd College did tax the facilities of the joint Claremont Colleges laboratory building quite heavily from the beginning of instruction. By the time our first students were juniors, however, we would need separate laboratories for chemists, engineers, and physicists. There was no conceivable way Claremont College, Claremont Men's College, and Scripps College could provide these; they had no such laboratories nor the space in which they could be placed.

Accordingly, plans were explored for the "science building" in the fall of 1957, and in February, 1958, the architect was authorized to proceed to final drawings. The total cost of the building was then estimated at $940,000, and another $200,000 was estimated as the cost of initial laboratory equipment. We had no notion where these funds were to be found.

Our task was made more complicated, and also made much more possible, by the interest and help of Claremont College on behalf of the Claremont Colleges. Each of our sister undergraduate colleges expected to need more laboratory space as the sciences became more important in undergraduate instruction. Some years before Harvey Mudd College was established, the Board of Fellows of Claremont College, aware of this growing need, had considered building common laboratory facilities to serve all colleges requiring them. The Cavendish Laboratory at Cambridge University in England, in which much of the experimental foundations were laid for our present knowledge of the atom and the nucleus, serves this function for the Cambridge colleges. Pomona College was at that time planning to expand its laboratory facilities, and the Board of Fellows proposed common planning and pooling of resources to centralize laboratories, just as the Claremont Colleges have a common library system. Pomona College in due course decided not to join a common effort. Claremont College, on behalf of Claremont Men's College and Scripps College, then secured the funds for the Baxter Science Building and built it on a central location belonging to Claremont College. At the time Harvey Mudd College was founded, laboratory instruction for these two sister colleges was offered in Baxter Science Building, and Harvey Mudd College had the good fortune to be invited to share in its use.

Claremont College thus had an interest in the Science Building we knew we needed. With forethought, it could be planned to serve more than one college. Accordingly, Claremont College had reserved a portion of its campus, adjacent to the west end of the Harvey Mudd College campus, for more laboratories. Indeed, the availability of this laboratory space was a reason for the campus property exchange we had had with Scripps College. Claremont College volunteered to provide the land without cost, provided that the plans be drawn and the building constructed under the joint supervision of the building committees of Claremont College and Harvey Mudd College, that Harvey Mudd College be responsible for funding the construction but that Claremont College had the right to contribute, and that if there were use of laboratory space by other colleges, the cost of maintenance would be divided according to use.[5] As of February, 1958, we still didn't know how we would fund the building, but we had plans, land, and a formal agreement covering possible use by other colleges.

As of July 2, 1958, we knew we needed to start construction in September to have the building available (if all went well) by September, 1959, a year later, when those students who needed laboratories would be entering their junior year. A frantic summer of fundraising followed. The board, acting as a committee of the whole, met eight times to assign solicitations of individuals, corporations, and foundations; by summer's end many such calls had been made by trustees. The Buildings and

5. As I write in 1990, the concept of joint laboratory facilities seems to me to have been a limited success. Claremont McKenna College, Scripps College and Pitzer College have established a joint sciences program serving all three student bodies. This program is clearly successful, and the demand for its services is rising. In accordance with the hope for shared facilities, the Joint Sciences building was constructed on Claremont College property, across the street from the Harvey Mudd College Science Building. No laboratories have been shared with Harvey Mudd College. There are many shared

seminars, some collaborative research, and students from one college enroll in laboratory courses in another, but these forms of sharing also occur with Pomona College, six blocks away. The Joint Sciences building is to be replaced with a larger building which will be located centrally for Claremont McKenna College, Scripps College, and Pitzer College, without reference to laboratory facilities at Pomona College or Harvey Mudd College. However the concept of shared laboratories may have developed, Claremont College provided Harvey Mudd College with the land for its laboratories, made it possible to fund the first laboratory building by borrowing when Harvey Mudd College had little visible collateral, and gave us a lecture hall!

Grounds Committee of the board reviewed several cost-cutting options: build the shell of the building, deferring until later the finishing of any space not immediately needed; build another dormitory and use it temporarily as a laboratory building; build and use a one story "warehouse" until funds could be found for a laboratory building. The conclusion was to build the shell of the building because the other options required too much in conversion costs. It appeared that the shell could be built for less than $800,000. On September 17 the board noted that $210,000 would be available, due primarily to a trust set up by Henry T. Mudd, and that commitments were probable from others. The Citizens Bank had agreed to loan up to $300,000 to Claremont College at prime rate, unsecured, and the same amount on the same terms to Harvey Mudd College. The board agreed with Claremont College that the two loans would be paid down equally, dollar for dollar, by Harvey Mudd College. The board voted to instruct its officers to enter into a construction contract with the firm of Secrest and Fish.

The next week the faculty and students of Harvey Mudd College held a ground-clearing picnic on the site of the new building and joyfully cleared away underbrush and loose boulders to make way for the foundation. At the board meeting of November 19, 1958, I was able to report that the contract had been executed and construction was under way.

A collection of strikes in the construction trades and some bad weather delayed the completion of the Science Building until December, 1959. Equipment was set up and experiments performed out of doors and in hallways of other buildings throughout that first semester. We felt secure in the knowledge that "real laboratories" were nearly ready. Indeed we were using the laboratory rooms planned for immediate use as soon as the paint was dry. Other rooms had neither paint nor plumbing. There was an elevator shaft, but no elevator. The exterior was unpainted concrete. The air conditioning system would come when we could afford it. A lecture hall designed for scientific demonstrations was on our "not now" list. To our surprise and delight, Claremont College added that hall at its cost as a contribution to our common effort.

The building may not have been on schedule, but it was completed under budget. We were able to pay off the loans ahead of schedule. Even as of June, 1959, we had made a beginning on reducing both loans—of course, "dollar for dollar."

As I write in 1990, that building has been completed, rebuilt, improved, and substantially enlarged. It is now the Jacobs Science Building, thanks to the generosity of Dr. and Mrs. Joseph J. Jacobs and their daughters. The core is still the one that gladdened our hearts in 1959. The building has brought "hands on" learning experience to 2,500 engineers and scientists, and contained much research over these years.

Raymond Hill resigned as chairman of the Buildings and Grounds Committee in the summer of 1960. The board noted that "Mr. Hill had planned the present arrangement of our campus and had participated in the selection of architects; that he had guided the decisions on building needs, scheduling, and function, and that the present and ultimate appearance of our campus will have been shaped largely by his judgment and wisdom." Reviewing this assessment thirty years later, I thoroughly agree.

He was succeeded as chairman by William B. Coberly, Jr., who served the college well in the next phase of its campus development, which required sensitivity to the hopes and expectations of donors as well as to the needs of the college. A patient and respected businessman with good design instincts, excellent taste, and a delightful sense of humor, Bill kept a common vision before us when it was not clear how we would get on with the development of our campus.

LANDSCAPING

When the college had selected its building architects, the firm of Cornell, Bridgers and Troller had also been selected as landscape architects. They had, in fact, had little to do over the opening years of the college because there were other needs more pressing than landscaping. Areas immediately around the buildings were graded and planted to grass. Our students were accustomed, during our first two years of classes, to hiking over rocks between buildings.

These students appreciated that the college needed help with campus clearing and landscaping. The first freshman class, before instruction began, spent an afternoon clearing the center strip of the new section of Twelfth Street. (Part of the motivation may have been to make our campus more attractive to the young women of Scripps College.) Later that year our students approached Mr. and Mrs. Garner, then the owners of the Padua Hills property, who contributed several sycamore trees; the students transplanted them to the courtyard of the initial dormitory. (These sycamores graced the area from which Garner Beckett had removed the proposed reflecting pool.) When the third dormitory was approved, an old barn stood on part of the required plot; student volunteers removed it. As our first class graduated, its members presented the college with another tree as their class gift. In short, our early faculty and students did improve our landscaping, without professional direction.

There were portions of the campus that did not yet need grading or planting. The several houses purchased from private owners were habitable and in most cases attractive. Those that were rented were continued with the same tenants if the tenants chose; three or four houses were rented to faculty families who understood that the growth of the college might force them to move elsewhere. In the meantime, those faculty families never lacked opportunity to invite students for dinner, a frequent occurrence.

However, much of the campus remained as we found it: rocks and chaparral, with an occasional native tree to add stature to the landscape. This was the state of affairs when the college was the beneficiary of a second unsolicited minor miracle.

Victoria Mudd (Mrs. Henry T. Mudd), who understood landscaping, made three major contributions. The first was that she set up a personal trust with income sufficient to make regular progress in landscaping and designated its income for that purpose. Secondly, she knew Thomas Church, a distinguished San Francisco landscape planner, and persuaded him to help under the same consulting arrangement between him and Cornell, Bridgers and Troller that we had found to work so well with Stone and Heitschmidt. Thirdly, she and Marian Garrett took a personal interest in seeing to it that our native live oaks and sycamores were preserved wherever possible, that the landscaping was generally simple, easily maintained, and effective, and that the campus developed a pervasive sense of natural beauty. We owe Vicki Mudd, Tommy Church, and the team they enlisted a major debt of gratitude.

Dedicating their gift in commemoration of the first HMC commencement: Peter Loeb '59 digs some dirt for the planting of a tree while Stuart Black '59 and Joseph B. Platt look on.

Office and Classroom Buildings

As of December, 1959, four years after Harvey Mudd College was chartered and in the third year of instruction, the campus buildings consisted of three dormitories, a president's house, a laboratory building, and the former Scripps College swimming pool. Our classes were held in Pitzer Hall North of the Claremont Men's College campus, which also contained most of our faculty and administrative offices. Our students had their meals at Collins Hall, also on the CMC campus. CMC, which was a generous host indeed, had plans to increase its own student body as space and finances would permit.

Accordingly the Board of Trustees of Harvey Mudd College had asked our architects to study possible building arrangements for classroom and office space. After consultation with faculty and staff, and working with the trustee Buildings and Grounds Committee, Heitschmidt and Stone proposed two U-shaped buildings facing each other, each two stories high, carrying the same distinguishing architectural features as our dormitories: flat roofs, open courts, integral color block walls with the characteristic fascia.

At the December meeting of the board in 1959 Dr. Sprague announced, on behalf of the Mudd family, that the Harvey S. and Mildred E. Mudd Foundation would provide $300,000, subject to matching, to attract gifts either to endowment or to building needs. Mrs. Frederick Kingston, Victoria Mudd's mother, announced the following February that she would provide $150,000, which, with matching funds, would make possible the office building, to be named for her late husband. The following July, Mr. and Mrs. Leroy A. Garrett also pledged $150,000 to make possible the classroom building, to be named for their parents, Mr. and Mrs. Ray Thomas and Mr. and Mrs. Ray M. Garrett. The architectural plans for the two buildings were complete in the fall of 1960, and both buildings were occupied in September 1961.

It was with a real sense of "coming of age" that our faculty and administration moved to the Harvey Mudd campus. We had thoroughly appreciated the privilege of living with relatives, but it is a joy to have a house of one's own. Trustees, faculty, and students dedicated these two buildings with a sense of homecoming that I still feel these thirty years later.

The courtyard of Thomas-Garrett Hall, at the time of dedication, had a good-sized olive tree as its centerpiece—the same one that graces it now in the 1990s. The tree had been planted before the courtyard was completed with the covered walkway that closes the U. When Kingston Hall was dedicated, the courtyard was pleasantly landscaped but there was no similar tree; that would have gone over budget. One of our trustees, not yet a donor to either building, felt an appropriate tree really belonged in the Kingston Hall courtyard and provided the funds necessary. The prob-

"Only God can make one, but we can fly it"—a student's comment when a specimen olive tree, not included in the initial funding, was added to the site plan and lowered into place.

lem was that there was no longer a way to move the tree into the court-yard. That problem was solved when the landscape contractor appeared with a huge crane that lifted a good-sized specimen tree over the building and deposited it in the courtyard, to the cheers of the entire student body. Student comment: "Only God can make one, but we can fly it."

THE CAMPUS CENTER

During the first five years of instruction, students at Harvey Mudd College had their meals at Collins Hall, a Claremont Mens' College facility. Indeed, CMC enlarged Collins Hall primarily on our behalf, with the expectation that by the time we had our own dining facility the CMC student body would have grown and would ultimately require the added space. The Harvey Mudd College board in 1958 thanked President Benson for this helpful arrangement and noted that it saw no prospect that we would have our own dining facility before 1962.

Our students would, of course, have welcomed having their meals on our own campus but were remarkably forbearing about the economies needed to start a new college—happily taking pride in their part in the building of the campus. But, by the time the campus included three dormitories, a president's house, a laboratory building, a classroom building, and an office building, it seemed clear to all of us that it would be useful to have a place of our own in which to eat.

My own intention had been to propose the building of a simple structure—a "mess hall"—in the early half of the 1960s. There was some hope of obtaining a federal low-interest loan to help finance the structure, and the income from student dining could help to service the debt.

Two circumstances raised my sights considerably. The first was that we had had much larger attrition than expected in the Class of 1962. I will report in another chapter about the multiple reasons we discovered for the loss before graduation of more than half of this class. We were clearly concerned, and greatly helped in understanding our problems by Paul Heist, a social psychologist from the Center for the Study of Higher Education of the University of California. Paul spent a substantial amount of time with our students, both in formal testing and in informal visits. He reported that some students were indeed proud of building a college, but many considered the college a workhouse from which the joys of the flesh and the spirit were systematically excluded. He urged that we build not only a dining hall but a real student union with recreational space, rooms for student government, a browsing library, to include but not be dominated by dining facilities. The trustees and the faculty paid attention to his recommendation.

The second encouragement came from the success of a new support organization: The Founding Friends of Harvey Mudd College, of which I will also have more to say elsewhere. In particular, a group of these new friends, including Charles W. Lee and Holmes Tuttle, were quite hopeful that much of the funding for the proposed building could be raised from persons not previously substantial donors to the college.

The Board of Trustees had voted on October 18, 1961, to begin the architectural study of the proposed student union. A loan application was submitted to the Community Facilities Agency for $696,000 in a thirty-year loan at 3.5 percent interest per annum, the board certifying that the college had credit or cash for another $290,000 in project costs. (In subsequent negotiation, the loan request became $810,000 with $100,000 cash certified.) On June 11, 1962, the board learned that the Community Facilities Agency had authorized the loan. The board voted to proceed with construction of the student union as a whole, not simply the dining portion of the building. Bids were opened on August 14, 1962, and the construction contract awarded to the James I. Barnes Construction Co., at a figure a bit under budget. Ground was broken on September 24,

1962. Construction was interrupted by strikes in two of the building trades, but a good portion of the building was usable by the opening of classes in September, 1963.

The student union was designed as a U-shaped building, facing the axis of the campus, but larger than the dormitories, Kingston Hall, or Thomas-Garrett Hall. It is essentially a two-story building with one story below grade; the lounges, recreation rooms, snack bar, mailroom, and similar student services are primarily on the lower floor, and the dining room, kitchen, large meeting room, student government offices, and other student services are on the floor at ground level.

I was surprised to learn, when it came time to arrange the dedication of the building at commencement time in 1963, that the board had determined to name the building the Joseph B. Platt Campus Center. Mr. Charles W. Lee had secured the permission of the board to solicit pledges on the building with this understanding and had done so. The board had not only accorded me this unexpected honor but wanted to know how the Platt family wished the dedication planned. Accordingly, the speaker at the dedication was Lee A. DuBridge, then president of the California Institute of Technology, who previously had hired me for my first teaching appointment at the University of Rochester and subsequently again hired me to work in radar at the Radiation Laboratory of the Massachusetts Institute of Technology. The minister who presided over the dedication was my cousin, Robert H. Beaven, chaplain of the University of Rochester. My wife's parents, my father and stepmother, and our daughters were present. Furthermore, we were surrounded by faculty, students, trustees, and donors who by then seemed to us an extended family.

At the June 8, 1964, meeting of the Board of Trustees, Charlie Lee could report that the Platt Campus Center program had pledges and payments totaling $612,000 and was seeking the remainder. I was impressed as well as honored.

THE FIRST TEN YEARS

The tenth anniversary of the founding of Harvey Mudd College came on December 14, 1965. The college could celebrate the occasion on its own campus: dormitories, a student union, classrooms, laboratories, offices for faculty and staff, and a president's house. More buildings would come, but we had our basic needs for a college of 300 students that was well-designed, well-landscaped, and functional. We had every reason to be proud and grateful.

Jean and Joseph Platt on the day of the dedication of the Platt Campus Center.

CHAPTER 5

The Faculty and Staff

A COLLEGE requires a faculty. Indeed, to a considerable extent, a college is its faculty. Good faculty members attract good students, and the combination attracts more of each. Accordingly, the Board of Trustees encouraged me to recruit the best available faculty members to begin our teaching at Harvey Mudd College.

What faculty members would we need when we opened our doors for instruction?

The answer was inherent in the idea of the college and in our plan to start with a limited number of freshmen and add a class each subsequent year. We were founding an engineering college in which all students would have a solid foundation in the basic sciences and mathematics and in which substantial emphasis would be placed on the humanities and social sciences. A number of representative curricula were given in *The Goals of Engineering Education*, mentioned in Chapter 2. Our freshmen would need instruction in mathematics and English, two essential tools of communication. They would also need a foundation in physics and chemistry as prerequisites for later work in the engineering sciences. It would also be useful to teach them some of the other essential tools of engineering: graphical representation, how one analyzes the components of a system, and perhaps some computational skills.

The Board of Trustees, which has final authority for faculty appointments, asked for my recommendation on the number, fields, and experience of the faculty we would need to begin instruction. I responded generally as suggested above. Not surprisingly, the members of the board had ideas too. I felt strongly that English—composition, writing, and public speaking—should have early and continued emphasis. Mr. Wig thoroughly agreed and added the importance of economics to engineering.

We soon found it would not be difficult to fill five years with subject matter every engineer or scientist should know.

After discussion we decided to use a four-year format, with the possibility of a fifth year for those who chose. The program we sketched that day required all students to have two years of basic science, mathematics, English, and history, leaving concentration in specific fields until the junior and senior years. More electives in the humanities and social sciences would be available at the upper class level as well. We were not too far from the four quadrants of Raymond Hill's educational model.

Accordingly I proposed, and the board agreed, that we appoint faculty members in English literature, mathematics, physics, and chemistry. We also agreed it would be desirable to appoint a senior engineering faculty member, even though most of the engineering teaching would come after the second year. We needed the advice of an engineer in planning other courses, and a good engineer might be able to help teach physics, mathematics, or English literature as well.

OUR FOUNDING FACULTY AND STAFF

I was eager to have on our initial faculty several "old hands"—persons who had taught for a number of years and were known to be excellent teachers; mentors who had learned elsewhere what needed doing at the beginning of an engineering education and what could be deferred until the student was well grounded in the fundamentals. It was of course necessary to have a general idea of the entire four years of the curriculum to know where to start, but the details could best be worked out once a knowledgable faculty could exchange ideas. The college was planned as a teaching institution, not a research institute, but I knew from personal experience that research can assist teaching by keeping the faculty interested in new developments and by involving able students with problems for which the answers are not yet known. Hence, I hoped for teachers with continuing interests in research and scholarship.

One other characteristic which I wanted was open-mindedness, flexibility, and the willingness to explore new methods of teaching. I needn't have concerned myself. I soon learned that anyone leaving a good job in an established university or college to help found a new college with an uncertain future—any such person was a risktaker. Everyone I met while recruiting faculty was interested in our venture and volunteered useful advice. The relative few who were also willing to leave secure positions in respected institutions to explore the luck of Harvey Mudd College were venturesome idealists. These were just what we needed.

How did I set about trying to find our initial faculty?

The first step was to ask knowledgable deans and department chairmen for nominations. Once these were in hand, I got in touch with the nominees—usually by telephone, followed by letter—to explore interest.

From this came a list of possible appointees, which I ordered and reordered as more correspondence and telephoning made us better acquainted. Then came interviews; I traveled to the nominees, spoke to them and (with their permission) to their students and colleagues. The remaining task was to persuade the candidate to come, which, for those unacquainted with the Claremont Colleges, involved visiting to see what was here and to meet with trustees or faculty of other colleges. If, after all this, we were mutually convinced that we fit, there came a formal offer, authorized by the board, and an acceptance.

At least, that was the plan that worked for much of the initial faculty. The others had heard of the new college, sought us out, and then we found a fit. We had some excellent "volunteers."

We were very fortunate in our first appointment: Professor J. Arthur Campbell. Art was nominated by Kenneth S. Pitzer, then dean of chemistry at the University of California, Berkeley.[1] Art had his doctorate in chemistry from Berkeley and had taught there before moving to Oberlin College. At the time we met he was full professor at Oberlin, on leave for a year to the National Science Foundation to direct its Program of Institutes. He knew the Claremont Colleges well, and I had learned that he was nationally respected as a chemist and teacher of chemists. Our first real visit was in Washington, D.C., where Dottie and Art invited me for dinner at their home. I knew in short order that we wanted the Campbells at Harvey Mudd College. Fortunately for us, the Campbells agreed.

Art was appointed professor of chemistry and chairman of the Department of Chemistry, which at the time consisted of him. Over subsequent years he built a distinguished department, taught many students who have gone on to first-rate careers as academic or industrial chemists, and is remembered by all our students, chemists or not, with respect and affection. The Manufacturing Chemists' Association designated him as an outstanding teacher of chemistry in the nation. He directed the CHEM Study, which upgraded the teaching of high school chemistry nationally. He also did whatever other tasks the college needed—student advising, the reorganization of freshman teaching methods, representing our programs to potential donors—with ability, great good humor, and vim. Of his many contributions to the college, he took particular satisfaction from the part he had played in leading our first students to adopt a constitution for their student government, and to adopt an honor system. Dottie Campbell baked I know not how many cookies for student parties, organized faculty wives to serve as hostesses at numerous commencements, and much else. I repeat: We were very fortunate in our first faculty appointment—really, our first faculty family appointment.

Our next appointment was Robert C. James, as professor of mathematics and department chairman. Bob was nominated by Herman H.

1. The reader may recall from Chapter 1 that Kenneth Pitzer had nominated Art Campbell and me as candidates for the presidency of Harvey Mudd College. Art declined consideration for that appointment, but wrote Ken Pitzer that he might be interested in the department chairmanship in chemistry, when and if that became available. Fortunately for the College, Ken remembered this comment when I asked him for candidates for our first appointment in chemistry. (Private communication, K.S. Pitzer to J. B. Platt, April 1991.)

Goldstine, a mathematician at the Institute for Advanced Study, where Bob had been invited to spend a sabbatical year. A Caltech Ph.D. in mathematics, Bob had subsequently taught at Harvard (as a Benjamin Pierce Fellow) and then at Berkeley before joining the faculty of Haverford College. He had done his undergraduate work at the University of California, Los Angeles, where his father had been professor of mathematics. Father and son were co-authors of *A Mathematics Dictionary,* which was then and is now a standard reference. Bob, a committed Quaker, was and is an excellent research mathematician who believes in the importance of teaching. He and his wife, Edith, decided that they could contribute to our new college—as they certainly did—and stoically turned down the expected year at the Institute for Advanced Study. We count among our graduates many able mathematicians in industry or academic life, and all of our alumni and alumnae have earned a sound basis in mathematics taught in the department that Bob founded. Bob served as our "senior mathematician" for ten years, resigning in August, 1967, to become chairman of the Department of Mathematics at the Albany campus of the State University of New York.

Our next appointment was a "drop in:" William H. Davenport, then chairman of the Department of English at the University of Southern California. Bill Davenport, a Dartmouth undergraduate and Yale Ph.D., had taught at Carnegie Institute of Technology before coming West, and, during World War II, had combined a full-time job at USC with teaching English courses and editing technical manuals at the California Institute of Technology. (He pointed out that this made an eighty-hour week.) How did he hear of Harvey Mudd College? In his words, "During Christmas vacation, 1956, my friend Paul Bowerman of the Caltech faculty dropped in to chew the fat and have a beer; during the course of the small talk he let on as how Harvey Mudd College was looking for somebody in English and that the gossip was that they were paying full professors between $10,000 and $15,000. I got on the phone to Joe Platt, who suggested an interview the next morning. We talked about two hours, Joe went on the road, I thrashed around for a few weeks, trying to weigh a chairmanship in a large university, tenure, a sabbatical, nineteen years' service to one institution, against a new school, Claremont, intellectual climate, and a decent faculty-trustee-student relationship—and decided to plunge, when, as, and if. Joe returned, laid it on the line, and the rest you know. Incidentally, the yarn about salary turned out to be just that, a yarn."[2]

The next "drop in" was George C. Wickes, then on the faculty in English at Duke University. George grew up in a French-speaking family, his mother a Belgian and his father a United States national. He earned his baccalaureate in philosophy from the University of Toronto and spent the years 1943-46 in the Army assigned to the Office of Strategic

2. Quoted from George Wickes' *The Harvey Mudd College Diary: September 20, 1957 -June 12, 1959,* Saturday, March 1, 1958.

Services, where he added Vietnamese to his languages and then spent a year in Vietnam in intelligence work. He earned his doctorate at the University of California, Berkeley, and he earned part of his doctoral support by working for the Fulbright program in Brussels. He had accepted a three-year terminal appointment at Duke and was seeking a teaching appointment on the West Coast. He visited Claremont and had interviewed at two of our sister colleges when another English professor remarked, "Say, there's a guy down the hall who is starting up a new college; maybe you ought to talk to him."[3] As it turned out, his department chairman at Duke had been a student of Bill Davenport's, whom Bill consulted promptly, to learn that the Duke Department of English would try their best to keep George. We, too, were much impressed, and fortunately George Wickes joined us, remaining until 1970, when he resigned to become University Professor of English at the University of Oregon.

3. Ibid.

I had asked Robert F. Bacher, then provost at the California Institute of Technology, for nominations, particularly in physics. He suggested Graydon D. Bell, a post-doctoral research fellow at Caltech. Gray had taken his baccalaureate degree in physics at the University of Kentucky and had taught for two years at Robert College in Istanbul, Turkey, before completing his doctorate at Caltech. As it happened, Paul Routly, one of Gray's friends on the Pomona faculty, had also suggested to him that Harvey Mudd College could be worth exploring. Accordingly, when we met, our searches were converging. Gray agreed to come. Caltech not only helped us find him but volunteered to let him continue his research program while using his apparatus at Caltech—accordingly, the first research program in physics to start at Harvey Mudd College was Gray's work in astrophysics.

The introductory course in chemistry would require several laboratory and recitation sections as well as lectures, and a similar situation existed in physics. Clearly we would need two faculty members in each discipline when we opened our doors. We had a letter of inquiry from Roy A. Whiteker, then on postdoctoral appointment at the Massachusetts Institute of Technology. Roy had earned his doctorate in analytical chemistry from Caltech. I quote his comments: "After a year and a half at a large Eastern institution where an analytic chemist rarely had an opportunity to talk to anyone except another analytic chemist, I began looking for a small liberal arts college in the West. Pomona College had no openings, but Corwin Hansch suggested that I write Joe Platt. I had been favorably impressed with what I had already heard of HMC, so I wrote Joe, was duly interviewed by Art Campbell, and could hardly wait to accept when an offer was made."[4]

4. Ibid.

It was harder to find a second physicist, and particularly one with at least a decade of teaching experience. I had about concluded that I might have to fill in for some laboratory and recitation sections, with no time to

prepare for them. Then, in late spring of 1956, who should walk in but Duane Roller. President DuBridge of Caltech had suggested to his old friend Duane that he talk to me.

Duane Roller was a Caltech Ph.D. in physics and was nationally known as a teacher of physics. In particular, he knew the philosophy and history of physics and related sciences as few physicists do. He had taught at Caltech, at the University of Oklahoma, at Wabash College, and at Hunter College. He held the Oersted Medal, presented annually to one nationally outstanding teacher of college or university physics. He was co-author, along with President Millikan and Dean Watson of Caltech, of the textbook in physics that had been for twenty years the standard for a rigorous introductory course.

Duane had left college teaching for some years at the request of a former student, Dean Wooldridge. Ramo-Wooldridge Corporation was given the task of overall design of the United States' guided missile sys-

Faculty and administration of Harvey Mudd College, first "pre-employment meeting," June 1957. From left: William H. Davenport, professor of humanities; Emery Walker, dean of admission; George Wickes, assistant professor of humanities; Roy A. Whiteker, assistant professor of chemistry; J. Arthur Campbell, professor of chemistry; Graydon D. Bell, assistant professor of physics; Robert James, professor of mathematics; Edward F. Little, assistant to the president; Joseph B. Platt.

tem, and their rapidly growing number of employees needed to learn a good deal about orbital mechanics quite promptly. Dean remembered Duane, the best physics teacher he had had, and persuaded Duane to set up training programs for the Ramo-Wooldridge Corporation. That task had been done, and Duane was ready to return to college or university teaching. I was most grateful to Lee DuBridge. Duane Roller and I had no trouble agreeing that we had a place for him.

As of June, 1957, we had appointed seven to the initial faculty: Professors Campbell and Whiteker in chemistry, Davenport and Wickes in English, James in mathematics, and Roller and Bell in physics.

We had also made some appointments to our staff. I concluded after several months that I could not work with architects, interview prospective students, make calls on foundations, and recruit faculty members without help. I needed an administrative assistant. About this time I heard from Edward F. Little, whom I had met in the Boston area. "Spif" Little, a Dartmouth alumnus with a master's degree in medieval philosophy from the University of Montreal, was at that time production manager for the Glastic Corporation, a Cleveland firm. The idea of a new college really intrigued him, and he suspected that with all those academics it might be useful to have one staff member with business experience and scholarly sympathies. With the board's consent, I had invited him to come. As of June, 1957, he had been with me for five months, working with building inspectors, finding housing for incoming faculty, keeping track of the finances, and telling potential students about Harvey Mudd College.

The next staff appointment was particularly welcome and was shared with Claremont Men's College. We needed help to recruit and admit students. That first winter, while Spif Little and I had visited high schools and answered telephone calls from youngsters wanting to know about the new college, Claremont Men's College had an admission officer, a retired preparatory school teacher named F. Donald Frisbie. He had handled the correspondence for our applicants as well as those for CMC, and he did his full part in visiting high schools or telephoning, but he did not feel comfortable about making the admission decisions for a technical college. Jean, Spif, and I made those decisions on our living room floor. We were most grateful for Mr. Frisbie's help in all of the preparatory work. Before that first year was out, Mr. Frisbie felt that the total workload suggested to him that he retire again.

At this juncture Emery Walker visited his old friend Stuart Briggs, professor of accounting and dean at Claremont Men's College. Emery was dean of admission at Brown University; he and Stuart were fellow Brown alumni. Emery was active in the College Entrance Examination Board (later becoming a trustee) and in the national Association of College Admission Counselors (eventually he was national president).

Stuart asked Emery's advice on staffing an ongoing admission office. Emery responded that he and his wife, Dorothy, had wondered what the West Coast might be like. I next heard from President Benson of CMC, who suggested that we might continue to share an admission office and offer Emery an appointment. We did, and Dean Walker accepted. Our next staff appointment in 1957, therefore, was a shared position for a dean of admission. This arrangement served both colleges well for twenty-five years. It is a real tribute to Emery's ability and evenhandedness that this is so; two colleges sharing an office of admission is a bit like having two families share a bank account.

By early summer Emery had found the initial staff for the Office of Admission, which included Bob Rogers, CMC '50, and a secretary. Bob served Harvey Mudd College ably and loyally as assistant dean of admission (later associate) for twenty-five years.

The other two staff appointments as of June, 1957, were my secretary, Frances Gentile, and Spif Little's secretary, Loretta Meyer. Accordingly, there were four of us on the full-time payroll at that time. The seven faculty, and additional staff, would be in place by September, when the college opened its doors.

Our first faculty meeting—a five-day affair—took place that May. Emery Walker and Roy Whiteker flew out from New England; George Wickes flew from North Carolina; Art Campbell flew from Washington, D.C.; Bob James flew from Philadelphia; and Bill Davenport and Graydon Bell drove over from Pasadena. (We did not yet know that Duane Roller would soon join us.) Spif Little met all airplanes and arranged the meetings, and Fran Gentile made sure we all knew what we were to do.

Emery Walker recalls that I opened our meeting with a brief prayer. I did, indeed. Five days later, at the conclusion of this meeting, we were agreed on what would be taught in the college's first year of instruction. We were also agreed on the program to introduce students to the college, on the schedules for the year, on how we would counsel students, and on who would do these things. Furthermore, we had all met our fellow adventurers, and we were pleased.

Two more staff appointments were made that summer. President Benson had told me that if he were to start Claremont Men's College again, he would have had a development office—a fundraising organization—in place as promptly as possible. Several of our trustees also felt that we needed a plan and a staff for this purpose as soon as we could. Alfred Thomas, one of our trustees, looked into the question of fundraising consultants and suggested that we get in touch with Paul H. Davis, a former Stanford University fundraiser now consulting for a limited number of clients. Several of us met with Mr. Davis and concluded he could be of real help to us. He advised us to employ a director of development as

soon as we could secure a good one. After a search for candidates, I recommended, with Mr. Davis's concurrence, that we offer appointment to
George I. McKelvey III, then vice president of the American Alumni
Council, whom I had known when George was an undergraduate and I
a faculty member at the University of Rochester. George accepted the
appointment. Accordingly, when the college opened, we also had a
director of development and a development consultant.

CHAPTER 6

Our Students—The Early Classes

I CAN see our first students now, arriving of a hot September morning in the parking lot the city required us to have and carrying their possessions down our one concrete sidewalk to the dormitory—not quite completely painted but nevertheless our own. We of the faculty and staff welcomed them and reassured their parents. We told them of the campus yet to come, which would replace the rocks and chaparral. And we had a full round of orientation lectures, placement examinations, and evening get-togethers to take the minds of these frosh off the homes and friends they had just left. Who were these students? How did they happen to choose Harvey Mudd College and the college choose them?

WHOM SHOULD WE ADMIT?
We planned the college to be an excellent place for the development of broadly educated engineers and scientists, and we hoped to attract students whose career aspirations fitted this pattern. Blessed human variety being what it is, not all would continue throughout life in engineering or science (some might even become administrators!), but most would find their backgrounds in technology and science an essential part of their outlook, professional competence, and way of life. We hoped for academically able students really excited about broad technical careers.

Rudolph J. Wig, our trustee, observed we were not the only institution interested in attracting able students. To get our share we should remember that not all qualified applicants can afford to attend a private college without financial help. The student should have savings from part-time work, and the family should contribute, but many families cannot provide the full cost of private higher education. Mr. Wig had earned his authority on admission questions. In 1953 the California legislature

1. *Rudolph James Wig,* by Clifford F. Drury, Arthur Clark Co., Glendale, CA. 1968; pp. 240–246.

authorized a study to explore the experience of other states with publicly supported scholarship programs to determine if such a plan could be of use to California. Mr. Wig became chairman of the study group. The group recommended, and the legislature in due course established, a state scholarship program available to students in both public and private higher education in California. The report stated: "There are at the present time physical facilities that are unused and available in the independent colleges and universities in California. These facilities can accommodate a substantial number of students of exceptional promise without expense or delay to the state other than providing scholarship funds."[1]

The California State Scholarship Commission was established in 1955. In the fall of 1955, shortly before the founding of Harvey Mudd College, Governor Knight appointed Mr. Wig as one of the nine commissioners. By the time we were considering the admission of students Mr. Wig was chairman of the commission. He probably knew more about admission questions than anyone not a professional admission officer.

He pointed out that to admit able students, whether or not from families of means, we would need scholarship funds of our own. The State Scholarship Program could help after we became accredited, but that could not happen until our educational performance could be evaluated—perhaps years. He not only advocated scholarship funds, but volunteered to provide a full tuition scholarship and invited other board members to join him. Ford Twaits promptly spoke up too, and in the following weeks other trustees contributed or solicited still more support. R.J. Wig's leadership was most helpful in setting our admission standards.

The board took another informal action that has helped to shape our student body. I had proposed that we admit sixty students in our first freshman class. The board shared that hope and planned accordingly. But, said Alfred Thomas, "We'll settle for six if they're the right six." There was no disagreement.

The board gave substantial time and thought to the admission of women. Some engineering colleges, such as the Massachusetts Institute of Technology and the Illinois Institute of Technology, admitted women, while others such as the California Institute of Technology and the Case Institute of Technology did not. Mrs. Mudd, as chairman of the board, appointed a trustee subcommittee to propose to the board which policy Harvey Mudd should adopt.[2] The subcommittee asked me to put my views in writing and to explore the reasons for the policies of other institutions. (One Caltech administrator told me Caltech would indeed admit undergraduate women in due course, but there needed to be a few well-placed deaths in the faculty first.) I recommended the admission of women, the subcommittee supported my recommendation by a two-thirds vote, and the board voted to admit women.

Those favoring the admission of women argued that: (a) a little more

2. The members of the subcommittee were Hugh L. Clary, chairman; Robert P. Hastings; and Raymond A. Hill.

than half the world's human brains are owned by women; (b) women are an increasing portion of the labor force and of college enrollments, and the numbers are expected to continue to grow; and (c) the numbers of women in the sciences and in the more recent branches of engineering are increasing. Hence more women students are interested in engineering and the sciences than once was the case, and alumnae stand a better chance of finding significant jobs. Those opposed countered that women are more likely than men to drop out of the labor force to raise a family, and that the very few women we could attract would require separate housing, supervision, and social arrangements. The fact that Scripps College could house a limited number of our women somewhat tempered the latter argument.

After the meeting Al Thomas said to me, "Joe, I understood the arguments and I voted to admit women—but I have an uneasy feeling about it. Who would marry a math major?" "Well, Al," said I, "I did."

THE FOUNDING CLASS OF 1961

As it developed, some 124 students applied for admission to the founding class of Harvey Mudd College. Many of these students could have been admitted to any university; some were quite unqualified but hoped a new college would have lenient admission standards. We admitted sixty-four students, of whom forty-eight accepted admission. It was a strong class by the admission standards of any institution of that time. And, obviously, it was a venturesome class!

Who were the first students to enter Harvey Mudd College? With all due respect to the college catalogue I had written and sent to thousands of high schools, the majority of our first class had heard of Harvey Mudd by word of mouth. Trustees, friends of friends, and high school counselors intrigued by a new college all spread the news, but the college was not yet well known at a distance. Two students came from the state of Washington, two from Oregon, and one each from Hawaii and Arizona. The rest were from California, and in most cases from less than fifty miles away.

Nearly all had excellent high school or preparatory school records. Most had done much other than study—they had been student body officers, and writers, and athletes, and musicians. We admitted a radio ham or two, a number of science fair winners, and many who had earned a portion of their college expenses.

Some did indeed come from families of means—corporate officers, a banker, two investment counselors. Others came from blue collar families—retired enlisted military, a bartender, machinists, a crane operator, a mechanic. Some were children of teachers, scientists, or engineers; one was the child of a minister.

We liked what we saw of the founding class during our first days together.

The final event of the orientation week was the first convocation of Harvey Mudd. I quote from George Wickes's *HMC Diary:*

> This date should go down in history as marking the formal opening of Harvey Mudd College—if not the birthday, at least the christening of the College, marked by the ceremony of our first convocation.
>
> Faculty and staff assembled—in borrowed or faded academic finery—in the patio of McKenna Auditorium (on the Claremont Men's College campus) and, with our ranks increased to decent proportions by several trustees and representatives of fellow colleges, marched in solemn procession into the auditorium and onto the stage. The audience, consisting of the student body and a dozen or two friends and relations, rattled a bit in the auditorium, but the occasion was none the less ceremonious for that.
>
> After the invocation and the national anthem, President Platt introduced several of the guests on the platform: Mrs. Harvey Mudd, Mr. Clary, Mr. Bernard, paying tribute to their roles in the founding of the College.
>
> Dr. Hard, speaking as provost-designate of Claremont College and as president of "your fair neighbor to the south" (Scripps College) brought the greetings of both colleges. He harked back to the inauspicious early days of Scripps, when the campus was nothing but sagebrush and wash, populated by rattlesnakes and gophers, and to the founding more recently of CMC in a disreputable neighborhood.
>
> President Benson, speaking next and welcoming us in the name of Claremont Men's College, could not allow President Hard's obloquy to pass without observing that Scripps College had owned several houses in the dilapidated and disreputable neighborhood which had since become the CMC campus. Drawing parallels to the early days of CMC, he went on to trace the founding of Harvey Mudd College during his term as provost. He told members of the Class of '61 that, like the early graduates of CMC, they would always have fond memories of the early days of the College.
>
> President Platt then turned to the future of Harvey Mudd College, inviting all present to look back from the vantage point of the year 2000 and consider what we might behold. Then he brought it home to us that the responsibility is ours: "The future of Harvey Mudd College is what we make it."
>
> After Chaplain Rankin had pronounced the benediction, we marched out into the sun again, feeling a little solemn and a little gay, and altogether pleased that our college was now properly launched.[3]

3. *HMC Diary*, Vol I, by George Wickes, pp. 5 - 6, dated Thursday, September 26, 1957.

Lee Pattison, a nationally distinguished musician and professor of music at Scripps, had volunteered to play the organ for our convocation. As the final speaker, I was disconcerted to discover as we left that he had chosen for the recessional Johann Sebastian Bach's "Sleepers Awake."

Academically the first months went quite well. Most of our students were interested and quick, all were excited that they were the pioneers and that every act became an instant tradition, and all were curious to try the intellectual independence they now had. There was a student government to organize. There were social events to plan, and both intramural and varsity sports to try (jointly with CMC). And they had more of an academic load than they had previously thought possible.

We did indeed have one lone young woman in the class—Jenny Rhine. She roomed at Scripps College and made herself a part of both colleges. Not surprisingly, the founding class promptly elected her social chairman.

There were some problems of adjustment which were familiar to experienced college teachers. Nearly every student had been at the top of most of his secondary school classes, and it rapidly dawned on many that half this group would now be in the bottom half. For some this shock required a change of identity: if he could not be the most promising mathematician, a student might settle for being the best bridge player or a guitarist or an organizer of midnight food forays. All of this is, of course, part of growing up, as even the most venerable of us can remember. The task of the faculty is to reassure the new student when worried, and give a pat on the back when a "well done" is earned. We were concerned that a number of our students found it a comfort to go home

Jenny Rhine '61, left, with Kenneth Stevens '61, center, and Donald Trapp '61. Although Jenny was the only woman enrolled in Harvey Mudd's first class, seven women were to follow her in the second semester of the 1957-58 school year.

weekends. Much entertaining in faculty homes and such outings as an all-college trip, including faculty wives and children, to the Mount Baldy ski lift and lodge for Sunday brunch (which of course was for several years a "tradition") helped to make Claremont more attractive and built a sense of community. The pervading sense that we were together in building a college was the major bond.

We had a group of students who rarely needed to be amused. In the second week of classes several noted a huge stack of building blocks across Twelfth Street from the dormitory, to be used in building the new Scripps College north wall. Nothing would do of a late evening but to build a wall without mortar, cutting straight across both lanes of Twelfth Street, from the Scripps campus north to ours. Later that evening a young man from a sister college, speeding back in his open sports car on Foothill Boulevard from a tour of its watering places, found himself chased by police. He knew a road they didn't, so he ducked down Mills Avenue and screeched onto Twelfth, to discover the new wall a bit too late to stop. The wall did stop him, and he bolted out of the car and got away. The car, its hood covered with building blocks, went nowhere.

Art Campbell, in his part-time role as dean of student activities, discussed the adventure with the class the next morning. The upshot was that the class put back all the blocks, replaced the broken ones, had the car repaired to the satisfaction of its owner, and decided among themselves how the costs should be divided. This learning experience (for all of us) began another tradition: Pranks are tolerated, but no one should be hurt, and it should be possible for the perpetrator(s) to restore the status quo ante.

We had one faculty member who was co-opted to live in the dormitory—Roy Whiteker, assistant professor of chemistry and at that time unmarried. Roy was of great help to the students, managed remarkable equanimity in the midst of chaos, and had the sympathy of the rest of us. George Wickes's report on our first Christmas party suggests that Roy knew how organize the chaos.

'Twas the night before vacation, and the dorm, which looks something like a Christmas tree at night anyway, seemed particularly festive as all assembled in the lounge for our First Annual Christmas Party. It was a family affair, with students, faculty, wives, even Mrs. Mudd and Mr. Platt senior on hand to start off the holiday.

The first half of the evening's entertainment was catholic, to say the least, with Joe Platt representing the sciences and humanities in song, Bill O'Brien (our master of ceremonies for the evening) evoking Broadway, and Bill Leppo contributing jazz on his harpsichord.

Then, just as carols were announced, the program was interrupted by a HO-HO-HO as Santa Claus Whiteker appeared on the scene, resplendent in a red nightcap and Andy Blodgett's red pajamas. From the depths of a Harvard Co-op bag he proceeded to draw forth all sorts of surprises, beginning with a feather head-dress for Big Chief Platt, ranging on through such suitable gifts as flying saucers, *Sputnik* spotters, water balloon shields, hi-fi ear plugs, and model airplanes—all distributed in the most appropriate direction—and concluding with a flying saucer shield for himself.

Then, winding up his superb performance with another HO-HO-HO, Santa disappeared, and all joined in the singing of carols. Finally the wives purveyed cookies and punch, and, as the party broke up, an impromptu jam session was getting under way, with Bill Davenport on the bells (a prehistoric instrument, he informs us, played in the twenties before we were born.)[4]

4. *HMC Diary,* Vol. I, by George Wickes, dated Thursday, December 18, 1957.

(A few program notes, please. Mrs. Mudd is Mrs. Harvey S. Mudd, who joined us for the evening. The "senior Mr. Platt" is my late father, William B. Platt. Bill O'Brien, Bill Leppo, and Andy Blodgett were members of the Class of '61. Most faculty families, including children, were on hand. And "flying saucers," then quite a novelty, we now call frisbees.)

By mid-year three members of the class had decided that engineering and the sciences were not for them. One had dropped out shortly after Thanksgiving, and two decided to transfer to Claremont Men's College the following fall. Of the remaining forty-five, ten (including Jenny Rhine) were on the dean's list, twelve were notified their academic work needed to improve, and the other twenty-three were making solid if unspectacular progress. In short, we were jointly learning how to teach and how to study in the setting of this new college.

The student government conducted a series of meetings on a possible academic honor system during the first semester, hearing from other institutions about the successes and problems honor systems provided them. In January, "Record attendance and extraordinary interest in English classes today, as we staged a series of debates. Student body officers sat in on all of them, listening attentively and taking extensive notes. Partisanship ran high, and the debate was carried on long after its formal ending. The subject: Resolved that HMC shall have an honor system."[5]

5. *HMC Diary*, Vol. II, by George Wickes, dated Monday, January 27, 1958.

The Associated Students of Harvey Mudd College did indeed choose to have an academic honor system, and it has served them, their successors, and the college well. It has been, and no doubt will be, periodically reviewed and fine-tuned by successive generations of students, but it is essentially the plan adopted by the Class of '61.

At the close of the academic year 1957-58 all but three of the class

The Class of '61, fall of 1957.

were admitted to sophomore standing. Ten were on the dean's list, and six were still on warning that their work needed to improve.

The remaining years at the college were busy ones for the Class of '61. In addition to organizing a student government and establishing a multitude of traditions, the class began the practice of building floats of great mechanical ingenuity to be paraded at football games. (The primary purpose was to involve young women from Scripps in the design and construction of these mechanical and artistic triumphs.) The intercollegiate competition in float building was finally discontinued because some HMC-Scripps team always won, and students of the other colleges saw no point in competing.

Each year the student government matured. It also showed growth in the sophistication of student officers. Dick Davis, '61, who was president of the Associated Students at Harvey Mudd College in the year 1959-60, was sent to a national meeting of student body officers. He arrived to discover the associated group was electing its officers. Dick correctly inferred that the president of the presidents would have to be from a major university, so the vice president would be from a small college; he lined up some support before others had figured this out. He became vice president of the presidents with attendant trips, visitations, and the privilege of planning the next year's program.

Of the forty-eight entering members of the Class of '61, thirty-three graduated, plus one additional transfer student (now Lori Ives, the wife of our Professor Robin Ives) who joined after the first year. The group now (1990) includes four owners and presidents of their own businesses, four who are senior corporate officers of large organizations, three who are faculty members (including Jerry Van Hecke, professor of chemistry at Harvey Mudd, and one professor of fine arts and another of drama, elsewhere) and many professional engineers and scientists. Fourteen have earned the doctorate and another nine have master's degrees. I am sad to report that two are no longer living, ending in both cases productive technical careers.

THE CLASSES OF '59 AND '60

The California State Scholarship Program, mentioned earlier, was tremendously helpful to Harvey Mudd students over the first decade of teaching. But, to be eligible for state scholarship help, our students needed to attend an accredited college. Accreditation was determined by the Western Association of Schools and Colleges, and accordingly I got in touch with the executive secretary, Dr. Mitchell Briggs, before we admitted students. I learned that WASC is an association of universities, colleges, and schools; that the state and federal governments delegate to it the authority to determine which institutions may grant degrees in its geographic area; and that the determination is made by a board of university and college faculty and staff members, on the recommendation of an accreditation team, also made up of faculty and staff. The accreditation team reads an extensive self-study prepared by the institution, and then

Associated Students of Harvey Mudd College, March 1959 (left to right): Dick Olson, treasurer; Don Gross, secretary; Tony Fallon, athletic chairman; Jim Barden, publicity chairman; Terry Beckett, vice president; Dick Davis, president.

visits the institution, to see at first hand what is being offered, by whom, and within what kind of facilities. The accreditation team has access to admission records, financial statements, faculty vitae, and whatever else can assist the team members to determine whether the college can perform as it claims to do.

Dr. Briggs knew the Associated Colleges of Claremont well, and assured me we could apply for accreditation as soon as we were in full operation. I asked him to define full operation. He replied we needed to have all four classes in operation, but that there was no requirement about the size of these classes. Accordingly, I planned to admit, with the Class of 1962, some juniors and some seniors, transferring from other colleges and universities. The problem was to attract good students, making excellent progress in established institutions. Furthermore, they needed to be students of mathematics; we did not as yet have the laboratories for advanced undergraduate courses in chemistry, engineering, or physics.

Emery Walker, our dean of admission, tried valiantly to recruit transfer students in mathematics, and he did locate Janet Cook, then completing her second year as a mathematics major at the University of Chicago. Janet, a National Merit scholar and an excellent student, wanted to transfer to a good California college because her parents were retiring to this area. Emery also located Thomas B. Peters, then completing his second year at Chaffey College, a Navy veteran hoping to become a teacher of mathematics, and we had two able students to constitute a junior class. But where were the seniors? As of the end of August, 1958, neither Emery nor anyone else had found candidates who had good undergraduate records in respected university or college mathematics departments and who could be persuaded to finish elsewhere.

Enter the public relations consultants, Braun and Company. (I will describe elsewhere how the college came to have the help of this excellent firm.) They felt that a little national publicity, discreetly placed, might call us to the attention of appropriate transfer candidates. The September 8, 1958, issue of *Time* magazine carried an article in its education section entitled "The Rise of Harvey Mudd College." It was a generally laudatory statement, reporting our progress to date, and it ended with a paragraph pointing out we would welcome senior transfer students to hasten our eligibility for accreditation.

The day that issue of *Time* hit the California newsstands, I received a telephone call from Stuart E. Black, a married veteran about to enter his senior year in mathematics at the University of California at Los Angeles. He inquired about the possibility of transfer, I put him in touch with Dean Walker, and I learned shortly thereafter he was indeed admitted. Some days later Dean Walker had another inquiry, this time from Peter A. Loeb, then about to enter his senior year at Reed College in Portland, Oregon. He was admitted on September 16, 1958. We had our senior class.

Both junior and senior students received tutorial instruction in all their courses. We applied for accreditation, began the task of studying ourselves, and hoped.

We had the benefit of a knowledgeable and sympathetic accreditation team composed of deans from Occidental College, Fresno State College, the California Institute of Technology, a vice president from San Diego State College, and a professor from the University of California, Riverside. Together they represented the disciplines we were teaching and proposed to teach. They also had many years experience in evaluating and promoting good teaching. The team pointed out, to WASC and to us, that not enough was yet in hand to make a professional judgment about the adequacy of the engineering program of the junior and senior years. Clearly planning had been done; as for the rest: "Nothing truly informative can be said at this time about the degree curricula in chemistry, mathematics, and physics, for they have not yet been developed. However, approval can be expressed for the soil from which these curricula will grow. . . . Therefore it is reasonable to assume that when the present program is expanded to cover all four years, the completed curricula will more than meet accreditation standards."[6]

I should add that the accreditation team knew our sister Claremont Colleges, knew the support available to Harvey Mudd College from them, knew the standards we were expected to uphold, and judged us in part on the strength of the group to which we belonged.

The Western Association of Schools and Colleges did indeed grant the college provisional accreditation, and all California students admitted after our second year were eligible for California state scholarships if they needed them. Their California upper classmates also became eligible. We were again inspected by WASC when our founding class was in its senior year, and reaccredited. This "act of faith" on our behalf by the Western Association of Schools and Colleges was tremendously helpful to us.

What happened to the four students who volunteered to become our first graduates? Stuart Black is on the faculty of mathematics of California State University at Long Beach, Janet Cook is on the faculty of mathematics of Illinois State University, Peter Loeb is on the faculty of mathematics of the University of Illinois, and Tom Peters teaches mathematics at Chaffey College in California.

And that is how Harvey Mudd College came to have classes of 1959 and 1960, admitted after the founding Class of 1961.

THE CLASS OF 1962

The Class of 1962 is a special class in the history of Harvey Mudd College. We of the faculty and administration learned a great deal from those who graduated and even more from those who did not. We had a much wider selection of students for admission than we had had for the

6. Western Association of Schools and Colleges, *Survey Report of Harvey Mudd College,* January 26 and 27, 1959.

Class of 1961. Our new admission team visited 233 secondary schools, far more than were seen the prior year. The academic records of the students admitted to the Class of 1962 were essentially identical to those of the prior class. Seventy-one students appeared as entering freshman, compared to forty-eight the prior year. Yet, of the first class, thirty-three graduated; of the second class, thirty. We faced what we considered an entirely unacceptable attrition of well-qualified students, who should have graduated no matter where they chose to go. What happened, and what could we do about it?

There are a few qualifying remarks I should make, but they did not comfort us then nor do they now. Nationally, less than half of the students who enroll in engineering or scientific curricula do graduate in those fields. In most universities or colleges, students who decide technical fields are not for them (a common decision) can change majors and graduate, say, in economics or literature; that option was not available for us. Engineering dropouts do not generally appear as attrition statistics for most universities for this reason. In our case, many of the students who left were accepted in good standing at other institutions, and graduated on schedule; in our bookkeeping they failed to graduate *from Harvey Mudd College*. Students whose interests change as they mature should be able to transfer to a school strong in the fine arts or journalism or whatever fits their developing interests. One always expects some attrition; family circumstances change, a few students fall seriously ill, and so on. To the best of my knowledge, no college or university in the nation graduates much more than 80 percent of its entering class, and few technical institutions come close to that figure. But 42.2 percent?!?

We were startled to discover in June, 1959, that twenty-two of the class had either not done acceptable academic work, or had chosen to leave. By June, 1960, another ten were gone, and a year later, nine more. We had regularly counseled students having academic struggles, and we had exit interviews with all who left for any reason. Fortunately we had Carnegie Corporation funds to help us learn how to build as good a college as we could.

We got help from Dr. Paul A. Heist, a social psychologist on the staff of the Center for the Study of Higher Education at the University of California, Berkeley. Paul consulted with us from 1961 to 1964 and taught us a great deal. He interviewed students, developed attitudinal profiles on every one of them using accepted psychological inventories, and really caught our attention when he was much more successful than we had been in predicting which students would stay, and which leave.[7]

Paul Heist told us we had students with a variety of interests, and we needed to bear that in mind when teaching. True, essentially all our students were from the top 2 percent of entering freshmen in the nation, but some of those we admitted learned much more rapidly than others.

7. The two research tools which Dr. Heist found most predictive were the Strong Vocational Interest Blank and the Omnibus Personality Inventory, although he experimented with a number of others as well.

What was even more important: some just loved to play with ideas, were highly theoretically oriented, and were interested in all sorts of fields; others, with equal or higher scholastic records, were pragmatic, interested in what one could accomplish with a new concept, and impatient with ideas of no apparent practical use. In teaching a class containing both types of students some attention must be given to both points of view if all the class is to remain interested. Paul taught both the staff and the faculty much more detail about the variety within our student body than I can report here; the outcome of his research and teaching was that we began to offer more varied methods of learning. Paul Heist had real support in this pedagogical revolution; several members of the faculty became strong believers, and we were greatly helped by Eugene Hotchkiss, our first full-time dean of students, who joined us in February, 1960. Gene, an historian, had been associate dean of students at Dartmouth College.

Paul and Gene confirmed our hunches (and disabused us of others) about various sources of attrition. As I mentioned in Chapter 4, the college had few facilities in its early years for student activities other than classroom and laboratory. This situation changed for the better with the coming of the Campus Center; things began to look less grim as soon as we broke ground for a building not just intended for study. The Class of '62 had one burden that later classes would not shoulder: they were for three years understudies of the founding Class of 1961. It could not have been easy to ship as crew on Columbus's second voyage to the New World, along with veterans of the first voyage. And, for both the classes of '61 and '62, those students who hoped to be engineers had two long years of science, mathematics, and humanities before any inkling of the art and practice of engineering was visible. The Class of 1963 found all freshmen exposed to some work in engineering problems, and this exposure has continued.

We all became aware of the range of interests of the students we taught. The faculty became sensitive to locating any student who wanted help. With due respect for rigorous academic standards most faculty members became partners, rather than taskmasters, in assisting students to meet those standards.

We substantially reduced attrition in the classes following the Class of '62; 65 percent of the next class graduated, and the fraction has climbed since then to the mid-1970s. As of the late 1980s, a bit more than 80 percent of our admitted students have been graduating.

Of the thirty who did graduate in the Class of '62, fourteen subsequently earned doctorates, and another six earned other advanced degrees, including two doctors of jurisprudence. (One of these lawyers is an economic counselor to the Department of State and the other a partner in a San Francisco law firm.) Eleven are on college or university faculties, from the University of Wisconsin to the Universidade Federal de Minas, Brazil. Included in this eleven is Dick Olson, professor of humanities at Harvey Mudd. The remainder are mostly in technical positions, ranging from group leader or section chief in governmental laboratories to senior positions in industries. One heads up an organization producing gallium arsenide semiconductor devices; another, a geologist, is president of Toyon Environmental Consultants. We have cause for pride in those who did graduate—and in a number of non-graduates with whom we have kept in touch, and who are doing very useful things.

COMMENCEMENTS

Each graduating class deserves a commencement. Accordingly, our first commencement for the Class of 1959 was held in the courtyard of our first dormitory, with an academic procession including faculty and trustees and special guests and a considerable audience of students and well-wishers. President Lee A. DuBridge of the California Institute of Technology was our speaker. Peter Loeb and Stuart Black received their diplomas from our board chairman, Henry T. Mudd. The idea of a commencement for two students attracted media attention; through the good offices of Richard A. Moore, president of station KTTV,[8] the ceremony was televised regionally, and a number of stations throughout the nation replayed the tape over the following months.[9] For a number of years entering freshmen reported they had first learned of Harvey Mudd College when they saw that commencement on television. A feature of this commencement was the charge to the Class of '59, given by John Murray, president of the Class of '61, congratulating the new alumni and reminding both that neither was a member of the founding Class of '61.

The next year the Class of 1960 had its own commencement. By this time the college had adopted its seal, which adorned the platform.[10] We also had an elegant mace, ingeniously designed, handmade, and given to us by Jack Miller, professor of physics at Pomona College, and David Davies, librarian of the Associated Colleges.[11] Our faculty marshal, Art Campbell, led the academic procession with the dignity this mace conferred.[12] Our speaker was Dr. Leonard Carmichael, secretary of the Smithsonian Institution and a distinguished psychologist. With the graduation of Janet Cook, Harvey Mudd had an alumna; Tom Peters became our third alumnus.

Clearly, the founding Class of 1961 deserved special recognition. After consultation with faculty and trustees, I placed the arrangements in the capable hands of Professor and Mrs. John B. Rae, with authority to tell the rest of us what to do. John, early in his academic career, had been administrative assistant to President Wriston of Brown University. We invited each of the colleges and universities in North America granting engineering degrees to send an academic representative to join us in our

8. Richard A. Moore, also a director of Times Mirror Corporation, was very helpful to the College, and we wished him well reluctantly when he left California to become Counsellor to the President of the United States.

9. Some months after this Commencement I was tossing and turning in an East Coast hotel at three in the morning, and turned on the television set. There I was, presiding over our first Commencement.

10. The Harvey Mudd College seal was designed by Thomas Jamieson, then of Claremont, after extensive consultation with faculty, students, and the Public Relations Committee of the Board of Trustees. The Board of Trustees adopted the design at its meeting of January 23, 1960.

11. In our first commencement our faculty marshal, J. Arthur Campbell, carrried in lieu of mace a piece of dowling perhaps a foot long, to which were tied ribbons in the College colors. Mrs. Campbell tells me these ribbons were not easy to press, or to tie.

12. Legend has it that the practice of having the faculty marshal carry a mace dates from the Middle Ages. The academic procession, as it wound its way through town, needed a mace wielder to protect graduating students from merchants concerned that the students would leave town with unpaid debts.

First senior class recruits, Stuart Black '59 and Peter Loeb '59, with Joseph Platt.

first full commencement. Seventy-three delegates came, representing a geographical spread from the University of Wisconsin in the north to Mexico City College in the south and varying in age of founding from Harvard University's 1636 to California State University at Los Angeles (then called Los Angeles State College), founded in 1947. Our commencement speaker was Kenneth S. Pitzer, then dean of the College of Chemistry at the University of California, Berkeley, and shortly to become president of Rice University. Ken, the son of Russell Pitzer who had committed the initial gift to Harvey Mudd, had been my superior at the Atomic Energy Commission, and was at that time serving as a trustee of the college. He spoke on "Man and Technology." The valedictorian was Robert C. Ashenfelder '61, (as of 1990, Bob lists himself as director/member technical staff, AT&T Bell Laboratories). In addition to parents, students, faculty, trustees, and delegates, many other friends attended the commencement and its associated luncheon and receptions. We made this milestone as notable as we could in the college's history. Thirty-two members of the founding class graduated at this time, and two others with some incomplete work graduated later.

The Class of 1962, its numbers augmented by students who transferred in after the freshman class was admitted, graduated thirty-six students. The number of alumni was thus doubled, to seventy-two. (No subsequent class can claim to have doubled our number of graduates.) The speaker was Donald J. Russell, then president of the Southern

The HMC Seal

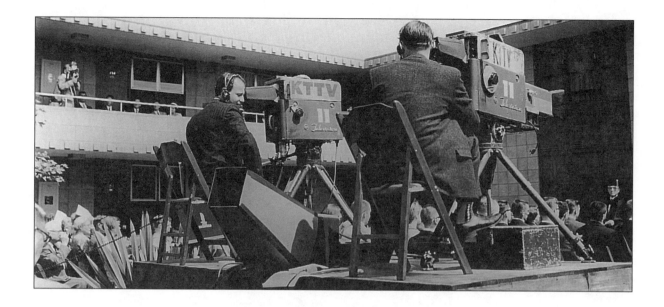

A commencement for two students attracts media attention.

Pacific Company, and the valedictorian was Richard G. Olson, '62, now professor of history and Willard W. Keith, Jr. Fellow in Humanities at Harvey Mudd.

With these four commencements, Harvey Mudd College was clearly "in full operation."

CHAPTER 7

Money

THE net worth of Harvey Mudd College, as of June 30, 1990, was $104 million. The reader may remember that at the time of founding the total funding "in hand or in sight" was about $2 million, and that I felt it would require about ten times that much to launch the college properly. In particular, I had estimated it would require about $10 million in plant and equipment, and another $10 million in endowment (in 1956 dollars) to do the job. The purchasing power of the dollar has decreased by about a factor of 5.3 from 1956 to 1990, so the initial estimate is not far from the current net worth of the college.[1] Where did all that money come from?

It came from many sources: individuals, foundations, corporations, and government agencies. It came in many forms: gifts, grants, contracts, bequests, and gifts in kind. The remainder of this chapter tells the story of accumulating these assets, without which there would be no Harvey Mudd College now.

Many people assume that the college was created and is maintained by the generosity of the Mudd family. Clearly Harvey Mudd College was founded, and has continued to the present time, with major financial support from the family and close friends of family members. Much of our endowment, as of 1990, can be traced to family sources. As we have seen, the initial commitments to the college were made before Mrs. Harvey S. Mudd was approached or the college was incorporated. Thereafter, in the year 1955-56, the Mudd family contributed 99.7 percent of the gifts to the college; for 1960-61 the fraction was 53 percent; for 1965-66, 39 percent; for 1970-71, 26 percent; and for 1975-76, 23 percent.[2] Substantial family help certainly continued; the growth was in other sources of support.

1. The initial estimate of the cost of the college was a very rough approximation. When I was approached about the presidency, I decided that before I volunteered my candidacy I should update my "Texas figure" for the resources required to found a college of engineering and science for 400 students, and find out whether such funds might be available. Accordingly I estimated square foot requirements for classrooms, laboratories, dormitory and dining space, and offices; then I multiplied each by the then typical cost of construction per square foot for that type of facility. The total came to about $10 million, excluding athletic facilities, faculty or staff housing, library, and other amenities. (I knew by then that The Claremont Colleges would provide without capital cost an impressive array of common services.) I then took the endowment per student for several engineering schools primarily offering undergraduate instruction, averaged them, and multiplied by 400 to find the required endowment for a new college,

again, in the $10 million range.

The change in the purchasing power of the dollar is also crudely estimated: I have simply taken the Bureau of Labor Statistics' Consumer Price Indices for the dates in question, and established the ratio. A more proper method would be to multiply building costs by the adjusted Construction Price Index, and the endowment figures (since the endowment purchases educational services) by the Higher Education Price Index. The building costs need also to be adjusted by the year in which the construction occurred; the $53 million in plant and equipment is an underestimate of the cost of replacing the entire campus in 1990. The 1989-90 Harvey Mudd College Annual Financial Report shows total costs of plant and equipment, entered at the times we actually did construct the buildings or purchase equipment, as about $25 million.

Accordingly, on both scores, these are rough figures in the text, intended simply to compare initial estimates with subsequent experience. We did not know in 1956 what we would need, but neither were we without clues.

2. The "Mudd Family" reported here includes Mrs. Harvey S. Mudd, Mr. and Mrs. Henry T. Mudd, Dr. Norman F. Sprague, Jr. and his wife Caryll Mudd Sprague, Mrs. Virginia Kingston (mother of Victoria Mudd) the M.E. and H.S. Mudd Foundation, the Seeley W. Mudd Foundation, and several trusts controlled by one or more of the preceding.

What is more, the family contributed leadership. Each member saw the college as a regional and national asset and welcomed others to join in making it possible. The members of the family had long records of community leadership in civic, educational and artistic activities, and others of similar interests and means were attracted. Mrs. Harvey S. Mudd corrected those who spoke of "her" college and invited them to join in the enterprise.

Very well. Where did the rest of the money come from?

Both the Board of Trustees and I knew we needed to raise additional money. George Benson told me before I arrived in Claremont that if he were starting Claremont Men's College again, he would be more prompt in establishing a development program. Alfred Thomas told his fellow trustees in the fall of 1956 the college needed to plan and staff a fundraising program, and he felt good consulting advice would be needed for a number of years. He volunteered to discuss the matter with trustees of other institutions and identify possible consulting advice.

Al returned in early 1957 with the name of Paul H. Davis. Mr. Davis had entered consulting on completing his service as chief development officer at Columbia University during Eisenhower's tenure as president there. Prior to that, Mr. Davis had served as secretary to the Board of Trustees of Stanford University. He began his professional career as a YMCA secretary. His modus operandi as a consultant was to serve five or six institutions at a time, each for a period of five years with one possible renewal on mutual consent. He was completing his service for another client and would consider Harvey Mudd College if we wished.

Paul Davis visited Claremont and met with a number of trustees, including Al Thomas, Leroy Garrett (then chairman of the Board Committee on Ways and Means) and me. I recommended to the board that we obtain the services of Mr. Davis and was given approval.

I knew very little about raising money, and colleges and universities in general had not yet developed the staff and procedures now widely familiar. Paul Davis seemed to me straightforward, factual, and much less given to hand-waving and hyperbole than some professional fundraisers I had known. Serving Harvey Mudd College well for nearly a decade, he not only taught us successful things to do but pointed out to us promptly when we failed to do them. (If we persisted in a failing, he told the board.) He told the trustees we would need to spend money to raise money, and told me we needed to build a full-time development staff and that he would help me find our first development professional if I wished, but that the choice was mine. What he did not recommend was that we ponder overlong about it.

We developed a list of candidates, one of whom I had known when I was a faculty member and he an undergraduate at the University of Rochester. After consultation, we approached the former student:

George I. McKelvey III. George was at that time associate director of the American Alumni Council, an association of directors of university and college alumni activities in Washington, D.C. Prior to that he had been director of alumni relations at the University of Rochester. I had become acquainted with him because I had been the faculty advisor to the student Board of Control, which authorized, monitored, and funded undergraduate organizations and activities, using student fees. George had decided the undergraduates needed a radio station covering the campus, and with modest funds he had built the station, recruited and managed the student staff, developed the programming, and built up a considerable campus following. I had thought this no small accomplishment for a history major, working part-time as volunteer founder. I learned he had served during World War II, prior to entering college, as radio officer on merchant ships. I too had served on merchant ships for some eleven months, in my case as ordinary seaman in the early 1930s. In short, his professional qualifications were sound, and I thought other factors in his background also suggested he might get things done.

I recommended his appointment to the board in July, 1957, with Paul Davis's endorsement. Bob Hastings suggested we invite him to visit Claremont and to meet trustees, to better our chances of attracting him and to make the people with whom he would work party to the choice. Bob and Roy Garrett volunteered to provide the airline tickets for his round trip and mine, so that I might come out with him. We were provided with first-class tickets, new in George's and my experience while flying on educational business. George visited in August, and all concerned agreed he "fit." He was offered the appointment, and accepted. He returned to Washington, sold his sloop on the Chesapeake Bay, and drove west, arriving September 15, 1957. On the way he visited the Esso Education Foundation, the United States Steel Foundation, and the Westinghouse Foundation, with each of which he had previous contact, to acquaint them with Harvey Mudd College.

Shortly after arrival Messrs. McKelvey, Davis, and Platt met together. Said Paul: "What do you think you should be raising? A million dollars a year?" George and I blinked, thinking he was baiting us. (He was.) How were we to raise that much new money? "Non-family gifts" approached a $200,000 annual rate the following year, and reached $1,000,000 nine years later. In 1976 the annual total was $3.5 million.

Paul Davis met with the board on October 17, 1957. The gist of his advice is preserved in the board minutes:[3]

3. Minutes of the Board of Trustees of Harvey Mudd College, October 17, 1957.

In connection with his work for another client, Mr. Davis has visited some seventy colleges and attempted in each case to identify factors promoting or limiting growth. To his surprise, he finds that the presence of money in hand, or the fame of the faculty or the president, are not primary factors.

In order of importance, Mr. Davis listed the following conditions as significant factors in determining the rise in stature of a college:

1. The existence of well-defined and generally recognized objectives.
2. A sense of mission in the accomplishment of these objectives.
3. The interest and involvement of the Board of Trustees, administration, faculty and friends of the college.
4. Boldness in planning and action.
5. Willingness to spend money to raise money.

Mr. Davis stressed the importance to the college of the funds it had in hand to start operations, but warned that the college must be alert that it does not become solely identified with a single family.

Thus, the development operation at the college began, in the sense of having a staff and formal program, by the time we opened the doors for instruction. It evolved, with the urging and full participation of members of the board, as a volunteer program. While the president and others of the staff have been known to ask potential donors for gifts, the usual solicitation is made by a volunteer. A businessman who knows the college introduces us to one who does not; the staff provides background material, a formal proposal when appropriate, and may arrange the meeting. Volunteers and staff together plan the fundraising activities.

Funds did not flow in forthwith. In Paul Davis's well-remembered words, "You can't put the reaper behind the plow."

At the December meeting of the board I reported on the student activities (including our first dormitory Christmas party, mentioned in Chapter 6) and on faculty recruiting. Since our books of account were kept by the common business office of the colleges, which was overworked and usually at least a month behind schedule, I did not know the college's current cash balance. I was startled, therefore, when the controller, Paul H. Burton, reported to the board that Harvey Mudd College had cash on hand to meet its payroll for another week at most. An awkward silence followed. Since no one volunteered any help, I had a great deal of psychological time to think about liquidating the college. Finally, after what may have been a minute but seemed to me a month, another board member raised a question about landscaping; once that had been answered, someone else moved adjournment. We all went home. I didn't sleep for the next forty-eight hours. Gifts did indeed flow in at year end in sufficient quantity to fund the college until the second semester's tuitions were paid. I decided we needed to know our current cash position more quickly, and that we urgently needed that development program.

The following January (1958) the board established several subcommittees of the Ways and Means Committee, each chaired by a trustee but authorized to add non-trustees to its membership. The Plans and Projects Committee, chaired by William B. Coberly, Jr., had as its task the identification of items of support which might appeal to a particular donor— such as a building, a scholarship, or a tree—and to establish the price and the specifications in each case, ready at hand if the opportunity for support should appear.[4] The Corporations Committee, under the chairmanship of James F. Davenport, was assigned the task of acquainting corporations with the work of Harvey Mudd College, and enlisting corporate support.[5] A Foundations Committee, tasked to identify foundations which might support the college, determine the interests of each foundation and the best method of approach, was established under the chairmanship of Dr. Norman F. Sprague, Jr. Finally, a committee was established to organize an "associates program," under the joint chairmanship of Edward R. Valentine[6] and Stuart O'Melveny.[7] The chairman of the Ways and Means Committee, now including these new subcommittee chairmen, continued to be Leroy A. Garrett.

FOUNDATIONS

The first of these subcommittees to become active was the Foundations Committee, chaired by Norm Sprague. Henry Mudd, George McKelvey, and I each made calls on major foundations based in New York City during the winter of 1958. These resulted in two grants which became available that summer—much more rapidly than a grant proposal is normally handled—and which were tremendously helpful in shaping the teaching at Harvey Mudd College. Other foundations we contacted at that time supported the college somewhat later. These first two major "outside" grants deserve individual comment.[8]

One was a grant from the Carnegie Corporation of New York, in the amount of $138,000, to enable the new college to employ faculty to develop course materials in advance of the actual need in the classroom; in effect, to make use of the latitude a new beginning provides for educational innovation. We were free to expend the funds in a period of years and were given wide latitude in their use; we could employ consultants if we chose, as well as free faculty for planning. (As we saw in Chapter 6, these funds proved most helpful to Harvey Mudd College when we ran into an unexpected attrition problem. We will learn in Chapter 15, on Educational Innovation, of other work the Carnegie grant made possible.)

Despite our need for funds, the Carnegie grant and the help of its staff meant much more than money. The Corporation had a deserved national reputation for using its funds where it had found real merit and

4. William C. Coberly, Jr., then president of the California Cotton Oil Corporation, was elected to the Board on August 8, 1957. Bill, a member of a well-established California family, was very well acquainted, a nationally ranked trap shooter, and a pillar of strength. A patient friend with a twinkle in his eye, he helped many donors decide exactly what it was they wished to do. Since he also had excellent business judgment and sound artistic taste, he helped both donor and donee.

5. James F. Davenport, an engineer by professional background, was at this time Executive Vice President of Southern California Edison Company. He also was elected to the Board on August 8, 1957. A Harvard graduate in mechanical engineering, he joined Edison in 1926, and remained with the company with two leaves of absence: he served as an Army Air Corps Colonel during World War II, and served the government again as Defense Electric Power Administrator during the Korean War. A loyal and a thorough trustee, he headed our Budget Committee for much of our first decade. When he reported to the Board, his fellow trustees knew all the proper questions had been completely answered. It was a privilege and a pleasure to work with him.

6. Edward Valentine was elected to the Board on August 8, 1957. He was at that time president of the Robinson Building Company; he had earlier been Chairman and Chief Executive Officer of the J.W. Robinson company. He was Chairman of the Board of the Huntington Hospital, a trustee of the California Institute of Technology, director of a number of corporations, and gave leadership to many civic enterprises.

7. Stuart O'Melveny, then Chairman of the Board of Title Insurance and Trust Company, was elected to the board on October 17, 1957. A lawyer and a graduate of the University of California,

Berkeley (elected to Phi Beta Kappa on junior standing) Stuart joined his father's law firm (now O'Melveny and Myers) in 1912. He moved to Title Insurance and Trust in 1923 as first vice-president, later becoming president, and then chairman of the board. He served as director of many corporations, had been a regent of the University of California, and had been president of the Caltech Associates.

8. "Outside" because the foundation in question had no overlapping trustees with Harvey Mudd College. The College had by this time received support from the Harvey S. and Mildred E. Mudd Foundation, and from the Seeley W. Mudd Foundation.

9. John W. Gardner was at the time president of the Carnegie Corporation and of the Carnegie Foundation for the Advancment of Teaching. He was Secretary of Health, Education and Welfare (1965-68), chairman of the National Urban Coalition (1978-80), founding chairman of Common Cause (1970-77) and a co-founder of Independent Sector. In the latter half of the 1980s he has done substantial research on the subject of leadership, leading to a series of papers, and then the most thoughtful book on the subject I have seen.

opportunity. Before the grant decision was made, we had the benefit of a visit by Jack Honey, of the Carnegie staff, who carefully reviewed our plans and told us what was going on elsewhere. John W. Gardner, then president of the Carnegie Corporation, not only gave us a hearing but gave a luncheon at his New York City headquarters at which he introduced me to a number of other foundation executives and introduced them to the story of Harvey Mudd College.[9] He later traveled to California to speak to the Founding Friends of Harvey Mudd College. The Annual Report of the Carnegie Corporation identified Harvey Mudd College as a promising educational venture. These endorsements from a recognized national authority were invaluable to a new college.

The second grant, in the amount of $28,000, was from the Fund for the Advancement of Education, a Ford Foundation subsidiary. The Fund was another foundation recognized nationally for its understanding of higher education. The money made possible a workshop, lasting through most of the summer of 1958, to which we invited a number of faculty members from other institutions whose innovative teaching we had learned to respect, and they, together with an equal number of our own faculty, explored how we might best use our opportunity to design the junior and senior years of a new curriculum. In particular, we hoped to make the most of our opportunity in engineering and in the humanities and social sciences. Here again, the "validation" of the fund was important to us as we went about the business of attracting faculty, students, and money.

In its first six months, the Foundations Committee could count two immediate successes, plus important gains in visibility with many other charitable foundations which would in time support us. Dr. Sprague reported to the board that over fifty foundations were under active research.

THE FOUNDING FRIENDS OF HARVEY MUDD COLLEGE

Two of the members of the Board of Trustees, both elected before 1958, joined with a particular plan in mind to raise money for Harvey Mudd College. They were Ed Valentine and Stuart O'Melveny, both widely respected, both trustees of the California Institute of Technology, and both friends and admirers of Harvey S. Mudd over much of his life. They had been active in promoting the Associates of the California Institute of Technology, an organization whose members made substantial annual contributions to Caltech. Harvey Mudd College, they suspected, could use similar help, and they volunteered. They enlisted the support of James Page, then chairman of the Caltech board, and called a meeting of friends and former colleagues of Harvey Mudd. Henry Mudd and I were also invited. Ed Valentine asked Henry to tell how his family became involved with Harvey Mudd College, and Henry gave this history. He then asked me to tell how far the college had progressed (as of May 17, 1958, the time of this meeting) and I did. He then said, "Every man in this room owes a great deal to Harvey Mudd. Henry has bitten off everything he can chew. I think we should pitch in and help." A week later Ed Valentine reported to the board that seven charter members had paid $1000 each, and eleven others had pledged to do so.

One of these charter members was Henry Duque,[10] a well-known lawyer. The Founding Friends organized a Board of Governors, and Henry Duque became chairman. Shortly thereafter, Henry was also elected to the board of Harvey Mudd College, where he served with distinction for many years. Eleven months after the charter meeting, Henry was able to report to the board that the membership of the Founding Friends stood at sixty-five, and was climbing.

The pattern for the Founding Friends was to hold two or more dinner meetings a year. At each meeting members heard a progress report from the college, met faculty members and students also invited to attend, and heard from a distinguished speaker. The first such speaker was Admiral Arthur Radford, then recently retired as chairman of the Joint Chiefs of Staff.

I might add that when the concept of the "associates' program" was first advanced, Paul Davis felt it was premature; the college did not yet have the constituency to support such a group. (However, he did not object to making the attempt.) He was of course correct: The college had not as yet earned many friends of the necessary resources and commitment. The late Harvey S. Mudd, on the other hand, had.

PUBLIC RELATIONS

Since Harvey Mudd College was new and little known, we needed help in developing better public understanding of what we were and hoped to do. Our problem was that we had very little money with which to employ a public relations firm. Paul Davis suggested we might find a knowledgeable firm to volunteer, as a public service, rather than serve for a fee. Accordingly Henry Mudd searched through his considerable corporate contacts to find a respected and effective firm we might approach.

I learned that good public relations counsel is quite different from an advertising agency, although counsel may suggest advertising and identify a good agency when appropriate. The task of public relations counsel is to identify the constituencies it is important to influence and devise the best ways to do so within the available resources.

Henry Mudd found that the firm of Braun and Company was universally respected, so he and I approached Theodore W. Braun to see if he would be interested in volunteering his own services and hopefully those of his firm.[11] Ted said he did not know whether he could or would be of help, but that if we would give him ten days or so he would decide;

10. Henry Duque was one of nine children of Thomas L. Duque, a banker who arrived in Los Angeles in 1888. The senior Mr. Duque, born in Cuba, also served as Consul for the Republics of Ecuador, Honduras and Cuba. Each of his children became prominent in the business and social life of the community. Henry Duque, in addition to having a thriving law practice and serving Harvey Mudd College and the California Institute of Technology, was active in a variety of other community affairs.

11. Ted Braun, a tall man, volunteered in World War I when somewhat under the legal age. He was gassed, and spent

two postservice years convalescing. By the time he was discharged he had fallen in love with Beatrice Banning, a nurse volunteer, and he went to the West Coast, where she lived. Starting as a box boy in a grocery store, he showed extraordinary talent for finding the right way to do things. By the 1930s he had established a reputation at Safeway Stores as having remarkable public relations skills (and had married Bea). In due course he set up his own firm, Braun and Company, which had a small and select staff, and a small and select group of corporate clients.

12. As of 1990, Clifford A. Miller was Chairman, Braun & Co., Executive Vice President, Great Western Financial Corporation, and Chairman of the Board of Trustees, Harvey Mudd College.

Theodore W. Braun

might he learn some facts about Harvey Mudd College on his own? We agreed.

We next heard from his two colleagues, Clifford A. Miller and Bruce Nathan.[12] Might they come out and learn about the college? They certainly might. Out they came, and interviewed faculty, staff, and students. They examined the college's financial statements and questioned the financial officers. They were friendly, interested, and thorough. Back they went to Los Angeles, to interview trustees and I know not whom else. I am sure they had developed an informed judgment of the college and its prospects and briefed Ted Braun thoroughly.

Ted telephoned Henry within the week to say he and his colleagues would be happy to help. Six weeks later Leroy Garrett, chairman of the Ways and Means Committee, reported to the board we now had a Public Relations Committee chaired by Ted Braun, that it had in hand a list of recommendations from Braun & Co., and that work to implement these recommendations would begin promptly. We set a consistent style for college communications; adopted a descriptive name identifying us as a college of engineering and science; and began a search for a professional writer to create a descriptive brochure introducing the college. We also defined the market for a newsletter and for news releases.

I have reported in Chapter 6 that an article in the education section of *Time* magazine, appearing some months after our Public Relations Committee was established, brought us the two senior transfer students in mathematics we needed to have the college considered for accreditation. I still do not know how *Time* came upon our story, but I suspect Braun & Co. may have helped.

There was one other public relations triumph early in the academic year 1957-58 which benefited all engineering colleges in the United States, but was not of our planning. On October 4, 1957, some three weeks after Harvey Mudd College began instruction, the Union of Soviet Socialist Republics launched the world's first globe-circling satellite, known as *Sputnik*. In the United States, public interest in the teaching of engineering soared.

CORPORATIONS

At the April, 1958, meeting of the Board of Trustees, Jim Davenport reported he and five other corporate officers involved with the college had each agreed to secure $5000 in corporate scholarship support for Harvey Mudd College students. Based on this commitment and other scholarship funds in hand or pledged, the board voted to commit the $64,000 estimated as needed for the next academic year's scholarship support.

All in all, the first six months of 1958 had been busy ones in establishing the development program of Harvey Mudd College.

CHANGES IN THE BOARD OF TRUSTEES

No review of these busy months in 1958 could be complete without noting two major changes that took place in the Board of Trustees. The board is responsible for all of the life of the college, not simply fundraising, so these comments go beyond the stated subject of this chapter. Mrs. Harvey S. Mudd submitted her resignation as chairwoman to the board on April 16, 1958. She was at that time in declining health. Four months later, on August 23, 1958, she died. We lost a great friend. In the words of the board resolution at its next subsequent meeting, "the board records with deep appreciation its indebtedness to her for her vision and leadership as colleague and chairman, for her participation in the affairs of the campus with both faculty and students, and for her generous support of the college." To this I would add my personal indebtedness for her friendship and understanding, and for her firm conviction that the college which bore her husband's name would become a significant source of the responsible technical leadership of subsequent generations.

The board elected Henry T. Mudd its chairman upon the resignation of Mrs. Harvey Mudd. Henry continued in this responsibility for the next twenty-three years.

The second major change was the board's growth in membership. During the academic year 1956-57 the board had grown by the election of Kenneth S. Pitzer, then dean of the College of Chemistry of the University of California, Berkeley; James F. Davenport, Joseph L. Hegener (then chairman of the board of the McCulloch Corporation), Edward L. Valentine, William B. Coberly, and Robert Hornby. Several of these new trustees, as we have seen, had taken major assignments in the development program. In the year 1957-58, the board also elected Stuart O'Melveny, Henry Duque, and Ernest J. Loebbecke. Mr. Hornby, who had expected to be in Southern California much of the time, found that he would not, and resigned.[13] In the year 1958-59, the board elected George Gose and Theodore W. Braun. Garner Beckett, a founding trustee, retired, and Edward R. Valentine (the Founding Friends of Harvey Mudd College well launched) resigned. The board thus gained eleven members (and lost four) over this three year period. I will discuss below the strong leadership the college had from the development activities of George Gose and Ernie Loebbecke.

THE DEVELOPMENT COUNCIL

As of September, 1958, the Committee on Ways and Means had several subcommittees, with more in prospect. These included the subcommittees responsible for the Founding Friends, for corporate support, for special gifts (earlier called Plans and Projects), for cultivating support from foundations, and for public relations. Programs for involving the help of parents, and for soliciting testamentary gifts, (known as deferred gifts)

13. Robert A. Hornby, then president of Pacific Lighting Corporation, had his headquarters in San Francisco. A civil engineer active in many civic activities, he had begun his career with Southern California Gas Company, a subsidiary of Pacific Lighting Corporation.

14. George B. Gose, Missouri born, earned his baccalaureate degree in 1931 at the University of California at Los Angeles, and his law degree at the same institution, three years later. He practiced law in the Los Angeles area for eight years. He joined Pacific Mutual Life Insurance Company in 1942. He served as a naval officer in World War II, returning to Pacific Mutual in 1946. He became general counsel in 1949 and executive vice president in 1955. He had been a leader in a number of business and community organizations prior to joining the Board of Trustees of Harvey Mudd College.

15. Minutes of Board of Trustees, Harvey Mudd College, July 29, 1958.

16. Dorothy C. Harris joined the staff of the Development Office in 1959, and served the College with diligence and high ability for the next thirty years. She has had nearly every responsibility within the development activity, including in particular the nurture of support groups. Educated at the University of Oklahoma, Dorothy came to know Southern California well, and made many friends in many different communities here.

were being planned. We clearly needed to keep these many activities coordinated and supported with adequate staff. Accordingly the board decided to reorganize the former Ways and Means Committee as the Development Council, the council members to be the chairs of the several subcommittees. Henry Mudd persuaded his friend George Gose, then executive vice president of Pacific Mutual Life Insurance Company, to join the Board of Trustees and to chair the new Development Council.[14] George became a tremendous pillar of strength.

George McKelvey was diligent in locating and persuading the additional staff we needed. Doris Ballard, formerly of the Alumni and Fund Office of Colgate University, joined the development staff in July, 1958, "to work on all phases of the development program."[15] Charles E. Persons of Los Altos was engaged that summer to prepare a brochure describing the college. Some months later Dorothy Harris joined the development staff to do research, beginning what proved to be three decades of able and devoted service to all the development constituencies of the college.[16] Zaner Faust, a New England newspaperman with a zest for adventure and a delightful sense of humor, was appointed in 1959 to head the college's news bureau. Richard Mason, an experienced fundraiser who had worked with the Cumerford organization, joined the development staff in July, 1959.

George Gose took a firm and friendly hand in moving things along. Once or sometimes twice a month, he played host to a luncheon—often in the executive dining room of Pacific Mutual—which introduced the college to corporate executives or other new friends. Both Henry Mudd and I were often present, and we would tell the college history and accomplishments to date. The group was small enough for open discussion and might lead to a subsequent visit to the college by our new friends. We involved many donors in this way, and also recruited friends who served the college as trustees, or who involved others who contributed work, wealth, or wisdom.

The two Georges—Gose and McKelvey—also kept each of us, volunteer or staff, informed about the progress of all facets of the development program. We knew which foundations and corporations were approached and what came of the approach. We knew of progress with the Founding Friends program, of notable public relations opportunities, and of individuals of means who were becoming interested in supporting the college. Success in one area increased the interest of each committee in proving it was "carrying its weight."

George Gose also found ways to help each of his subcommittee chairmen. If we needed help in securing a speaker for a Founding Friends dinner, or were searching for an introduction to a trustee of a particular foundation, he was ingenious and persistent in finding a way to accomplish the task.

I overstepped his patience only once. Jean and I invited Mr. and Mrs. Gose for dinner in Claremont, followed by a dance program at Bridges Auditorium. It is a long way from the Gose home in Palos Verdes to Claremont, and George's interest in national dance forms was less intense than I had assumed. He later thanked us for the evening and said that he thoroughly enjoyed working for the college, but "please, no more Spanish dancers."

The "Futures" Program

Over the long term, most colleges and universities find that many of their larger gifts come by bequests or other instruments for distributing estates. Many people who wish to support a college are reluctant to commit any substantial portion of their assets until they are sure their own lifetime needs, and the bequests they hope to make to others, are first attended to.

Charitable organizations, attorneys, and accountants have developed a variety of methods for transferring a portion of a person's assets to the charitable organization following the death of the donor. These forms of giving are often referred to by the euphemism "futures." Harvey Mudd College needed to establish a "futures" program.

Indeed, such an essential program had been established by Mr. and Mrs. Harvey S. Mudd before I had ever heard either the Mudd name or the "futures" expression. Much of their assets were used to fund the Mildred E. and Harvey S. Mudd Foundation. Upon the founding of the college it became Mrs. Mudd's intent that the foundation continue to support the college, which it did. In this sense Mrs. Mudd's determination, and her generosity, have supported the college many years after her death.

A frequently used mechanism for such gifts is the life income contract (the forerunner of today's unitrust). Under this arrangement, the donor gives assets to the college with the agreement that during his or her lifetime, or others the donor designates, the income from these assets is paid to the person(s) designated. On the death of the last designee, the unexpended balance of the gift becomes the property of the college for whatever purposes the donor and the college had mutually designated— for example, for scholarship support of students at the college. A variation on this arrangement is the annuity contract, under which fixed payments are guaranteed the designee for life, which may require the distribution of some part of the initial principal.

Harvey Mudd College was not at first legally able to write either life income or annuity contracts. The law requires (properly, I believe) that a charitable organization have years of experience in handling investment assets, and in demonstrating fiduciary responsibility, before the organization is authorized to accept such contracts. Accordingly Claremont College volunteered, by action of the Board of Fellows on June 7, 1958, to accept and administer such contracts on behalf of Harvey Mudd College. The Harvey Mudd College board agreed to use these good offices, and grateful we were.

At its December 17, 1958 meeting, the Harvey Mudd board accepted our first two life income contracts, and transmitted them to Claremont College for administration.

The first of the two was written for Mr. and Mrs. M. Guy Edwards of Pasadena. (Mr. Edwards, a distinguished exploration geologist, also happened to be brother to an aunt of mine). The second was written for Paul H. Davis, our fundraising consultant, who told us he planned to return to the college all fees we had paid him, subject to life income reservation. He made good on that generous plan. He also personally checked out whether we had a workable scheme for accepting life income funds!

The first essential step in our futures program was to recruit Ernest J. Loebbecke, then president of Title Insurance and Trust Company.[17] When Ernie was elected a trustee of the college on August 12, 1958, he joined with the intention of helping the college develop a futures program. He knew everybody in the business community, and a great many people involved in helping others plan their testamentary giving not only knew Ernie but did business, or hoped to do so, with Title Insurance and Trust.

Ernie's first move was to recruit two able colleagues: Jack Charleville and Miles Flint. Jack, a trust officer with Title Insurance and Trust Company, was widely acquainted with estate attorneys, particularly in the San Gabriel Valley area.[18] Miles Flint, another old friend of Ernie's, headed the trust department of the Citizen's Bank. The three of them made up the first lists of attorneys and accountants to be cultivated.

Ernie took on his new responsibilities with characteristic energy. He acted as host for luncheons in downtown Los Angeles, and also in Santa Barbara, San Diego, Phoenix, San Francisco, Portland, and Seattle (to give a partial listing). Each such luncheon was attended by lawyers, accountants, and trust officers, who heard from me about the mission and history of the college and from Ernie about the importance of the college to the future of the communities represented. On many occasions Henry Mudd also shared in the presentation. We had receptions on campus for the same clientele and took two sizeable groups of them to Henry Mudd's ranch, Saddle Rock, in each case for half a day's outing. Needless to say, the presentation was part of each affair.

It is not easy to quantify the help Harvey Mudd College has had from the futures program. One never knows how an individual may have become interested in a college, nor which advisor had the confidence of the trustor. But in many cases we can trace who said what to whom and what then happened; we can trace some, but not all, of our bequests to those meetings that Ernie hosted. In 1978, twenty years after the program was initiated, the college had received over $2 million in "matured futures gifts," and had been informed of another $5 million of which the college was the intended beneficiary. None of these funds was "in hand or sight" when the program began. It remains true that much of the college's endowment and much of the plant and equipment came into being through testamentary gifts.

Alumni

George McKelvey had come to Harvey Mudd College from the American Alumni Council. Accordingly, as soon as the college had seniors, he began the work of keeping in touch with alumni. In the early years, faculty members corresponded with our few graduates to learn how they were faring in employment or in graduate school. The Alumni

17. Ernest J. Loebbecke grew up near Chico, California, and studied business administration at the University of San Francisco (aided, if I recall correctly, by a football scholarship.) He took further education in law and accountancy following graduation. He joined Title Insurance and Trust Company's Accounting Department in 1934, subsequently becoming treasurer and vice-president, executive vice-president, president, and chairman of the Board. He has been active, and is currently active as of 1990, in more civic, business and philanthropic organizations than we have space to list here, and has been designated an outstanding citizen by several major organizations.

18. Jack Charleville later joined the staff of Harvey Mudd College as the Futures Program grew in scope, and this began a multifaceted relationship between Harvey Mudd College and Jack's family. His daughter, Billye, was married to Captain Lefteris Lavrakas, who in 1960 commanded a destroyer squadron based at Long Beach. "Lefty" Lavrakas, a careeer Naval officer, had served on the destroyer *Aaron Ward,* which had the unenviable distinction of having engaged some 25 kamikaze aircraft off Okinawa on May 3, 1945, destroying five, taking hits from five, and reaching port the next morning with the help of a towing vessel. (This story is told in the book *Brave Ship, Brave Men* by Lt. Commander Arnold S. Lott, Bobbs Merrill, 1964.) Upon his retirement from the Navy, Lefty Lavrakas took his doctorate in education at Claremont Graduate School, and became a secondary school administrator. Their son John Lavrakas, HMC '74, also taught secondary school after graduation, and is now (1991) in the satellite navigation business.

Association dates from 1965; by that time our graduates were dispersing, and wanted to keep in touch with each other and with the college. The early meetings of the Alumni Board of Governors were devoted to deciding what, if anything, the alumni really wanted to do together. The goals which were in due course adopted included moral and financial support for the college; keeping alumni in touch with each other; job placement for graduates; and help in student recruitment. Alumni Days and Homecoming Days were early ventures, and these events were organized and directed by alumni; they were more successful, of course, in reaching the graduates living in Southern California than they were with those living at a distance. A next felt need was for a current list of alumni names and addresses. The alumni were interested in giving to the college, even in the early years when few had much to give; sports equipment for intramural teams, or scholarship grants to specific students, were examples of early projects that involved a number of alumni. Once there was an organized Board of Governors representing the alumni, it became possible for them to assign alumni representatives to work with committees of the Board of Trustees, to assist in corporate relations, to help in the recruiting of students, and to serve the college in other ways.

A consequence of this closeness is that the Board of Governors has been able to claim, ever since its founding, that the fraction of graduates who participate annually in the Alumni Fundd is in the top 1 percent of colleges and universities in the nation. (In most years more than 50 percent of our alumni contribute.) This evidence of interest and loyalty has been very welcome in its own right, even in the early years when the amounts were modest, and has enabled the college to say to other donors that those who know the college best are very loyal indeed. And, as the number and the prosperity of graduates have increased with the decades, so has the annual size of the Alumni Fundd. Alumni contributions include work and wisdom as well as wealth. Since 1970 the college has had formal alumni representation on its Board of Trustees, alumni regularly return to give seminars or recruit employees or work with the Engineering Clinic, and many other kinds of alumni support regularly enrich the life of the college.

THE GALILEO SOCIETY

It became evident early in our fundraising experience that the college had a number of friends who would be happy to contribute gifts ranging up to several hundred dollars, but who were unlikely to contribute the thousand dollars that was the minimum entrance fee for the Founding Friends of Harvey Mudd College. Ted Braun suggested we form a support group for such potential donors. John Luhring, then vice-president of Union Bank and a friend of the college, volunteered in 1960 to organize such a group. Since Harvey Mudd College had no alumni in 1960, it seemed appropriate to name the group the Honorary Alumni, its members contributing more or less as would alumni of longer established institutions. The Board of Trustees authorized the forming of the Honorary Alumni in September of that year. Within several months a number of new friends joined. Most of these new supporters were from the Claremont area. They were close enough to attend college functions, meet our students and faculty, and form friendships with these Claremont newcomers. Others also joined. Some were from Southern California, but more distant. A parents' group had been organized under the leadership of Llewelyn Barden, father of our student Jim Barden, and a number of these parents became members of the Honorary Alumni.

Over the next two years several trends evolved. We had, by then, alumni who had earned degrees with four years of hard work, and they were displeased with the name of the Honorary Alumni, which to them sounded as though the college were peddling honorary degrees.[19] It was straightforward to keep in touch with the growing local membership of the group. The more distant ones were hard to reach for meetings and were in any event contributing to the college whether or not affiliated with a formal group. The year 1964 was the four hundredth anniversary of the birth of Galileo Galilei, who did much to begin the scientific revolution of the early Renaissance. The Board of Trustees agreed on the desirability of a name change. The Board of Governors of the Honorary Alumni, after discussions with faculty members about possible names, requested the Board of Trustees to change the name from Honorary Alumni to the Galileo Society, and the trustees agreed.

Over the next decade the Galileo Society flourished and grew. Under the leadership of Gerald R. Case,[20] many friends were introduced to the college who in time contributed substantially beyond the level required for nominal membership. Members of the Galileo Society held luncheons and dinners at which they met the students they supported and heard from the faculty and administration. Field trips to NASA installations and similar points of interest gave the members opportunity to see first hand some of the technical developments then in the news. We of the faculty and administration, in turn, felt we were surrounded by interested friends. Indeed, we were.

ARCS

The news of the Soviet *Sputnik* was broadcast throughout the United States. In particular, it reached the ears of Mrs. Florence Malouf, as she drove from Palm Springs to her home in Los Angeles. She, along with many others, was shocked that the USSR was outstripping the United States in technological accomplishments that might have military applications. Furthermore, she decided she should do something about it. Some days later she presented herself at the office of President DuBridge of the

19. Years later, the Board of Governors of the Harvey Mudd College Alumni Association would decide to award the title of Honorary Alumnus (or Alumna) to a few people, ususally retiring faculty, of their choice.

20. Gerald R. Case, a certified public accountant, had his own accountancy firm in the city of Pomona. He also was a leader in many local activities, an organizer of corporations, a world traveller and first-class photographer. He was elected to the Board of Trustees in the mid '60s.

California Institute of Technology and told him she proposed to found a women's organization to raise money for science scholarships. President DuBridge encouraged her to do so. In another week Mrs. Malouf had established Achievement Rewards for College Scientists (ARCS), was recruiting members, and had applied to obtain status for ARCS as a tax-exempt organization.

ARCS is now a national organization with many local chapters, following the initial one in Los Angeles. It is not an organization affiliated with Harvey Mudd College or any other single institution, but it has been important to a number of centers of scientific education in Southern California, including our college. Many of our constituents—wives of trustees, faculty members, alumnae—have worked diligently and effectively as ARCS members to recruit new members, organize fundraising banquets, conduct campus and plant tours, and much else. The ladies of ARCS have been our most consistently helpful scholarship donors, and (as of 1990) 248 of our graduates have had their education at Harvey Mudd College supported in part by ARCS. This report on fundraising would be incomplete if it lacked a salute to these determined ladies.

STAFF

The reader will have detected that by 1965, ten years after the college was founded, we had established a fundraising organization with many effective volunteers. Such a group requires reliable staff support. George McKelvey had not only to manage the recruiting of volunteers but also to find the staff to give them help.

I have reported on the first of the development staff members: George McKelvey himself, Doris Ballard, Dorothy Harris, Zaner Faust and Richard Mason. Doris Ballard left in 1961. David Lavender began his career in development here in 1961, leaving in 1963 to become director of development for Carleton University.[21] As the futures program grew, Jack Charleville joined our staff.[22] Jack, a trust officer and former city manager of Pasadena, was appointed to assist Ernie Loebbecke in March, 1962. Dick Mason left in 1961 to return to a professional fundraising firm. Michael Kearney, another experienced fund-raiser, joined our staff in August of 1964, to remain for four years, returning again to Harvey Mudd College in 1977, and later completing his development career at the University of San Diego.

No listing of the development staff would be complete without adding our internal "volunteers"—the president and his wife, Dean Gene Hotchkiss and his wife, Sue, Spif and Nancy Little, and any number of our faculty and their spouses.

21. The Development Office of Harvey Mudd College became a training ground for many who went elsewhere to head development programs; Colgate University, the University of Iowa, the University of Oregon to name but a few.

22. Minutes of the Board of Trustees of Harvey Mudd College, March 10, 1962.

SOCIAL NOTES

Working with our volunteers very often turned out to be just plain fun. There was, of course, great shared satisfaction in bringing in money for our new college. In addition, those of us on the staff had the privilege of working with people of good will, extensive knowledge, and great good humor. George McKelvey and I remember with glee one such meeting in Northern California. Several of us traveled with Charlie Lee (in his corporate Lockheed Lodestar) to a two-day planning session at George Gose's mountain cabin at Squaw Creek. We accomplished a great deal during those two days, including a reorganization plan for the committee structure of the Board of Trustees, but the six of us who were there also did some fishing, hiking, our own cooking and housekeeping.[23] I took a brief swim in Squaw Creek (which must have originated in a glacier some five miles upstream), and later we all enjoyed singing and storytelling. There were many other meetings, formal and informal, with trustees and other volunteers. We built the college, and we also built many happy friendships.

SUMMARY

In this chapter I have attempted to tell the story of the fundraising for Harvey Mudd College from the inception of the college to the mid-1960s. I will return in another chapter to the story of the next decade. Perhaps the briefest way to summarize the importance of the development program to that time is to note we had constructed much of our campus by 1965, and the cost of instruction for a Harvey Mudd student for the academic year 1964-65 was met by three sources: 38 percent by tuition, 5 percent by income from endowments, and 57 percent by gifts for current operations.

23. Bob Hastings writes (March 25, 1991) "About George Gose's Squaw Creek Cabin: I forgot exactly how many were in that party but I do very distinctly recall that you and Charlie and one other outstanding engineer tried to fix a butane heater, George having failed completely himself. As I was no help at all, I took a walk, and along the trail I met a woman who seemed a frequent camper in that area. I happened to mention to her the problem we were having with the butane heater and she remarked that George and his friends who were wont to use the cabin always had the problem and never knew how to fix it. I countered that we had a group of men who were topflight engineers and scientists and she allowed that they probably weren't much better at fixing things than any of George's previous guests, and volunteered to fix it herself. She walked with me to the cabin, entered it, gave the heater one hell of a swift kick on the side, the burner ignited, and she departed, with a knowing smile on her face." (Private communication to J. B. Platt.)

Saddle Rock!

1. There was also one urgent isssue:
How to meet the next week's payroll?
See Chapter 7.

A
T the meeting of the Board of Trustees of Harvey Mudd College held December 18, 1957, some three months after the college had opened its doors, the board had before it a number of issues that would require action within months.[1] What faculty appointments should we make for the next academic year? How many freshmen should we recruit for the next entering class? Should we increase tuition? What physical facilities would we require next year? The next five years?

I proposed that the board consider an all-day retreat, together with faculty and staff, to consider these matters. Henry Mudd invited us all to hold the retreat at his family's ranch in the Malibu mountains. The board voted to accept this generous invitation and to express its gratitude to Mr. and Mrs. Mudd.[2] The board also voted to hold a prior meeting in Claremont, early in January, to inspect our current campus and facilities, and to consider what information it would wish available for the discussions at the retreat.

My suggestion, and Henry Mudd's invitation, were not completely unprompted. Another trustee, Rudolph J. Wig, was thoroughly convinced of the value of such retreats in building confidence and mutual understanding among the constituencies of a college, and had himself sponsored such retreats for Pomona College and San Francisco Theological Seminary, on whose boards he also served. He had suggested this approach to Henry and me and had volunteered to help.

The board met in Claremont, at the Claremont Colleges Faculty House, on January 7, 1958. (Mrs. Mudd was pleased; the Faculty House was the last project she and "her beau," Harvey Mudd, had made possible for the Claremont Colleges prior to his death.) Fifteen of the nineteen board members were present. We toured our one dormitory, looked over the otherwise unoccupied eighteen acres of our campus, and visited the facilities Claremont College and Claremont Men's College were making available to Harvey Mudd. We then convened again at the CMC board room for our formal meeting.

The faculty and staff had prepared a formidable amount of material to outline what would be needed, at what times, if the college were to grow to 185, 278, or 372 students. I spoke first (I had set the agenda!) and noted that the United States was currently graduating 35,000 engineers and scientists per year, with a need for 60,000. We could expect to fulfill less than 0.2 percent of the overall demand. But, if we did our work well, "we will contribute many times our share of the technical leaders." We should give our highest priority to attracting and retaining the best faculty we could find and then give them effective working conditions. We should subordinate enrollment increase, when necessary, to the establishment of the best teaching standards we could attain.

Emery Walker, our dean of admissions, pointed out that some 100,000 young people had turned eighteen that year in California. By 1970 the number would rise to 250,000. Not more than 1 percent of these potential freshmen would have the combination of interest and abilities required to do the work of Harvey Mudd College, and we would compete with many established universities for these students. (Our market would no doubt extend beyond California, but so would our competition.) As of 1958, our laboratory facilities would limit us to an entering Class of '65. By 1960, given a new laboratory building, we could, if we chose, admit the 111 students required for an eventual student body size of 372. As both the applicant pool and the reputation of the college grew, we could expect our selectivity to increase. Tuition could also be expected to increase, and the need for scholarship funds as well; outside sources could be expected to give more scholarship help once the college was accredited. A lively discussion followed.

Bill Davenport, professor of English, reported on our projected faculty needs. Quantitatively, the college expected its faculty members to prepare for classes as well as to meet them, to counsel students and grade papers, to do research and to publish, and to serve both the Claremont Colleges and the larger community. (Four of our seven faculty members held responsibilities in national educational or scientific societies.) One could assign hours to each of these requirements, and knowing the classes to be met and assuming a forty-eight-hour work week, calculate the faculty size we would need. A student body of 185 would require a faculty of 22, one of 278 would require 34, and one of 372 would require 42. A new college, intending to develop new methods of instruction, could expect a larger workload and would need either to add faculty or impose a longer work week. Qualitatively, our ability to attract and retain faculty of stature would depend on our salary scale, on the provision of good teaching and research conditions, and on the caliber of our students. He concluded with the hope that we could hire some faculty members a year in advance of classroom need to take advantage of our opportunity to develop a new curriculum. The college would need to establish policies for sabbaticals and for promotion. The current faculty salary scale ($9,000 "and up" per year for full professors!) was appropriate and competitive, if we made astute use of the "and up." He added that he felt the college rated well in faculty estimation and that the faculty was confident this situation would continue.

I reported that the State of California expected to need 40,000 new faculty members in the coming decade and that the *nation* was currently producing 9,000 Ph.D.s per year, not all of whom would go into teaching. The coming competition for faculty would be brisk.

Art Campbell, professor of chemistry, reviewed our building needs. We had plans in progress for a laboratory building and for the additional dormitory we would need for a student body of 185. If Claremont College and Claremont Men's College continued to make available the space we were then using, these two new buildings were all we would need for a student body of that size. Going to 278 students would require us to provide our own dining facilities, another dormitory, and some classroom space beyond that available at CMC; 278 students, with upperclassmen in four different fields of study, would severely strain our planned laboratory facilities. For 372 students we would also require a fourth dormitory, another laboratory building, and substantially more classroom and office space.

George McKelvey consolidated these presentations in charts representing enrollment, buildings, operating expense, plant expense, and the required annual gift income until "full size" was attained, for each of the three enrollment levels under consideration. He had found that the differences in operating gifts required for the three levels were relatively modest. The major differences were in the building costs required at the larger enrollments. In response to a question, he summed up the cumulative building costs: for 185 students, $2.6 million; for 278 students, $4.7 million; and for 372 students, $6.0 million. He added that of these totals, some $1.5 million was already spent, was in hand, or was pledged. The totals did not include the equivalent cost of space contributed by our sister colleges. (We also shared in the use, but not the capital cost, of some $7 million in central facilities such as the Honnold Library.)

The board instructed the staff to prepare more detailed figures for the forthcoming retreat, based on an assumed 278 students. We could expand or contract from that level depending on finances. We then adjourned to the Faculty House for cocktails and dinner.

SADDLE ROCK! #1

We met again on January 18, 1958, at the ranch of the Henry T. Mudd family, known as Saddle Rock Ranch. It was located in the mountain range which runs east and west, some ten miles inland from the coast in the Malibu area. The ranch included a double-headed peak resembling a Western saddle; hence its name. It was a glorious area, most of it in pasture and woodland, occupying perhaps two square miles. There were cattle and horses. The mountain valley lying below the peak included the ranch house, the manager's home some half mile away, and the barns. The ranch house had a living room which held twenty people comfortably, with a large fireplace; there was a large, well-equipped kitchen, and a bedroom. An ell on the ranch house contained bunks for another dozen people. Some hundred yards from the ranch house stood a guest house, with its own living room, kitchenette, and bedroom. A swimming pool and tennis court were between the main house and the guest house; there was an expanse of lawn surrounding the house.

Saddle Rock Ranch played an important role in the life of Harvey Mudd College. The ranch passed out of the hands of the Mudd family about 1980 and the buildings were lost in a subsequent forest fire, but any college retreat is still called "a Saddle Rock" and recalls the excitement and anticipation that the ranch brought to those of us who were its guests.

Trustees, faculty, and staff began arriving at the ranch about nine o'clock on that Saturday morning, to be greeted by coffee and sweet rolls. When we were assembled, Henry welcomed us, and presiding board Vice Chairman Roy Garrett reviewed the highlights of the prior meeting concerning the possible rates of growth of the college.

The ranch house at Saddlerock.

The group then divided into four subcommittees, each including trustees as well as faculty and staff. (The eighteen trustees outnumbered the fifteen faculty and staff, three of whom served all the Claremont Colleges.) One committee considered buildings and grounds questions; another, admissions and scholarships; a third, faculty and curriculum; and the fourth, "ways and means."

A morning of lively discussion followed. Shortly after noon we broke for a buffet luncheon, to gather in small groups on the lawn and to continue our visiting while eating. Henry suggested that some of the more hardy of the group might enjoy climbing Saddle Rock. Off went about half the group, to climb up 800 feet or so to the top. The climbers were rewarded with a beautiful view of the Pacific Ocean and the Channel Islands.

The entire group met on the lawn after lunch, with board Vice Chairman Bob Hastings presiding, to hear the reports of the subcommittees. Trustee Raymond Hill reported for the building and grounds subcommittee. Its major concern was the urgency of getting on with the first science building, which would be needed by the fall of 1959. This building of some 30,000 square feet would provide adequate laboratory facilities for 278 students and should meet our needs for the next four to six years. Funds were on hand for the next two dormitories, and for a president's house, and progress was on schedule. With the help of Claremont Men's College we could postpone constructing our own dining facilities until the enrollment reached 278. With some crowding and the help of CMC we could also defer construction of classroom and office space until we reached about that size. The ultimate plan involved four dormitories, two laboratory buildings, two classroom-administration-office buildings, and a combined student union and dining hall. We might also eventually need a dormitory for women.

R.J. Wig, the trustee reporting on admissions and scholarships, said that his group recommended that we admit sixty-five freshman students for the Class of 1962; that the admission standards be at least as high as they had been for the first class; and that the college seek accreditation at the earliest possible date. The group referred to the president its recommendations that no tuition increase be instituted for the academic year 1958-59, but that an increase be considered the following year; that some of the general funds of the college be used as loan funds; and that no repayment of scholarship or loan funds be required in 1958-59. To the ways and means committee they recommended that a permanent revolving loan fund be established. Finally, they placed before the board the recommendation that enrollment should total at least 250 by the academic year 1961-62, and that the ultimate goal for enrollment should be at least 400.

Trustee Kenneth Pitzer, (then dean of the College of Chemistry of the University of California, Berkeley) reported the conclusions of the faculty and curriculum subcommittee. He stated that the enrollment should be at least 278 by 1961-62 in order to attract and hold a high caliber faculty. It would be important that the faculty have time for thoughtful planning of courses, and funds should be made available for faculty members to plan curriculum during the summer. Recruiting of faculty for 1958-59 should proceed without delay, especially for the senior appointment in engineering. He then added some personal remarks, emphasizing the college's opportunity for educational leadership and the vital importance of a first-rate faculty. He urged that the salary scale be increased to keep pace with leading institutes of technology, raising the class sizes a little if necessary.

Vice Chairman Roy Garrett reported for the ways and means subcommittee, which had included faculty, staff, and eight of the eighteen trustees. The group had felt that operating funds could be raised in sufficient amounts to balance the budget. Their chief concern was to raise the funds for the science building, with the help of Claremont College and any donors either board could identify and persuade. If necessary, the college would borrow funds. He also reported that the group had studied various ways to raise funds, and had allocated responsibilities for developing these ways. Jim Davenport had agreed to serve as chairman of the Corporations Committee. Bill Coberly volunteered to serve as chairman of the Plans and Projects Committee. Ed Valentine and Stuart O'Melveny had undertaken to organize a program such as the Caltech Associates. And he, Roy Garrett, would take responsibility for special gifts.

The board voted that the student body should reach 250 students by the academic year 1961-62.

Robert J. Bernard ("Mr. Claremont Colleges") added closing remarks, which I quote from the board minutes: "He thanked Mr. Mudd for the opportunity to study the college's problems in beautiful and detached surroundings. Touching on the enormous significance of the college and its prospects, and describing the exhilaration of this kind of enterprise, he concluded that this college has as promising a start as any in Claremont."

We thanked our host, got into our cars, and wound our way down the mountain road, pleased with the day, with our prospects, and with each other.

SADDLE ROCK! #2

The third Saturday of 1959 fell on January 17, and again our trustees, faculty, and staff were convened at Saddle Rock. This year the faculty and staff outnumbered the trustees: sixteen trustees were present, as were thirteen faculty members on Harvey Mudd College appointment plus three on joint appointment with Harvey Mudd and Claremont Men's Colleges.

We had in attendance five members of the Harvey Mudd staff, plus the treasurer, controller, librarian, and chaplain of the Claremont Colleges. We also had two guests, one of whom, Cliff Miller, would later become a trustee and then board chairman.

Following the invocation, Henry Mudd noted the progress of the decisions made a year earlier at Saddle Rock: (1) The building program that had been proposed was on schedule except the third residence hall was a year ahead of schedule; ground would shortly be broken for the President's House. (2) There were three times as many inquiries for admission to the college as there were the previous year. (3) As a result of the admission of junior and senior transfer students, the college was eligible for and was seeking accreditation. (4) Faculty recruitment was on schedule. (5) Considerable national recognition had come to the college through the grants from the Fund for the Advancement of Education, the Carnegie Corporation, and the National Science Foundation, and through faculty activity and publications.

We then divided into subcommittees which met separately. As in the prior year these considered educational planning and faculty employment policy; student admissions, scholarships and loans; buildings and grounds; and development (money raising, formerly known as ways and means.)

Luncheon was again given enough time to include climbing, visiting, and wandering. When we reconvened in the early afternoon, trustee Jim Davenport reported on the summer curriculum study, financed by the Fund for the Advancement of Education, which he had visited in August. The engineering curriculum, and the program in the humanities and social sciences, had been the two foci of the study. Some two dozen people had participated in the study, drawn from our own faculty and from a variety of institutions and disciplines. The outcome had been a clear statement of goals for the engineering program, with a variety of possible methods of reaching these goals from which the engineering faculty could choose; and several possible ways of organizing the work in the humanities and social sciences to educate people able to make broadly informed decisions and to continue learning in the humanities and social sciences after graduation.

Art Campbell, professor of chemistry, reported to the group on the development of extracurricular activities at the college. The student body had established a student government, including a dormitory council and a student court; it had drawn up and adopted a constitution and elected officers. The honor system was, in Art's opinion, the most significant achievement of all. Although the students had needed time and effort to learn the arts of self-government, Art felt they were making excellent progress.

A number of questions were raised concerning our students and their progress. Emery Walker reported our students complained about being overworked but were otherwise very pleased with the college. The transition from high school to college was a challenging one for top high school students and continued to be for our second class. About a quarter of our students worked part-time at paying jobs on campus, and nearly all of them earned a portion of their costs through summer employment, mostly off campus. The college had helped our first class find summer jobs that had value as professional education.

We then moved to reports of the morning's subcommittee meetings, and their recommendations for board action.

Trustee Kenneth Pitzer reported for the subcommittee on educational policy. A number of decisions needed to be made on terms of employment for faculty. The fraction of the retirement benefits paid by the college, and that paid by the faculty member, were being modified in other Claremont Colleges, and we needed a decision on this issue. What tenure policy should the college adopt? (Thus far faculty members had been appointed on an annual basis, with the understanding that a tenure policy would be adopted when we had a faculty to participate in the decision.) What should be our policy on sabbatical leaves? It was the recommendation of the group that the board appoint a subcommittee consisting of faculty and trustees, to explore the policies of the other Claremont Colleges and to propose to the board appropriate policies for Harvey Mudd.

We were agreed that faculty research would be advantageous for the faculty member and for students. Space would shortly be available, but research also would require equipment and operating funds. Policies on faculty research, on funding, and on consulting should also be developed. External funding could be attracted once research became established, but initial support usually would be required from the college if research were to flourish.

One of our trustees, R.J. Wig, had pointed out that the Claremont Colleges would benefit from graduate work in the physical sciences, mathematics, and engineering. Under our intercollegiate agreements such graduate work is the responsibility of Claremont Graduate School, but the undergraduate colleges with science faculties could furnish much of the initial graduate instruction, certainly through the master's degree level. Mr. Wig felt funding might be secured for such graduate instruction. The sense of the subcommittee was that graduate instruction in these fields would benefit Harvey Mudd College, and that we should cooperate with Claremont College (Claremont Graduate School) on request.

Emery Walker, reporting for the subcommittee on student admissions, scholarships, and loans, said the group had considered the need for more scholarship funds if tuition were to be increased; we might otherwise "price ourselves out of the market." With our anticipated accreditation, we could expect perhaps a quarter of our next entering class to bring California State Scholarships with them, and there would be other external scholarship donors as well. However, the need for scholarship funds from the college would continue. The sense of the subcommittee was that some part of the cost of educating a student could appropriately be borne by loan funds, but that the student should not borrow more than one year's tuition over the four years of college attendance. The subcommittee had reviewed a staff paper on estimated enrollment and the scholarship needs required by that enrollment. The paper was submitted to the full board with the subcommittee's endorsement.

Trustee Raymond Hill, reporting for the subcommittee on buildings and grounds, stated that the next buildings on the campus master plan were an office building, a classroom building, and a student union. The sense of the meeting was that planning should begin on these buildings and on some landscaping; the actual commitment of funds for construction could await the raising of money for the purpose.

Trustee George Gose reported for the development subcommittee. The goals adopted for the coming four years' fund raising were $1,500,000 for 1959-60, $781,000 for 1960-61, $729,000 for 1961-62, and $592,000 for 1962-63. The large total for 1959-60 included about one million dollars for the laboratory building. That cost could be retired over several years by borrowing, if necessary. The augmented costs associated with greater faculty fringe benefits, research support, and added scholarship funding had not been included in these projections, and the goals should be increased accordingly. The major sources of funds were expected to be special gifts, corporations, and foundations. Liaison should be established between development subcommittees so that each individual volunteer was kept aware of overall progress.

As the afternoon drew to a close it was clear to all of us that we were growing up. Much remained to be done in building our campus, recruiting students, securing faculty, and raising money. But we were also moving into problems of institutional adolescence; the student body was setting its patterns, student aid needed to be increased according to agreed ground rules, we needed to codify the policies for the attraction and retention of faculty, research needed to be established, and it was not too early to consider what graduate study in the sciences might be like. We were also showing some signs of becoming conservative; we now had more students, more faculty, and more national recognition to conserve.

SADDLE ROCK! #3

On January 23, 1960, Harvey Mudd College held its first Saddle Rock! meeting away from Saddle Rock Ranch. We were the guests of Mr. and Mrs. Van Renssalaer G. Wilbur at their gracious and commodious home in Montecito. Trustee Wilbur had generously offered the use of his home at the prior Saddle Rock meeting, and the board had accepted with gratitude. The Wilbur home was capable of seating fifty of us together in one room, other rooms were available for separate discussions, and out of doors there were delightful gardens in which to wander.

Mr. Wig offered the invocation. Henry Mudd summarized the present position of the college, and noted the accomplishment of the faculty and trustees in bringing the institution to the national standing it was assuming. Nevertheless, we still had much to do. We would spend the morning in subcommittee meetings dealing with faculty policy and research, with admission and scholarship matters, and with development.

We did indeed have a series of lively and helpful discussions, some of which were concluded early enough to permit wandering about the grounds of the Wilbur home before luncheon. Cocktails were served, including Mr. Wilbur's delicious, well-refrigerated, full strength martinis, which we learned to treat with respect. After a pleasant luncheon with much visiting, we reassembled the entire group of seventeen trustees, twenty-four faculty, and seven staff members.

Trustee Kenneth Pitzer reported for the subcommittee on faculty policy and research. He noted that it is customary for a college to offer tenure to its faculty, that Harvey Mudd College had arrived at a point in its history where it should enact tenure regulations, and that the faculty and administration had had the matter under discussion. The subcommittee recommended that the board approve in principle the adoption of a faculty tenure program, and instruct the president to present a detailed program for board consideration. Since a number of our faculty had held continuous tenure at their prior institutions before joining Harvey Mudd, the president should also present whatever tenure decisions he considered appropriate once a tenure program was in place.

He also reported the committee's recommendation that budget provision be made for the establishment of faculty research.

Trustee R.J. Wig, reporting for the subcommittee on admission and scholarship, recommended that tuition and fees remain unchanged for the coming year, but that increases in both should be considered for the year after that; the scholarship budget for 1960-61 should be $80,000, exclusive of funds from outside sources; and thought should be given to increasing the fraction of student aid for junior and senior students to be offered as loans rather than as outright grants.

Trustee George Gose reported for the development subcommittee. He noted that the fundraising goals for calendar year 1960 included $350,000 in funds for current operations and $780,000 in capital funds. Our newly established futures program might produce $500,000 in deferred gifts. The capital funds goals included a portion of the cost of the laboratory building, and part of a total of $600,000 that would be needed for classroom and office buildings.

In the following discussion, R.J. Wig asked about progress in developing a unique curriculum for science and engineering students. I replied we had made good progress in the curricular offerings in mathematics, chemistry, and physics; the engineering program was also "on track" but this was the first year in which engineering courses had been offered; and we still had much to do to develop the upper-division courses in the humanities and social sciences. Fortunately we had splendid help in these fields from our sister colleges.

Warren Wilson, chairman of the engineering faculty and then in his first year at the college, said the juniors majoring in engineering were taking courses in the engineering sciences, such as materials engineering, mechanics, and introduction to electrical engineering. Next year, when we would have senior engineering students, they would take another engineering science course, a design course, and would have elective options that would permit a small degree of specialization toward electrical, mechanical, chemical, or civil engineering. Kenneth Pitzer expressed his satisfaction that the design course came after a thorough exposure to the basic and applied sciences. Raymond Hill spoke with feeling on the importance of the humanities and social sciences in the education of engineers—the founders of the college had in mind not accomplished technicians but broadly educated leaders of scientists and engineers.

After faculty members left, the board members reconvened briefly in formal session. They instructed me to include an item for faculty research in the next year's budget, to present my recommendations for a tenure system at a forthcoming board meeting, and to recommend individual faculty members for tenure consideration. The board adopted the development goals reported above. It also attended to several matters not on the Saddle Rock agenda: it approved two new faculty appointments, legally adopted regulations concerning life income contracts, elected five new trustees, and authorized what became our official college seal.[3]

We did indeed adopt a tenure program, mutually agreed upon by faculty and trustees, at the February board meeting.[4] Six of the seven initial members of the faculty were granted continuous tenure; the seventh, Professor Duane Roller, on medical leave because of health problems and engaged in writing a text, was continued on annual reappointment at his request. Research support was included in the 1960-61 budget. While the Saddle Rock meetings were advisory to the trustees and to the faculty, both groups made use of the advice.

SADDLE ROCK! #4

The fourth annual Saddle Rock conference saw us again at Saddle Rock Ranch on January 21, 1961. Preparation for this meeting, however, started a good three months in advance, and involved many of our trustees and faculty. There were two complications. One was that I had been asked by the National Academy of Sciences to act as science advisor

3. Minutes of the Board of Trustees of Harvey Mudd College, January 23, 1960.

4. Minutes of the Executive Committee, Board of Trustees, Harvey Mudd College, February 24, 1960.

to the United States delegation to the biennial meeting of the member states of UNESCO, and the board had granted me leave for the purpose. Since I would be in Paris for November and much of December; my contribution to the planning had to come months ahead of time.

Much more important, in terms of the future of the college, was a division of opinion within the faculty about the methods of teaching engineering. It had been our hope to appoint an engineer as a member of the initial faculty, but I had not succeeded in that assignment. Warren Wilson had accepted appointment as of January, 1959, eighteen months after we had commenced instruction and five months following the summer study in which we had explored what the engineering curriculum might be. Over the prior two years I had been in touch with 130 possible candidates for the position, had interviewed thirty, had brought at least ten to campus, and had learned from these candidates, all of whom were interested in our venture, a great deal about engineering education. But Warren was the first in whom we were interested who would leave a secure position on an established faculty, with excellent consulting connections, to risk building a new and unorthodox engineering program in a college that might or might not succeed. Warren, who had a distinguished record in engineering education as professor, as dean, and as president in fine institutions and who had led major teaching reforms in established programs, was willing to leave a good job to venture with us. He subscribed to our emphasis on the humanities and social sciences, was thoroughly in agreement on the need for a strong base in the sciences and mathematics, and felt that a small, and new, unspecialized engineering program could be an important national experiment.

What had divided the faculty was how one might teach the art and practice of engineering. An engineer is characterized by interest in solving a problem, and he derives internal rewards from seeing new ideas work in practice. A scientist, on the other hand, draws satisfaction from understanding a situation, not necessarily from altering it. This is of course an oversimplification; much of our initial faculty, including me, had had experience in research as well as in design of new systems. Warren, and the engineering faculty he had attracted, were experimenting with giving student teams new problems to solve. A freshman project had indeed been useful in keeping the interest of some potential engineers who might otherwise have chosen not to endure two years of pure science. The design sequence for upperclassmen was now proposed by the engineering faculty to concentrate on such team solving of unstructured design problems. Much of the science faculty—"old hands" by now, with their own experience in developing new courses—were unwilling to concede academic credit for an unstructured design experience which might, for all they knew, turn out to be blocks and sand piles. A major feature of the engineering curriculum required the consent of a majority of the faculty. I left for Paris with a small but determined engineering faculty frustrated by many of their colleagues in mathematics and the sciences, and conversely.

Saddle Rock seemed to me an excellent opportunity to compare our views of what the college might become in the 1970s, and to air—we hoped to resolve—our disagreements. We had our share of trustees who were engineers of stature and vision. We especially needed their detachment, their wisdom, and their understanding.

The board established a steering committee under the chairmanship of trustee Bob Hastings which included four trustees, three faculty, and three staff to plan Saddle Rock! #4. This committee in turn established five subcommittees, each with trustee, faculty, and staff participation: academic planning and evaluation, buildings and grounds, development, fiscal planning, and research. Each of these subcommittees met in advance of the Saddle Rock meeting, and the steering committee itself planned to meet at Saddle Rock Ranch on the evening before the general meeting, to coordinate their presentations.

We met at Saddle Rock Ranch on January 21, 1961, another glorious day. After coffee and visiting we again met to set the day's program and divided into subgroups to consider what each subcommittee had presented. In the afternoon we heard and discussed the reports of each subgroup—beginning with the least controversial.

Bill Coberly noted that the college had expended or committed about $3.6 million for our three dormitories, the laboratory building, the president's house, and for Kingston and Thomas-Garrett Halls, then under construction. To reach "full size" we would need another $2.5 million for a fourth dormitory, a student union, and a second laboratory building—perhaps 15 percent of this funding was "in hand or in sight." Architectural studies of the student union were beginning.

Bob Hastings said the fiscal planning committee recommended the expenditure of $100,000 to equip the new laboratory building. (The trustees, meeting as a board in late afternoon, approved this recommendation.)

George Gose reported that the development council was making good progress in raising the necessary gifts for operating purposes for the current year's operations; it might also be possible to equip the laboratories. No major donor had yet appeared for the student union. R.J. Wig added that the Claremont Colleges had made a collective appeal for major funding (subject to matching) to the Ford Foundation.

Dean Wooldridge observed that the faculty had made good progress in establishing research; it would be important to our faculty and students to continue some financial support and to reduce the teaching load for faculty members starting new research. We also were developing a policy for patenting inventions made at the college.

Gene Hotchkiss, then in his first years as our dean of students, discussed attrition—students transferring out of Harvey Mudd College. He had interviewed nearly all of our students, whether planning on staying or leaving. He found that our students were working hard, but often without as much personal satisfaction as he or they would hope. More opportunity for recreation, or for some change from study, might help. It would also help if students derived more satisfaction with their substantial academic progress. Trustee Alfred Thomas observed it might be important to the college and our students to plan good recreational space for our student union—it should be more than a dining hall. He also thought we should not postpone construction of the building unduly.

We then came to the controversial issue of "objectives of the college." How much latitude should the engineering faculty have in the development of the engineering curriculum, especially in teaching the "art and practice of engineering"? Many points of view had been aired in the morning's group discussion; these were reported, and others added, in the afternoon's full discussion. How could one be sure of a rigorous intellectual challenge in a problem from some industry? If a student takes a course in higher algebra, a faculty member can test whether or not the student has understood the subject; what equivalent certification can one have if the student has spent a semester on an open-ended engineering task? The faculty in engineering pointed out that many professions have the same ambiguities: a musician judges other musicians, a lawyer judges another lawyer's interpretation of the law. The trustees, including those who were professional engineers, listened and asked many questions of the faculty. They concluded that the business of the college was to educate both engineers and scientists, with as much cross-fertilization as possible. The trustees had no intention of directing the faculty on the best ways of accomplishing these objectives, provided that they were in fact accomplished. Later that afternoon the board directed the president to draft a statement of purpose and circulate it for board consideration.

At day's end we of the faculty and staff were reasonably satisfied we could work out our academic disagreements and that we would do so with the understanding and support of our trustees.

The faculty held evening meetings in the subsequent weeks and decided to authorize the engineering faculty to develop the program in engineering design as they deemed best, subject to review by the full faculty after a period of years. The story of the subsequent development of the Engineering Clinic—a major success—is told in a later chapter.

After these faculty discussions I drafted the following resolution, which the board adopted by mail ballot:

> *RESOLVED, that the trustees of Harvey Mudd College reaffirm the intent to educate engineers well trained in the physical sciences and scientists familiar with engineering and to provide both with sufficient training in the*

*social sciences and humanities to assume leadership in their fields with
understanding of the impact of their work on the rest of society. The trustees
expect that a substantial portion of the graduates of the college will follow
engineering or related careers, but that many will elect graduate study in
other scientific fields. The trustees hence recognize that the curriculum must
be flexible and that new approaches must be made in the teaching of science
and engineering; they note with satisfaction the time and thought the faculty
has given to the solution of this challenging problem. Accordingly, the Board
of Trustees determines to continue the joint faculty-trustee committee on academic planning and evaluation with instructions to carry forward studies and
experimentation to the end that graduates of the college will have the
breadth of training envisaged.*

Today we would probably use the phrase "natural sciences" rather
than "physical sciences," but this statement of purpose and procedure
would otherwise still hold.

SADDLE ROCK! #5

The fifth Saddle Rock! conference—again at Saddle Rock Ranch—was
held on January 22, 1962, attended by twenty-four trustees, eighteen faculty, eight staff, and several guests. It was another beautiful day. The prior
June we had graduated our first entering class. Our campus now had
three dormitories, Kingston and Thomas-Garrett Halls, a laboratory
building, and a president's house. In fact, it was now a recognizable campus. We knew what we were currently teaching and would teach the following year. Some research was under way. We were, of course, financially stretched, but we were managing to do more things than
previously, and the development program was making regular progress.
We were still concerned about attrition, but we understood the causes
somewhat more adequately, and our statistics were improving. It seemed
a good year to take stock and look ahead.

Under the chairmanship of trustee Roy Garrett, we spent most of
the morning in four discussion groups, each looking ahead to the 1970s
to assess the career requirements that would be important to our graduates building their professional careers in those years. Eight of our trustees
present were managing substantial technically based corporations,
(Hughes Aircraft, North American Aviation, Ramo-Wooldridge, Cyprus
Mines, and Southern California Edison, among others) and such fore-
casting was familiar to them. After luncheon, the chairmen of the four
groups reported to all of us the similarities and differences in their fore-
casts. We then split into new discussion groups: one to discuss the art of
teaching and in particular new methods of getting students involved in
their own education; another on a more general review of motivation,
with attention to new psychological evidence on what does and what

doesn't encourage creativity; a third to reflect on the overall changes expected in the Claremont Colleges and ponder what Harvey Mudd could contribute to our sister colleges, or expect them to contribute to us; and a fourth to concern itself with checkpoints along the way, such as what we should watch to know how well or poorly we were progressing.

We concluded that good technical managers can anticipate and prepare for change and that keeping abreast of technological advance is an essential part of this skill. Indeed, we felt the best of the technical managers not only create the changes they find desirable in their own organizations, but in fact change the marketplace itself; a number of success stories were recounted and some horror stories were also analyzed. We observed that the computer revolution could be expected to reach the Claremont Colleges in the near future. (Indeed it did!) And, finally, we decided that Harvey Mudd College should systematically keep track of the subsequent careers of our graduates and of those who had attended but not graduated; from this evidence we might deduce what we were doing well and what needed improvement.

Henry Mudd closed the afternoon by pointing out that we had done much better in building the college than we had any right to anticipate in 1957. Part of our success had been due to factors not of our making: a nationally recognized need for engineers and scientists better and differently educated than their fathers; great help from others of the Claremont Colleges; and the particular demand for engineers and scientists in Southern California. We had required courage, dedication, and hard work from students, faculty, and staff. We had had beginner's luck and naïveté; we might not so readily have set about the task of founding a new college had we known how tough it is to do so. The college might now be doing a relatively first-rate job but, for all our self-examination and despite sometimes agonizing change, perfection always lies tantalizingly just out of reach.

Saddle Rock! #6

Saddle Rock! #6 was held on January 26, 1963, again preceded by a caucus the prior night of faculty, trustees, and staff who planned the meeting. The college had had the benefit of substantial support from the Carnegie Corporation, the Fund for the Advancement of Education, and the National Science Foundation. Some of these funds had been used for evaluating how well we were doing what we had set out to do. Our trustee Dean Wooldridge, then recently retired from the Ramo-Wooldridge Corporation, chaired the steering committee which had organized the meeting, and he had also chaired Saddle Rock! #5. Fifteen trustees and nearly thirty faculty and staff were on hand for a very lively discussion indeed.

The faculty and staff had a plethora of data to produce. We knew who had graduated, and where each graduate was employed or pursuing graduate degrees. We had had reports from most of these graduates on how they were faring, what they felt to be the significant gaps in their undergraduate education, and what they felt were their strengths.

We also had a good deal of information on those who had left the college before graduating. In many cases we knew to which institutions they had transferred and what progress they were making in their new places. We knew the reasons the departing students had given for leaving the college. We also knew some of their strengths and weaknesses.

The third body of data we had compiled dealt with other universities and colleges. What other educational ventures were being tried, and where? How did these institutions evaluate their success, or lack thereof? Conversely, what did other institutions make of new methods we were trying?

In the discussions which followed, these points emerged:

The majority of our alumni were still in graduate school. All seemed to be making adequate progress, although a number reported that their fellow graduate students were better prepared in some technical areas than they. Trustee Fred Lindvall (chairman, Division of Engineering and Applied Science, California Institute of Technology) observed that this was a familiar complaint of engineers: two years out, they felt the need of more technical detail; ten years, more management skills; and twenty years, more humanities and social sciences. The students who had gone directly into employment seemed to be doing well; here again, some were finding areas in which they needed to do considerable learning.

Dean Hotchkiss had been in touch with 106 students who had left Harvey Mudd without graduating. Of these, 65 had voluntarily withdrawn and 41 had been declared ineligible to reregister. Eighty-eight of these students had responded by mail and their comments had been evaluated by an independent consultant. The largest single group of complaints concerned the workload, which was well beyond what they had expected. Most had transferred to other universities or colleges (35 into the University of California system, 7 to other Claremont Colleges, and a total of 88 to all other institutions) and in general were making satisfactory to good progress. About half were still science or engineering majors; the others had shifted fields in their new institutions, primarily into the social sciences. A number of trustees commented that while these students may have been lost to Harvey Mudd College they clearly weren't lost to higher education.

We were beginning to improve our retention of students. A variety of reasons—or speculations—were advanced about what we might now be doing more nearly right. The development of a visible engineering major was encouraging to students who hoped to be engineers. A student union was under construction, giving some hope that not every college building would be dedicated to work. Furthermore, a number of Harvey Mudd graduates were now out in the great world and seemed to be prospering; students in college learned from these predecessors that the work of the college did have rewards. And the faculty, for its part, was less concerned about setting rigorous academic standards, since these standards had in fact been established, and more concerned about helping students develop their abilities to meet these standards. We still had a way to go, but we were less baffled about how to improve.

The remainder of a full day was spent in group discussion of how best to teach. No final conclusions were reached, but it was clear our trustees were much interested in the development of self-starting engineers and scientists and all the participants had experience of good teachers who had been important in their lives. It was also clear there was a common interest in making the most of the funds available for instruction. Trustee Lee Atwood summarized the afternoon's discussions by observing "it is very refreshing to see a faculty so self-critical and self-analytical as this one is. Naturally it is very stimulating to me. On the other hand, I hope that it doesn't lead to any feeling of running scared as I don't think there is any reason for this at all."

We left Saddle Rock reluctantly at the end of the day, most thankful for the sense of common concern with the importance of teaching.

SADDLE ROCK! #7

We met for the seventh time at Saddle Rock Ranch on January 16, 1964 with twenty-one trustees, eighteen faculty members, nine staff members of Harvey Mudd or other Claremont Colleges, and nine guests, including advisors and potential trustees. (The meeting had been preceded the prior evening by a caucus of trustees and staff involved in fundraising or in planning the next day's conference. That caucus had been useful, and it had also been an unqualified social success.) The planned purposes, for this Saddle Rock, were, in the words of the announcement, "for faculty, trustees and staff to become better acquainted. The specific purpose this year is to formulate a check list of facts and preliminary decisions which must be obtained before we can propose a timetable for enlarging the college to full size." Trustee Ernie Loebbecke presided over the day's program.

We had agreed, in 1958, to develop the college to an enrollment of 270 students, or 75 percent of the "ultimate size" we had in mind. As of Saddle Rock! #7, we had eight buildings (and an elegant swimming pool), 255 students, and 37 faculty. (By now only a portion of the faculty was invited to Saddle Rock, the invitations staggered so that each faculty member attended at least once over a period of three years.) In the coming year we could expect our 270 students—in fact, we projected 277. Accordingly, we divided into four groups, each including trustees, faculty, and staff, to consider what it would take in financing, in buildings and equipment, as well as in faculty. Also, from the points of view of education and student life, did we wish to become bigger? What were the expected gains and penalties?

The day began with a pleasant surprise. Dr. and Mrs. Norman F. Sprague, Jr., who had been called away from California, had authorized me to announce that they would provide funds toward the design and construction of a library, to be located on the Harvey Mudd campus and owned by Harvey Mudd College and which would also serve as the science and engineering library of the Claremont Colleges.

The morning's discussions were summarized by their several leaders: We could, indeed, decide in a year's time whether or not to move toward full size. A critical issue, as Henry Mudd pointed out, was the student-to-faculty ratio we approached as we became bigger. We expected the college to remain residential, coeducational, and of high academic standards. Our current ratio was about eight students per faculty member, where the faculty count included those on research assignments, supplying teaching services to other Claremont Colleges, or on sabbatical leave. If we could move that ratio toward ten to one as we grew, the economics looked much more possible than if the eight-to-one ratio were maintained.

We also heard, in the afternoon, from Paul Heist, of the Center for the Study of Higher Education at the University of California, Berkeley. He reported on the three years' study he had made of the characteristics of Harvey Mudd students. His evidence showed that although our students all entered with similar academic records, they were in fact a mixture of varying personalities: some highly pragmatic, some theoretical in outlook; some introverted, some extroverted. In teaching and in planning the range of activities of the college, we needed to be aware of these differences in student motivations.

At four o'clock the faculty and much of the staff thanked the Mudd family, and left. The trustees held a brief meeting, and adopted a new set of board bylaws which delegated a variety of powers to its committees. (The recommendations came from an ad hoc board committee which had weekended at trustee George Gose's cabin at Squaw Creek, on Mount Shasta.) It appeared that the board would have a good deal to do, and it was time to streamline its procedures. We also had our homework to do with faculty and staff to determine how, and when, we might go to "full size."

It had been a full and productive day and a happy one. Its main purpose had been accomplished: to outline what we still needed to do to plan our next years.

Saddle Rock! #8

The eighth Saddle Rock meeting, and the final one on which I will report, was held at Saddle Rock Ranch on February 6, 1965—nine years and two months after Harvey Mudd College was chartered and seven years, five months after our first students had arrived. The primary issue before us was whether to commit the college to an enrollment of about 400 students by the eary 1970s. We had done as much analysis as possible; now we needed to decide. We were also concerned, as usual, with maintaining our zest for curriculum innovation, with fostering student research and design experience, with student life beyond the classroom and laboratory, and with evaluating our successes and shortcomings in a systematic way. We concluded that, at whatever size, the college should continue to insist on the highest possible caliber of students and faculty, and should continue to experiment with methods of improving teaching and learning.

The afternoon ended with the entire conference asserting by voice vote that it was time, in accordance with past hopes and plans, to commit the college to grow to a 400-student enrollment, and that we should develop the necessary plant and other assets to make this expansion possible. The actual commitments would be made by the Board of Trustees and the faculty. Both groups subsequently acted as agreed in the voice vote.

These first eight Saddle Rock! meetings, and the subsequent twelve of our first twenty years, are important because they established our plans and common aspirations for the college; the initial ones provide a glimpse of the concerns of our early years. Each was a highlight of its year, uniting the college's constituencies in purpose and dedication. We developed common understandings about the growth of the college, the importance of research, appropriate ways for introducing students to the art and practice of engineering, our need for an agreed tenure system, and methods of improvement of teaching. We also developed a common concern for the financing of the college, together with growing confidence that financing could be found.

I will not report individually on the next twelve Saddle Rock! meetings. They influenced actions by students, faculty, and trustees that will be part of this history.

CHAPTER 9

The First Ten Years—A Summing Up

THE preceding chapters have reported major facets of Harvey Mudd College. We have learned of the idea of the college, the trustees, the faculty, the students, the campus, the financing, and of our common planning at the Saddle Rock meetings. The idea of the college, happily, has not changed since its founding. The development of our campus has been described as of 1965, as has the financial status of our venture. But we have now met only those trustees who were serving at the time the college opened its doors, except as we find specific trustees appearing in various chapters to perform useful miracles; we have been introduced only to the initial seven faculty members and the initial staff, and we have met only the student classes of 1959, '60, '61, and '62. A college is basically a collection of people, gathered for a common purpose. As of September, 1965, Harvey Mudd College had attracted an impressive group of such people. Here they are.

TRUSTEES

When Harvey Mudd College began instruction the trustees were either family members or close friends of Harvey S. Mudd, or they were experienced trustees of our sister Claremont Colleges, helping to start a new college. (The two exceptions were trustees Raymond A. Hill and J. Leland Atwood, both distinguished engineers.) As the board developed experience, it was planned to have the overlapping trustees drop off gradually, to make room for new members. This was, in fact, what happened.

In the academic year 1957-58, our first year of instruction, Mrs. Mudd, our board chairwoman, felt it would be useful to add a trustee who was a faculty member of another institution, to give the board as a whole the benefit of the academic perspective of a scientist or engineer of stature not directly involved on the faculty or staff of Harvey Mudd. We have subsequently been privileged to have a succession of such trustees, all but one of whom has either studied or taught (or both) at the California Institute of Technology. The first of these was Kenneth S. Pitzer, then dean of the College of Chemistry at the Berkeley campus of the University of California. Ken, elected shortly after our first class had arrived, had been director of research for the Atomic Energy Commission, and I had served on his staff. He also was the son of Russell K. Pitzer, whose gift to Claremont Men's College had helped to launch Harvey Mudd College. An outstanding theoretical physical chemist, he served this college diligently, and with the highest of academic standards, until June, 1961, when he resigned following his appointment to the presidency of Rice University. We had by that time elected Dr. Robert F. Bacher, then chairman of the Division of Physics and Astronomy at the California Institute of Technology. Bob, another old friend, had been on the faculty of the Department of Physics at Cornell University when I was a graduate student there. Later, Bob was a member of the Atomic Energy Commission when I was on its staff. Bob had helped Harvey Mudd College in its initial faculty searches before joining the board. He too resigned because of a change of duties; in 1962 he became provost of Caltech. Our next "academic" trustee was Dr. Frederick C. Lindvall, elected in March, 1962. He served Harvey Mudd faithfully and well for the remaining twenty-seven years of his life. Fred understood science, engineering, research, and teaching. He had been president of the American Society for Engineering Education, kept us informed of what others were doing to advance the teaching of engineering, and added a touch of humor and a great deal of good sense to every discussion of how we might best carry out "the idea of the college." The one exception to the Caltech succession of academic trustees was George W. Brown, a Harvard undergraduate and a Princeton Ph.D. in mathematics. George was dean of the Graduate School of Administration at the Irvine Campus of the University of California, and succeeded Fred Lindvall for a period of years while Fred, after Caltech retirement, served as vice president for John Deere Corporation. George, wise in academic matters and an expert in the rapidly changing computer field, was of great help to HMC in planning what use we should make of computers.

Harvey Mudd College continues to be fortunate in the independent educational advice it has had on its board. At the time of this writing (1991) we have as a member of our board John J. Hopfield, educated as a physicist, now professor of biology and chemistry at the California Institute of Technology.

The Board of Trustees began to increase its membership of business and community leaders who could speak effectively for Harvey Mudd College. In our first year of teaching we added William B. Coberly, Jr.,

1. Dean Wooldridge became an effective and hardworking board vice chairman, and his involvement with the college requires some telling. Dean was an undergraduate at the University of Oklahoma. He had entered as the high school state typing champion and was enrolled in a pre-law course. In his junior year, he needed to meet the graduation requirement for a course in natural science. Not one to avoid a challenge, he opted to take physics. The lecturer was Duane Roller, one of the best introductory physics teachers the United States has seen in this century. Dean decided to major in physics and managed enough work in the remainder year and a half of his college years to graduate with his degree in physics. He then went to Caltech for graduate work (as did his later partner, Si Ramo.) Dean kept in touch with his professor Duane Roller over the intervening years. When Ramo-Wooldridge needed a person to set up a course of instruction on the physics underlying the performance of guided missiles, Dean sent for his former teacher, who developed the orientation programs for Ramo-Wooldridge employees. This done, Duane came to Harvey Mudd to start our teaching program; Dean's interest followed Duane to us.

James F. Davenport, Joseph L. Hegener, Robert A. Hornby, and Stuart O'Melveny.

The reader has met each of these new members in Chapter 7, where we considered who raised the money needed to build Harvey Mudd College. In the same chapter we met Theodore W. Braun, the architect of the college's public relations program. He too was elected to the board in the academic year 1957-58.

In the academic year 1958-59, George B. Gose, Ernest J. Loebbecke, and Henry Duque, each also a mainstay of our development program, joined the board.

Dean Wooldridge, of what was then the Ramo-Wooldridge Corporation (now TRW Corporation), became a member of the board in 1959-60.[1] Dean, no stranger to the art of persuading technical people to work effectively together, was the trustee who led us in establishing our research policy, patent policy, and much else. Kenneth Julin, an electronics entrepreneur with a flair for organizing technical corporations and also for interesting people in a fledgling technical college, joined the board that academic year and served with drive, diligence, and imagination for the remaining decades of his life. Milbank ("Bud") McFie, member of a long-established California family and well known in the business community, became a board member and introduced us to another segment of our present constituency.

In the academic year 1960-61 the board added to its membership Clifford Tweter, then chairman of California Bank (now First Interstate Bank); Philip S. Fogg, chief executive officer of Consolidated Electrodynamics Corporation; Richard A. Grant, then head of California Portland Cement Company; and Clair L. Peck, Jr., one of the area's leading building contractors. Each of these trustees took a substantial part in the planning and support of the college. In particular, while his own firm built none of our buildings, Clair Peck saw to it that we found contractors who did excellent work at very fair prices.

In the year 1961-62 we elected to the board L.A. ("Pat") Hyland, then general manager of Hughes Aircraft Company, who would play a very significant role in the next decade of the life of the college.

The school year 1962-63 saw two additions to our board: Charles B. ("Tex") Thornton, chief executive officer of Litton Industies, and Charles W. Lee, chairman of the Vinnell Corporation. (Our readers have met Charlie Lee in Chapter 3; he headed the drive that raised most of the funds for the Campus Center.)

In the summer of 1963 one of our founding trustees died. The memorial resolution stated, "We, the Board of Trustees of Harvey Mudd College, unanimously record our gratitude to Leroy A. Garrett for his companionship in the building of the college, and express to Mrs. Garrett and their family the sense of loss we share with them. Through his unselfishness the college has been given ideals, policies and possessions which will shape the lives of our students for years to come."[2] Indeed, many decades.

The academic year 1963-64 saw three additions to the board. Mrs. Leroy A. Garrett (Marian Garrett had in fact been one of the group that founded the college) and Gerald G. Kelly, a lawyer who had been a partner of Mr. Garrett's in the firm of Musick, Peeler, and Garrett were elected in September. Later that year George J. O'Brien was elected; George was then vice president of California Portland Cement Company and had earlier been a senior executive of the Chevron Corporation.

The last academic year of our first decade was 1964-65. In that year the board elected Oliver C. Field, who together with his wife Ruby, was instrumental in making skilled aircraft pilots of many score Harvey Mudd students; and David X. Marks, a real estate investor, an able and determined tennis player, and a person with a compassionate interest in young people.

The reader may assume that by now the board had nearly fifty members. It had, in fact, revised its bylaws in 1965 to raise its permitted membership from thirty to thirty-three members. We had also lost members over the decade—four by death and six by retirement or resignation.

Our first loss by death was our first chairwoman, Mrs. Harvey S. Mudd, the senior member of the Mudd family, primary founders of the college. She lived to see the college through its second year of teaching and knew our students, faculty, and staff. Ford J. Twaits, another founding trustee, died in 1959, having helped to plan and build our campus and having established some of our first scholarships. Van Renssalaer G. Wilbur, who had been our host at the college's second Saddle Rock conference (the first not held at Saddle Rock Ranch) died in 1962. And, as we have seen, Leroy A. Garrett died in 1963. Each of these initial trustees helped to bring Harvey Mudd College into being.

Most of the group who were trustees of other Claremont Colleges before joining to help found Harvey Mudd had planned to leave after a few years of double service. The first such trustee to resign was George C.S. Benson, in the summer of 1957. Mr. Benson, as president of Claremont Men's College, had helped to secure the initial gift that made Harvey Mudd College possible and had recruited its president. Under his direction Claremont Men's College was providing the space to teach our classes, feed our students, and house our laboratories. George was clearly a founder of Harvey Mudd College! But we would shortly be entering into a number of additional joint ventures, and George was wise to point out he should not be representing both colleges. The board accepted his resignation with a vote of gratitude for his many services.[3]

Others found it more difficult to leave. William W. Clary, a founding trustee and also the chairman of the board of Claremont College, ten-

2. Minutes of the Board of Trustees of Harvey Mudd College, September 25, 1963.

3. Minutes of the Board of Trustees of Harvey Mudd College, August 8, 1957.

dered his resignation in June, 1957. The board promptly voted to make the chairman of the Board of Fellows of Claremont College an ex officio member of the Harvey Mudd College board. In 1964 Will Clary left the chairmanship of the Board of Fellows, and the Harvey Mudd board elected him an honorary member.

Robert J. Bernard, whom our readers met in Chapter 1 as "Mr. Claremont Colleges," also declined re-election in 1961. The board promptly elected him an "Honorary Trustee for the remainder of his lifetime."[4]

4. Minutes of the Board of Trustees of Harvey Mudd College, June 5, 1961.

Garner Beckett, another founding trustee of the college and chairman of the board of Claremont Men's College, retired in 1959. He remained an interested and loyal friend for the remainder of his lifetime.

A longtime friend and admirer of Harvey S. Mudd who had taken much of the initiative in establishing our Founding Friends' program, Edward R. Valentine, resigned in 1959, having accomplished that mission. His "teammates," Henry Duque and Charles Lee, remained on our board.

Accordingly, by 1965, Harvey Mudd College had nearly its statutory limit of trustees, plus several honorary trustees.

FACULTY AND STAFF

The growth in our faculty and staff was even more rapid. In Chapter 5 we were introduced to the initial seven faculty members and the five of us on the administrative staff at the time the college opened its doors. The 1965-66 Claremont Colleges Directory of Faculty and Staff lists a faculty of sixty-three (including three emeriti and five persons on leave) and a prodigious number of us on the staff—perhaps eighty, including the president, the dean, the groundskeepers, the registrar, the secretarial staff, the Claremont Colleges medical staff, the plumbers, and all the rest it takes to operate a college. All of this for a college of 270 students! Where did all these people come from, and, for that matter, why are so many people needed to teach so few?

There really weren't that many. We shared programs with our sister Claremont Colleges—programs in drama, music, and physical education. The faculty appointed to these programs were paid from funds contributed by the participating colleges in proportion to use. Harvey Mudd College "owned" about one-third interest in a physical education staff of five, or about one and two-thirds persons. When these joint appointments are weighted, and those who were retired or on leave subtracted, our full-time (equivalent) faculty consisted of thirty-five people. Of these, some were supported by funds given to teach aeronautics, to conduct research, or to write books.

(Our students, on the other hand, had access through our sister colleges to much more educational opportunity than Harvey Mudd alone could have provided.)

We began our second year of teaching intentionally overstaffed through the help of the Carnegie Corporation. Its grant underwrote the costs of additional faculty to make use of the opportunity we had to create a new curriculum and new teaching materials. The faculty of Harvey Mudd College did create a program designed for our particular goals. The same faculty has written its share of textbooks and other teaching materials used elsewhere as well as here. By 1965 we had begun this process.

One other preliminary comment: colleges and universities began receiving the first of the post-World War II "baby boom" in the early 1960s. As predicted, qualified faculty members were in short supply and much sought after. The University of California, for example, was in the process of creating and staffing four new campuses at that period. We lost some faculty members to more senior appointments elsewhere; in my opinion it did the college no harm to become known as a "stepping stone" for academics on the upward move.

To begin with our faculty in the humanities and social sciences: Our initial appointments, reported in Chapter 5, were Bill Davenport and George Wickes, both in the field of English literature. In 1958 we added, on a half-time basis, W. Henry Cooke, who had retired as professor of history at Claremont Graduate School. Henry was a first-rate teacher and historian. Also, more weeks than not, he and his wife Jenny invited students for an "evening at home" in their home not far from campus, for refreshments and discussions. In addition we added, on a part-time basis, John D. Seelye and Langdon Elsbree, both doctoral candidates in English at Claremont Graduate School.[5] Together with our sister colleges, Scripps and CMC, we appointed Jesse Swan in the field of drama. I should add that a number of our students took work in the humanities and social sciences in our sister Claremont Colleges.

The next year, as our students looked for more choices, we needed to offer a wider array of courses in humanities and social sciences on our own campus. We sought, and found, an experienced scholar-teacher who could design programs which took advantage of our students' interests and background in the natural sciences to lead them into other branches of knowledge. John Rae, a distinguished historian of technology with nineteen years of service on the faculty of the Massachusetts Institute of Technology, joined us as professor of history.[6] We then appointed David S. Sanders, at that time not long past his doctorate, an able scholar of American literature.[7] A number of our students were interested in learning German, and early in the life of the college we persuaded Emilie Wagner, former professor of German at Scripps College, to help us on a part-time basis. Katherine Hoskins was appointed instructor in English on a half-time basis.

In 1960 we added a philosopher to our faculty: Richard H. Popkin,

5. Following completion of his doctorate, Dr. Elsbree joined the faculty of Claremont McKenna College and has remained a colleague through the following three decades.

6. John Rae, a Scotsman by birth, took his three degrees at Brown University and served as assistant to President Wriston of Brown before moving to M.I.T. He was a founder and later president of the Society for the History of Technology. He became a nationally recognized authority of the history of the American automobile industry, then of the American aircraft industry. A prolific author, he was also an effective and beloved teacher.

7. David S. Sanders, B.A., M.A., and Ph.D. from the University of California at Los Angeles, served from assistant professor to full professor and chairman of the department of humanities and social sciences over the years 1959 to 1991, except for a period of three years when he held a similar position at Clarkson University in New York State.

8. Ted Waldman, a mainstay of the program in humanities and social sciences at Harvey Mudd College, was an undergraduate and master's student at Washington University (St.Louis) and took his doctorate at the Berkeley campus of the University of California. He came to Harvey Mudd from the faculty of Arizona State University.

9. June Tapp was on one-half time appointment. She left Claremont two years later for appointment at the University of Chicago. She returned to the West Coast perhaps a decade later, as provost of Revelle College of the University of California at San Diego.

then on the faculty of the University of Iowa. Dick, a stimulating teacher and an active scholar, soon had a number of our students questioning how one knows anything, and we also found we had become the temporary home of the *Journal of the History of Philosophy*. We were able to keep him only three years; he left in 1963 to become first chairman of the Department of Philosophy at the San Diego campus of the University of California. Dick's contributions brought home to us the necessity of including a philosopher in our faculty. Dick helped us persuade his friend and former colleague Theodore Waldman to join the college in 1963, and many generations of Harvey Mudd students lead more carefully examined lives for that reason.[8] We also gained strength in the field of history from two administrative appointments, both of whom taught part time: Eugene Hotchkiss, then associate dean of the college at Dartmouth and a Cornell Ph.D. in history, joined us as dean of students and lecturer in history. Also my assistant, Edward F. Little, who held a master's degree in medieval history and would later earn his doctorate, volunteered some teaching services.

The year 1961 saw us add one more discipline to our faculty. June Tapp was appointed visiting assistant professor of psychology, a post she held for three years.[9] By this time Paul Adamian, a doctoral candidate in English teaching at the Graduate School, was with us on a part-time basis. Over the next two years our joint venture in drama was augmented by two new recruits: Mike Harvey, a Harvey Mudd alumnus, and his wife Anne-Charlotte, a Scripps alumna. Both Harveys interrupted graduate work in drama at the University of Minnesota to help us for a year. Tad Beckman, who joined our faculty in 1961 as assistant professor of chemistry, changed his interests over the next several years and became a teacher (and then professor) of philosophy.

In 1965 we had a full-time faculty of five in the humanities and social sciences, plus a number of appointments in drama and music shared with other colleges, plus several part-time appointments. Our students took a portion of their studies in our sister colleges, and students from our sister colleges came to Harvey Mudd for some of their work in literature, history, and philosophy.

The department of chemistry got off to a flying start, as I have reported, with Art Campbell and Roy Whiteker here to greet our first students. The next year we added two more chemists. William G. Sly, a Caltech Ph.D. in physical chemistry, brought us a variety of talents; prior to deciding on a teaching career he had served in the Navy, had learned to be an excellent machinist, and played first-rate baseball. Generations of Harvey Mudd alums remember him for a demanding introduction to physical chemistry, and they also remember him attending nearly all athletic contests in which they were involved. Bill served as the faculty representative to the Southern California Intercollegiate Athletic Conference for most of the years in which the Stags (the joint Claremont McKenna College–Harvey Mudd College athletic program) have been conference members.

Kenneth M. Harmon, who held his doctorate from the University of Washington, also joined us and promptly got students involved in his active research program. Over the years the Department of Chemistry has earned a substantial national reputation for undergraduate involvement in research. This process began as soon as we had laboratories in which research could be done.

Nineteen fifty-nine brought us Mitsuru Kubota, a University of Hawaii undergraduate with his doctoral degree from the University of Illinois. (As of 1992 he is the chemistry department chair.) Scores of Harvey Mudd alumni trace their early experience with research in chemistry to Mits's lab. In 1960 Philip C. Myhre, another University of Washington Ph.D., joined the department he would later chair. Nineteen sixty-one saw Tad A. Beckman, a University of California Ph.D. with two postdoctoral research appointments, join the Department of Chemistry; he, too, in time became a department chairman, but, in his case, of the Department of Humanities and Social Sciences! Stephen V. Filseth, a University of Wisconsin Ph.D., arrived in 1962. Arthur Breyer, a Rutgers University Ph.D., was with us as visiting professor for the academic year 1963-64 on leave from Beaver College. That year both Art Campbell and Roy Whiteker were on sabbatical, having served the first six years of teaching at Harvey Mudd College.

We had two postdoctoral fellows in chemistry who elected to spend a year at Harvey Mudd: Robert D. Witters, who had his doctorate from the University of Montana, and Ronald E. Bowen, who was finishing his doctorate at Kansas State University. As I recall, both were Research Corporation postdoctoral fellows.

Thus, when the college was ten years old, we had an able and productive Department of Chemistry.

The reader may recall our first appointment in physics was Graydon Bell, a Caltech Ph.D. with several years of predoctoral teaching experience at Robert College in Istanbul, Turkey; our second was the nationally recognized teacher of physics, Duane Roller. Duane unfortunately suffered a heart attack in 1958 which placed him under doctor's orders to leave classroom teaching; he could and did write and continued through the remaining eight years of his life to produce an excellent introductory college physics text. I was eager to secure another very senior teacher of physics. Happily, we persuaded Thomas B. Brown to join us on a post-retirement (three-quarters time) appointment. Tom, a Cornell Ph.D., had been for forty years on the faculty of George Washington University, most of that time as chairman of the physics department. He had given particular time and thought to the development of laboratory equipment and headed the team of the American Association of Physics Teachers that produced a manual that became the national standard for good undergraduate laboratory teaching. He could do more with wire and a meter stick than most of us can with a rack of elegant electronics; Tom was at home with either. He taught and oversaw our laboratory development from 1958 until 1962, when his heart gave out. He and his wife Lea were open and generous to students who were willing and able to work; theirs was another faculty home to which students were welcome. We also added, in 1958, Robert Ward, a Harvard Ph.D. in physics who was a pillar of strength in developing new teaching materials. Bob left in 1962 to teach at Williams College. (He later worked for UNESCO in the Philippines, developed new teaching materials while at the University of Chicago, and is now at the University of Northern Iowa.)

In 1959 we had a stroke of good fortune which shaped the next decades of the Department of Physics. I was at that time a member of a committee of the National Academy of Sciences that advised the Navy on techniques for naval mine warfare measures and countermeasures. Another member whom I came to know and respect was Alfred B. Focke, at that time the Navy's technical director for the Pacific Missile Range. I learned that Al had grown up in a faculty family; his father had been dean of the Case Institute of Technology. Al took his bachelor's degree at Case and his doctorate in physics at Caltech. He had been a National Research Council postdoctoral fellow at Yale in the early 1930s, when there were very few such NRC fellows. He then had been on the faculty of Brown University until World War II came along when he became a physicist for the Bureau of Ordnance of the Navy. The Navy had moved him along through several levels of responsibility as technical director of one laboratory after another during World War II and more than a decade thereafter. He was ready to return to teaching, which is what he had really planned to do, and was about to seek a teaching appointment.

I knew just the place. Al joined us in 1959 as professor of physics and department chairman and served the college with distinction until he retired in 1971. He built our seismological laboratory and could be found at work in it for many more years.

We had two new appointments in physics in 1960. Alonzo E. ("Ted") Stoddard, a University of Michigan Ph.D., had been working as a geophysicist for an oil company and wanted to teach. He and his wife Marjorie and their children were a tremendous addition to our college "family." Ted was a first-rate teacher and research man, both were interested in students, and the Stoddard home was another in which students were frequently found. Ted, a remarkably lucid lecturer, died in 1986 of a heart attack, and the college, urged on by alumni, named the advanced physics laboratory for him. The second appointment of that year was

Albert V. Baez, a Stanford Ph.D. working at that time with a Harvard program for the improvement of physics teaching.[10] Al had a number of things on his agenda: He was writing an introductory college textbook in physics intended to interest non-physicists in physics, and he wanted to teach from it to see what worked and what didn't. A physicist at Claremont Men's College was to be on leave that year, and so half of Al's time was committed there. Also Al was much interested in the improvement of science teaching throughout the world; a year later UNESCO, a specialized agency of the United Nations, appointed him to its division of exact and natural sciences to work with member states interested in the improvement of teaching in the natural sciences. His stay with us was accordingly brief. He has continued through much of his subsequent life as a teacher of teachers, here and abroad.

In 1961 we added Jack Waggoner, an Ohio State Ph.D., to our faculty in physics, where he is teaching, serving on faculty committees, and arranging colloquia as of 1991. Enos Wicher, a theoretical physicist with graduate work at Wisconsin and a decade of subsequent teaching experience, also arrived that year. (A chess master, Enos promptly earned the respect of students who considered themselves chess experts.) In 1962 we added another theoretical physicist, Thomas M. Helliwell, a Caltech Ph.D. whom I had first known during his senior year at Pomona College. (Tom had done some theoretical calculations for me when I was still naive enough to think I could be a college president and find time for a little research in physics.) Tom subsequently has led any number of Harvey Mudd students into the mysteries of relativity, has served as department chairman, and now (1991) serves as (elected) chairman of the faculty.

Following the loss of Tom Brown, I persuaded another nationally noted teacher of physics to join us on post-retirement appointment: Ray Lee ("Pop") Edwards, who had for decades chaired the Department of Physics at Miami University (Ohio) and had a remarkable list of former students who had subsequently earned their doctorates in physics. "Pop's boys" by the scores were scattered around the United States, well placed in academia and in industry. Ray taught for us three years (1962 through 1965) before his second retirement.[11]

Bennet E. Robertson, also an Ohio State Ph.D., joined us in 1962. He remained until 1970, when his wife's family's interests called him back to her native Guatemala. Eldred F. Tubbs was appointed in 1963. A Johns Hopkins Ph.D., Eldred has a great laboratory knack for making optical systems, electronics, and combinations thereof work. Eldred left in the 1970s, and now performs these miracles for the Jet Propulsion Laboratory. Nineteen sixty-three also brought us William H. Sandmann, a University of Utah Ph.D., who became our first astrophysicist.

In 1965, we were joined by another widely known teacher of

10. You're right; Al Baez and his wife Joan have three daughters, one of whom is the folksinger Joan Baez. (Another is Mimi, who also can do very well with folksongs.) Al's father was a Mexican orphan, raised in Mexico in a Methodist orphanage, who subsequently became a Methodist minister. Al's childhood was spent in part in the Hell's Kitchen area of New York City, where his father was pastor of a Spanish-speaking church.

11. The reader will have noted that we were clearly enriched by the nationally respected teachers of physics who joined us on a part-time basis after an initial retirement. I was not always successful. One, who did not join us, told me, "Joe, I've had several such offers, and the only way I'd know it's part-time would be when I saw my paycheck."

12. Ro Rojansky's personal history was also amazing. A White Russian Army cadet in the Russian Revolution, his unit was chased across Siberia. He escaped to Harbin, Manchuria, finally earning enough money to pay steerage passage to Seattle. He found work on a wheat farm in eastern Washington, learned enough English to study at Whitman College, and in due course became one of three physics majors in his class. (The other two also did well.) He took his doctorate at Wisconsin and began a long and fruitful teaching career. In the 1950s he joined the staff of the Ramo-Wooldrige Corporation, (as had Duane Roller). The health of his wife had been one factor in his move West. Ro, a marvelous raconteur, would hold forth on what must have been grim experiences with the greatest of good humor.

physics, Vladimir ("Ro") Rojansky, for many years chairman of the Department of Physics at Union College, and author of perhaps the most widely used text on quantum mechanics of the 1930s, when that field was new and amazing.[12] Ro brought to our faculty both wide competence in theoretical physics and a gentle and sparkling wit. He and his wife Milla were also frequent and generous hosts. Ro taught with us for seven years and wrote and published a new textbook on electricity and magnetism thereafter.

Accordingly, as of 1965, we had a functioning Department of Physics and could boast more undergraduates majoring in physics than can most large universities. With the help of industrial gifts, war surplus property, kits of laboratory equipment that could be assembled by students, and some outright purchases, we had workable laboratories for teaching and for some research. We were on our way.

Our initial appointment in mathematics was Robert C. James who had kept in touch with the best of his students at Haverford. One was Robert Seeley, then completing his doctorate in mathematics at M.I.T. He and his wife decided to come, and were of great help for four years, when they were called back from our smog to the University of Massachusetts. The second was Robert T. ("Robin") Ives, who also came in 1958. Robin had earned his doctorate at the University of Washington and was at that time teaching at the University of Virginia. Robin celebrated his fourth year of teaching by marrying Lori, at that time a senior majoring in mathematics, a musician, and a fellow backpacker. Robin and Lori are still part of the college "family" as of this writing.

In 1959 we added Courtney S. Coleman as assistant professor of mathematics. Courtney, a Princeton Ph.D., was at that time on the faculty of Wesleyan University. Over his years of distinguished service at Harvey Mudd College he also has served as department chairman, as chairman of the faculty, and has written (and is currently writing) books which are widely used. We also added John M. Gary, then Bateman Fellow in Mathematics at Caltech, who held his doctorate from the University of Michigan. A year later the college granted John a year's leave of absence to accept a fellowship in applied mathematics at the Courant Institute at New York University, to be extended to two years if mutually agreed. Alas, he did not return.

Nineteen sixty-one brought to us another long-term pillar of our Department of Mathematics and our topologist, John Greever. John, a University of Virginia Ph.D., was at that time on the faculty of Florida State University.

Nineteen sixty-two saw three additions to our faculty in mathematics. Herbert Walum, a University of Colorado Ph.D., came as assistant professor, to move on in 1964. Alvin M. White, a Stanford Ph.D., also was appointed assistant professor. Al and his wife, Myra, have been another faculty couple whose home has seen many student guests, and does to this day. The third new mathematics appointment was Alden F. Pixley, a Berkeley Ph.D. who had had a hitch as a naval officer and a tour in the computer industry following completion of his master's degree, plus more than the usual teaching experience after his return to graduate study. Pix, a mathematician who can teach all sorts of things, is an internationally recognized authority in the field of universal algebras.

The faculty in engineering had the most difficult task of any faculty group, and had less time to accomplish it. I mentioned in Chapter 8 we had hoped to appoint an engineer to our initial faculty, but it had taken eighteen months to fill that key position. Because of our commitment to the humanities and the social sciences, and to a strong foundation in mathematics, physics, and chemistry, the engineering content of the curriculum needed to be contained in about one-third of the curriculum. Most engineering educators felt this simply wasn't enough time, however laudable the concept might be. Furthermore, the one we wanted was almost certainly well placed in an established institution and did not need to risk his or her professional future on an educational gamble that might not succeed. Dean Grinter, the principal author of the "Grinter Report" (see Chapter 2) suggested I might get in touch with Warren Wilson, then dean of engineering at Pratt Institute, and I did. Warren, an undergraduate at Lehigh University, had graduate degrees from Cornell, Caltech, and the University of Iowa. He was educated both as a civil and a mechanical engineer. He had been dean of engineering or department chairman in several universities. He had been president of South Dakota School of Mines. He had led successful reforms in engineering education at two major institutions. He was intrigued with the opportunity to build our engineering program, and while he also was not sure the task could be done in the available time, his view was, "Let's try it. If it won't work, we can always change the program later."[13]

Warren, a restless man, accepted appointment in February, 1959. Two months later I was able to report to the Board of Trustees that two more faculty members had accepted appointments in engineering. Jack L. Alford, who holds bachelor's, master's and doctoral degrees in mechanical engineering from Caltech, was at that time on the staff of the Jet Propulsion Laboratory. Jack, later to be James Howard Kindelberger Professor of Engineering, serving as clinic director and as chairman of the Department of Engineering, has been a mainstay of our engineering program. (Furthermore, as an avid sailor, he knows how important a mainstay is.) Our second appointment as associate professor of engineering was Richard Smith, who holds his doctorate in electrical engineering from Carnegie Mellon University and was at that time with the Westinghouse Solid State Electronics Engineering Department. Our three engineers were shortly in the business of developing the courses

13. I learned when I interviewed Professor Wilson that he too had been invited to candidacy for the presidency of Harvey Mudd College. I do not know whether or not he agreed to be a candidate. He did tell me, "If I come, you can be president." And indeed he was very supportive of me over our years together.

our engineering students would be taking in their junior year, some months later. The same trio began development of a freshman introductory engineering course to offer all freshmen some familiarity with the tools and concepts of engineering design.

In 1960 Harry E. Williams joined us as assistant professor of engineering. A University of Santa Clara undergraduate, Harry holds master's and doctoral degrees from Caltech in mechanical engineering. He, too, was employed at the Jet Propulsion Laboratory. Generations of Harvey Mudd students have learned vibration theory and much else from Harry. In 1961 we were joined by Murray Mack Gilkeson, at that time associate professor of chemical engineering at Tulane University, a University of Michigan Ph.D. in chemical engineering who would over the years take many faculty responsibilities at Harvey Mudd and also use his flair for engineering design to help develop industries in Brazil and India. Dick Smith decided to return to industry. We had the good fortune to attract James E. Monson, who has his three degrees in electrical engineering from Stanford University. Jim, another pillar of our engineering faculty, has been Harvey S. Mudd Fellow in Engineering and has also served as department chairman. Our final triumph of 1961 was to attract Sedat Serdengecti, once a Turkish Army officer, who has his undergraduate degree from Syracuse University and his master's and doctorate from Caltech.

Arnold Ruskin joined us in 1963, to remain for eleven years and contribute many ideas to the college. Arnold, who held all three of his engineering degrees from the University of Michigan, was an expert in materials, but he also was interested in library automation, in new methods for the teaching of design, and in much else.

Accordingly, by 1965 we had a well-established engineering program, unique in the United States, with new concepts in general education and in the teaching of the art and practice of engineering. We were beginning to attract attention from other institutions developing new concepts in engineering education; in 1965 we had our first (followed later by many another) visiting professor, Dr. Charles V. Bell. And we had the cadre of people who pioneered the engineering clinic program: Jack Alford and Mack Gilkeson, each now retired after more than a quarter century of service to Harvey Mudd College; and Harry Williams, Jim Monson, and Sedat Serdengecti, each actively teaching after more than a quarter of a century of service here. I will deal in a later chapter with the extent to which the program they created has been copied in this country and abroad.

We also had joint ventures well established, in some cases with one or more of our sister colleges, and in another, with a foundation.

In the academic year 1957-58 (our first year of teaching) our students were taught physical education by Pomona College's staff, as the students of

Claremont Men's College had been for a decade. Those students of either college who played intercollegiate sports were members of the Pomona College teams, and most of the competition was with other members of the Southern California Intercollegiate Athletic Conference, which at that time included Occidental, Redlands, and Whittier colleges, and Caltech. When we tried to renew our Pomona College arrangement for a second year, SCIAC balked. Our fellow conference colleges had chafed a bit when Pomona managed to increase its pool of available players by recruiting CMC, and they had no intention of permitting a three-headed monster to compete in the conference. After some negotiation, it was agreed that Pomona might maintain its own program of intercollegiate athletics if the two new colleges would establish a second and independent program.[14] Claremont Men's College and Harvey Mudd College began to build a physical education staff and create facilities in which the staff could teach.

We were able to persuade William B. Arce, then associate professor of physical education (and baseball coach) at Pomona College, to become department chairman and director of athletics for the new program. Bill, who has his three degrees from Stanford University, managed to get enough part-time help to offer both physical education and intercollegiate athletics our second academic year. He also started recruiting a full-time staff! I remember our first football game; it was against Chino Men's Institute, a nearby correctional facility, and (unsurprisingly) the game was played there. Chino had some excellent individual players, but very little teamwork, and we competed rather better than I had dared hope.

Claremont Men's College aggressively began fundraising for a gymnasium and athletic fields. A major early gift ($100,000) from Henry T. Mudd established Harvey Mudd College's share in our joint facilities. By the academic year 1959-60 Bill Arce had recruited two more able, full-time members of the physical education faculty: Lawrence (Ted) Ducey, who produced many first-rate basketball teams before his untimely death in a flash flood, and S.F. Vincent Reel, a track coach who would later coach Olympic teams for several nations.

We found we had a threefold physical education program. After considerable faculty discussion, the college decided on basic physical education for all students, and intramural and intercollegiate athletic competition for those who could and would compete. This pattern remains to the present (1991). Many of our students point out that, with the academic workload at Harvey Mudd, they can't manage intercollegiate competition. Indeed, we do have a larger participation in such individual sports as track, tennis, or swimming, where the student can set the practice schedule, than we do in the team sports. But for some of our students intercollegiate team sports have been an important part of their lives. We have our share who have done well and have the records to prove it.

The remaining question: What to call an athletic team from the

14. Following the establishment of Pitzer College in 1963, Pitzer joined forces with Pomona, so there are now two groups in intercollegiate competition in The Claremont colleges: the Stags and Athenas, and the Pomona-Pitzer combination.

Claremont McKenna College–Harvey Mudd College Joint Athletic Program? The easy solution was to adopt a mascot and let the name of the mascot designate the team—and the men's teams have been called "Stags" since the beginning of men's intercollegiate competition, as the women's teams (which include Scripps College) have been called "Athenas." Both have had their share of intercollegiate successes. Announcers at intercollegiate games would often call the Stags "Claremont" in the early days of competition. In case after case, in a matter of minutes, the announcer would be visited by President Benson of CMC, who would point out the team was from Harvey Mudd College as well. George Benson had had a decade of hearing CMC athletes identified as from Pomona College, and he wanted no part of permitting misidentification of HMC athletes.

We had other joint ventures as well. We were involved, along with CMC, with programs in music and in drama which were jointly supported, but managed by Scripps. Beginning quite early in the history of the college, a number of Harvey Mudd faculty members were invited by Claremont Graduate School to teach or to serve on doctoral committees, and they did so. Of course, we participated in the use and support of the Honnold Library system and in perhaps another dozen "central services" as well. These services, ranging from the chaplaincy to electricians and plumbers and security force, are supported by each college in proportion to use and make possible a range of services we never could have supported alone.

Iris and Howard Critchell

Mr. and Mrs. Varian S. Green of Claremont beside the Cessna Skymaster they donated to Harvey Mudd College. At the left is George I. McKelvey, vice president of the college and a trustee of the Bates Foundation for Aeronautcial Education.

The most unusual "joint venture" which started in our first decade was the Bates aeronautics program. Isabel Bates, a lady of some means but of retiring disposition, learned to fly in her middle years. She found this a very liberating experience indeed. She was fortunate in her choice of instructor: Iris Critchell, who had served in World War II as a WASP pilot, ferrying military aircraft to military bases. Iris had continued as a flight instructor following the war and was married to Howard Critchell, an airline pilot who also was a flight instructor. The two had high standards and great skill in bringing initially terrified students to capable and confident performance as pilots. Mrs. Bates had found her new flying skills increased her self confidence and gave her an introduction to an exciting new world. She coveted the same experience for able but reticent young people.

We met the Critchells through Oliver Field, one of our trustees, and his wife, Ruby. They too had flown with the Critchells. We learned that Mrs. Bates was interested in establishing a flight program, at her cost, for college students who might also profit from the experience. A period of exploration followed. The fledgling Harvey Mudd College was in no position to assume the financial responsibility, nor the possible liability, of a flight program, but we were certain we had students who would leap at this opportunity and we suspected Mrs. Bates was correct about the collateral educational benefits of such a program. The solution turned out to be to establish the Bates Foundation, which owned the aircraft and assumed the liabilities, and for the college to make space available for an office, for ground school teaching, and to join in the selection of students.

The Bates program has been an unqualified success. Several hundred Harvey Mudd students have learned to fly through its good offices and learned well enough so that federal examiners have told us students examined for the private pilot's license have skills comparable to the usual candidate for a commercial license. The program was not intended to produce professional pilots, although a number of its graduates have gone into careers related to aeronautics—with NASA research installations, in a few cases as airline pilots, and in one case as an astronaut. My own hunch is that a number of graduates who might have become capable scientists or engineers have also developed confidence that has led them into positions of broader leadership or entrepreneurship than they might otherwise have attained. After a period of some years Mrs. Bates found that she could no longer continue to support the program, but by this time enough other support had materialized so the program continued until 1990. The end came when the Critchells retired; try as we would, we could find no more Critchells.

The staff of the college also grew over the years 1957 to 1965, a bit less rapidly than the faculty or the student body. When the college opened its doors, we had a president; Edward F. Little was assistant to the president, and George I. McKelvey was director of development. The three of us and the faculty shared four secretaries, although the president wasn't very forthcoming about sharing the help of Andrea Parker, his secretary. Our one dormitory was managed by Steven and Yolanda Belmont, and Paul Hsu, recently arrived from Taiwan, was the technician who helped set up the teaching laboratories. The rest of our staff was shared with other colleges. As we have seen, we shared with Claremont Men's College an Office of Admission, which consisted of Dean Emery Walker and his associate Bob Rogers plus their secretary, Edith Schroeder. Katharine Lowe (now Mrs. George C.S. Benson), then the CMC registrar, served as our registrar as well. We had no full-time dean; Art Campbell, in addition to his responsibilities as chairman of the department of chemistry, served as dean of student activities, and Bill Davenport, in addition to chairing the department of humanities and social sciences, served as dean of student counselling. Through our membership in what was then the Associated Colleges of Claremont, we shared in the use and support of the staffs of the business office, security force, chaplaincy, and much else, but our share was modest indeed. In essence, when we opened the doors, we had a non-teaching staff of nine of our own appointment, including technician, housekeeping staff, secretaries, and president. (Well, the president did teach, a little.)

The next year we had two dormitories and had more than doubled the size of our student body. We were building our development program, and, as mentioned in Chapter 7, Doris Ballard joined our development staff. Margaret Thompson became secretary to the office of development. We had strained the capacity of the CMC registrar's office beyond its limit, and Katharine Lowe helped Spif Little become registrar for HMC, in addition to his responsibilities as assistant to the president. (What this really meant was that Katharine was training Spif's secretary, Evelyn Town, to become our registrar. Evelyn served as registrar with efficiency and grace for many subsequent years. In the course of this transition Spif and I learned how essential a good registrar is to the operation of a college.) With the new dormitory we added another housekeeper, Jannelle Huggans. We also now had a campus landscaped in places with plant material other than chaparral. Oskar Soolepp, a recently arrived refugee who had been a lawyer in his native Estonia, became our groundsman, and later head groundsman. He needed, and acquired, the college's first vehicle, a third-hand Model A Ford pickup truck painted blue. Oscar set a standard for diligence and attention to detail, and made a great improvement in the appearance of our campus, much of which he personally planted.

In the academic year 1959-60 we added a third class, moved into our own laboratory building, and had a third dormitory under construction. We also needed more money. The development staff grew with the addition of Richard N. Mason and Dorothy Harris. Dick would serve us well for two years and later return to help with our campaign. Dorothy served with distinction for more than thirty years. Mary Quist also joined the office, as secretary. With the new buildings we required an additional housekeeper, Delfina Huerta, and another custodian, Pedro Gonzales. Our technician, Paul Hsu, resigned to found the Phoenix Restaurant, which, I am pleased to report, did well. George Gillette began his term of keeping the chemistry laboratories in order, with substantially more laboratories to establish and tend.

A major addition came with the appoinment of Zaner Faust as director of our news bureau. Zaner, an experienced reporter and editor, came to us from New England, where he had been editor of a regional newspaper. He knew what was news (and what wasn't) and he was ready and eager to learn from faculty, students, and even administrators what we thought was happening. Any number of editors of newspapers or magazines came in time to respect Zaner's judgment of stories of interest, and we came to respect the coverage he earned for Harvey Mudd College. Furthermore, Zaner, with a boundless supply of anecdotes and a rare sense of humor, was remarkably good company. Zaner secured a second experienced newswriter, Mary Post, and Marian Gabler also joined his staff as secretary, office manager, photographer, and lady of all work.

I also had a small revolt on my hands. Bill Davenport and Art Campbell pointed out this was their last year as part-time deans, and that the load was now sufficient to keep a full-time dean well occupied. I began a search for a full-time dean of students.

As the reader has learned, I succeeded. The academic year 1960-61 brought us Eugene Hotchkiss III, previously associate dean of the college at Dartmouth College. Gene, whose doctoral thesis was in the history of higher education, also was appointed lecturer in history, and taught each year he was here. He served as dean of students for two years, becoming dean of the college as I transferred to him the responsibilities I had carried as dean of the faculty. I believe the many students and faculty whose trust he won and whose friendship he won join me in thanking Gene—and Sue, the wife he married in 1962—for their years at Harvey Mudd. The Hotchkisses left in the late 1960s when Gene became provost of Chatham College in Pennsylvania; they then moved to Lake Forest College in Illinois, of which he has been president for over two decades.

The year 1960-61 saw another change: The Chemical Education Materials Study came to our campus, with Art Campbell as director. I will deal with this remarkable program in another chapter. For a time, this program had a budget, supplied by the National Science Foundation, approximating that of the rest of the college. In its first year it had a staff of three professionals and would grow rapidly in the next years.

We also added, as groundsman, Josef Lorincz, another refugee who would in time succeed Oskar Soolepp as head groundsman. With the addition of a third dormitory, Homer Grimm joined us as residence hall supervisor.

In the next year I began a practice that served me well for the next two decades: Tom Holland became the first of several graduate students to serve as my administrative assistant on a half-time basis. Tom organized and helped plan Saddle Rock meetings, did the research I needed for the many speeches I gave, and much else. Phyllis Colclough became secretary to Spif Little, as Evelyn Town took on all the registrar's responsibilities. David Lavender joined the development staff, which also grew by one more secretary, Frances Wiles. As the student body grew, we added Consuela Capaceta to the residence hall staff; as the laboratories grew we added a machinist, Bill Schaufelberger, and Bill Hoesen, who did whatever needed doing in the physics laboratories. We were becoming a source of textbooks and other writings. Jointly with Claremont Men's College, we established a printing and addressograph office with Gerald Burns as printer, and Betty Chase managing the addressograph.

Another major addition to the staff this year was Hilda Larson who became secretary to Dean Hotchkiss and mother confessor to generations of Harvey Mudd students. Hilda later established our placement office, which has launched many graduates on their subsequent careers.

In the year 1962-63 Phyllis Colclough became my secretary when Edith Gaulding left, and Margaret Radley became Spif Little's secretary. Dick Mason left the development staff and Jack Charleville joined that staff. The "faculty secretarial pool" dispersed; Marcia Myers was by that time established as secretary to the department of chemistry, Norma Kruger as secretary to the engineering department, Evelyn Lee ("Aunt Evvy" to scores of physics alums) to the department of physics, and Marion Snyder did double duty serving both the humanists and the mathematicians. We added Raymond Gonzalez to the grounds staff. We were nearly staffed for the student body we then had. The staff of the CHEM Study grew to eleven, not counting part-time consultants, summer participants, and many others who gave less than full time to that project.

The 1963-64 school year saw the opening of our campus center, and Frederick Chamberlain arrived as director. Margaret Thompson left the development office to help him, and Virginia Blackwell joined the development office as secretary. Venus Martinez became secretary to our registrar, Evelyn Town. The Bates Aeronautics Progam had grown to require a secretary, Norma Raiguel. Our joint admission office with Claremont Men's College added another admission officer, Mike Holmes, a CMC alumnus.

The academic year 1964-65—the final year I will report in this chapter concerning staffing—saw the addition of Mike Kearney to the development staff, and May Weiser began a long career as secretary in the same office. Margaret Thompson returned to the academic side of the house to give the humanities and social sciences department its own undivided secretary, and Dorothy Pidhany became secretary to Fred Chamberlain in the Campus Center. The department of chemistry appointed its own undivided laboratory assistant, George Glonka. Kingston and Thomas-Garrett Halls acquired a custodian, John Thompson, who served Harvey Mudd College well for decades.

Mike Holmes left the office of admission, to be replaced by Dave Goodsell, an HMC alumnus. Dave remained several years before moving on to become headmaster of a private school.

The staff of the CHEM Study disappeared. The development phase of this operation was concluded, and it remained to administer the program as it was adopted throughout the United States and other nations. The administration of the program moved to the Berkeley campus of the

University of California, our joint venturer in the study. Happily for us, Art Campbell remained at Harvey Mudd.

We now had the necessary staff for a college of 270 students, housed, fed and taught on our own campus.

In summary, Harvey Mudd College had by 1965 a faculty and staff well matched to the educational tasks we had undertaken, and our students had also gained access to a number of educational and developmental activities beyond our initial hopes: intercollegiate programs of sports, drama, and music; much access to coursework in our sister colleges; and a flight program designed for Harvey Mudd students.

STUDENTS

What were our students like, as of 1965? In Chapter 6 we traced our students through the Class of 1962—the trailblazers of Harvey Mudd College. By July, 1965, we had graduated three more classes, and by September, 1965, we had admitted seven more. Our students had made the transition from instruction primarily on the Claremont Men's College campus, and dining in Collins Hall on that campus, to a self-contained existence on the Harvey Mudd campus, with such excursions to the other Claremont College campuses as a student chose.[15]

Clearly the anxious days about the acceptability of an HMC degree were over. The Class of 1965 graduated fifty-two students, including two women. As freshmen, the class had numbered ninety-six, so we were retaining more of our students than we had in the Class of 1962, although we still had much progress to make. Most of the graduating class planned on graduate work, forty having been admitted for the following year. Four were entering the University of California system, four Stanford, three Caltech, three the Ivy League universities, nine the Big Ten, and the remainder a variety of institutions, including M.I.T., Rice University, and at least a dozen other graduate schools. Eleven had accepted industrial jobs, and one was entering the Peace Corps. A growing fraction of the graduating class had majored in engineering, the visibility of the engineering program having increased since the days of the earlier classes. In short, the academic progress of our students, and the welcome they were receiving from industry and graduate schools, was encouraging.

A glance at the yearbooks for the classes of 1962 through 1965 reveals life at the college included more than the formal curriculum. Some of the earlier "traditions" of the college were still traditional. The annual college-wide trek continued to the top of the Mount Baldy ski lift. Brunch at the restaurant at the top, followed by snowfights when there was snow or, for the hardy, a hike to the peak of Mount Baldy with or without snow, filled much of a Sunday most happily. Those who made it to the top issued each other certificates, and lorded it over the rest of

15. In June, 1961, the Board of Trustees of Harvey Mudd College unanimously adopted the following resolution: *Resolved, that the trustees, faculty, students and alumni of Harvey Mudd College deeply appreciate the counsel and courtesies extended by Claremont Men's College over the past four years. The offices, classrooms and laboratories which were loaned to Harvey Mudd College in Pitzer Hall North have been vital in founding the College. Harvey Mudd College looks forward to continuing its harmonious relationship with Claremont Men's College through cooperative use of facilities, especially the joint athletic program, and through other cooperative efforts in whatever fields are appropriate in the years to come.*

Harvey Mudd students would continue to eat in Collins Hall, on the CMC campus, for another two years, and many appropriate fields for cooperation have indeed been found in subsequent years. The first president of Harvey Mudd College completely subscribes to the board action he has quoted.

us. (The 1963 yearbook has photographs of the sixth consecutive, and perhaps the last, of these Baldy brunches.)

The undergraduate fascination with water continued. The annual freshman–sophomore tug of war was held over a trench dug for the purpose and filled with water, plus crankcase oil, chicken heads, dry ice, and other embellishments—the losing team being dragged through the trench amid loud guffaws from the victors. Wastebaskets of water flew during many impromptu dormitory "study breaks," and considerable ingenuity went into the propulsion of water balloons. The best device, as I recall, was a slingshot made of some yards of surgical rubber, the ends fastened to the rail posts at the entrance to external steps leading to a dormitory basement. When the bombardiers extended the slingshot the length of the stairwell it could project a water balloon across the Scripps campus to reach the CMC dormitory area.

Students or faculty members occasionally announced intentions to become engaged to be married. Several dozen students, once the word was out, would abduct the newly engaged person, escort him (I remember no female victims) to the Seal Pond on the Scripps campus, and toss him in. Dean Hotchkiss was so honored, as were a number of other faculty members, and so were (and are) several students per year. By 1965 this practice was well established.

There were the standard pranks, some still noteworthy. One crew assembled a Volkswagen in a dormitory corridor, leaving three-quarters

The annual Mt. Baldy Trek (left to right): Mrs. Dorothy Walker, Mrs. Catherine Lowe, and Ms. Lori Wilcox '61 (now Mrs. Robert Ives).

16. Our special relationship with Churchill College was initiated by our trustee Robert P. Hastings, who also served on the Board of Trustees of the Churchill Foundation.

of an inch clearance on either side. Another removed the contents of a dormitory room and stacked them against the outside of the door.

Churchill College, one of the most recent colleges of Cambridge University and one with many scientific and engineering students, came into being a year after Harvey Mudd College was chartered.[16] The first master of Churchill College, Sir John Cockroft, visited Harvey Mudd College in May, 1962; he and I exchanged visits in the early 1960s, and several Harvey Mudd students have subsequently undertaken postgraduate study at Churchill College. As it happened, the graduating Class of '62 had declared themselves a beach holiday that Saturday, and were off campus. The Class of '63 had taken the opportunity to empty the seniors' dorm rooms of bedding, furniture, clothing, books, and whatever else was moveable; these impedimenta made up a heap extending to the second floor of West Dorm, and filled its courtyard. I, all unknowing, was conducting Sir John on a campus tour when we turned the corner to the courtyard. "Ah yes," said Sir John, "the rites of spring."

Another conversation I recall from that period was with Chris Haugeland '66, now professor of philosophy at the University of Pittsburgh. This again was in the spring, in this case of Chris's freshman year, and he was sitting in a corner of the campus that was barely land-

Life consisted of more than just study (1966).

scaped, looking disconsolate. I stopped by and asked him how things were going; he guessed they were going well enough. I then asked if the college had been misrepresented to him. He thought a moment, and replied, "No. You told me this was a college where I wouldn't get lost. You didn't tell me it was a college where I couldn't get lost." I thanked him, and left.

We had a problem for some months with students, expert at lock-picking, who had made soap impressions of a variety of campus keys, from which they had correctly adduced the shape of the master key, and made several copies. They were then able to come and go as they chose, to administrative or faculty offices, food lockers, or wherever, which they did with some bravado. We changed the keying, which bought us several weeks of time before their next effort again succeeded. Dean Hotchkiss had a better idea. He brought in the appropriate student leaders to discuss the problem and advised them that it is illegal to permit an unauthorized person to have access to student records, and, besides, much of the laboratory equipment is costly, and its disappearance casts suspicion on known master-key holders, and so on. It soon became an honor code violation to enter an unauthorized area by use of a key, and unauthorized entry stopped, with a single exception; the door to the dean's office disappeared. It developed that no key had been involved. A midnight crew had entered through a window, removed the pins in the hinges, and slid the door out. The door was paraded around campus to considerable acclaim and returned the next day.

Oil, chicken heads, dry ice, and other embellishments await the losers of the Fresh/Soph tug of war (1966).

Once a semester or so, in the days when students of both Claremont Men's College and Harvey Mudd were using Collins Dining Hall, the students of our host college served a "formal" dinner (coats and ties, please) with a dinner program. On those nights the Harvey Mudd students would be served an earlier meal. One such spring evening the after-dinner speaker was President Benson of CMC, reporting on the state of that college. His back was to the large picture window, which gives those dining at Collins a good view of Mount Baldy on clear days and of the campus approach to the dormitory area on almost any day. The students, of course, were facing President Benson.

Down the walkway to the dormitories, dressed in workmens' uniforms, came four Harvey Mudd students, carrying a mop, two buckets, a twenty-inch pipe wrench, a sledgehammer, cold chisel, and other paraphernalia. Three minutes later, when President Benson was well into his introductory remarks, the "workmen" reappeared, moving in the opposite direction with one bucket and a large porcelain toilet bowl. They disappeared stage right, to return five minutes later marching again to the left. Another three minutes, with President Benson into the subject of faculty publications, and they reappeared with an ostensibly second (actually the same) toilet bowl. President Benson's speech lasted long enough to permit the apparent removal of four toilets, and the after-dinner program had the rapt attention of the student body of Claremont Men's College.

Many Harvey Mudd students also participated in more organized extracurricular activities such as music, drama, and athletics. Through the year 1965 one of the more popular semi-organized activities was the building of floats to be paraded at halftime at home football games. Most of these floats were animated; if it were a ship, smoke poured from smokestacks; if an airplane, it moved on an overhead wire. Ingenious and attractive as some floats were, the real purpose lay in the building, which was a great icebreaker for the students of Scripps and Harvey Mudd colleges. Alas, as mentioned earlier, the other Claremont Colleges in the floatbuilding competition had given up by the late 1960s.

We had our share of athletes, particularly in track, and some of the Stag records set by HMC students in the early 1960s still stand. For several years, beginning in 1965, Harvey Mudd students contributed more than their share of varsity basketball players on teams that did well in the Southern California Intercollegiate Academic Conference. We also had students participating in most intercollegiate sports, some of whom did well in our conference, and others who did less well. In addition to intercollegiate athletics, many more students took part in intramural games, whether scheduled or impromptu.

In summary, the students of Harvey Mudd College were making commendable academic progress by 1965. And life consisted of more than study.

CHAPTER 10

Going up in Size—Impact/72

W HEN Harvey Mudd College opened its doors in September, 1957, we had enrolled forty-eight freshmen and no other students. It was our plan to admit sixty students each of the subsequent three years, for a total student body (after normal attrition) of perhaps 180 persons. Four months later, as the reader may recall from Chapter 8, at our first Saddle Rock retreat, trustees and faculty discussed how many students we should have, and on what schedule they should be admitted. Since our first dormitory held about 90 students, we thought in terms of adding similar dormitories for possible totals of 180, 270, or 360 students. (Married students, and others who would choose to live off campus, might swell these totals slightly.) We had decided to plan on 278 students by the early 1960s and actually enrolled 273 students in September of 1963, and 284 in September of 1965. By that time the Engineering Clinic was in operation, and could have accommodated more students; there was also research available for more students in chemistry, mathematics, and physics. Accordingly, our faculty was ready and eager to enroll more students. We were also quite aware that a few more faculty members could help to round out our curricular offerings.

What were the arguments for a size increase?

A basic argument for size increase is that if some is good, more is better. The purposes of higher education are to provide students with the knowledge and skills they need to function effectively as persons, citizens, and productive members of the society, and to provide the community at large with the people needed to produce its goods and services and manage its affairs. In our case we were concerned especially with the education of potential technical leaders. By the 1960s our first graduates were establishing excellent initial records in employment or (more frequently) in graduate study. We had both the demand and the supply for more such graduates.

In any university or college, more students create a requirement for more faculty, and more faculty can offer more specialties, whether the specialties be number theory or microeconomic theory, Old French literature or photochemistry. Most specialists can teach the introductory material in a general field, but to teach advanced material requires a range of scholarly specialties.

There are some economies of scale. The size of an institution may double, and while deans may be added, the institution still needs only one president. In our case, our Campus Center had been designed to accommodate more than 360 students. Several students, by taking turns, may read the same book, so library holdings need not increase proportionately to student body size. Conversely, for a new institution without many facilities, some increase in size could make it more possible to afford the operating costs of such "luxuries" as an available library, or lecture auditoria designed to include scientific demonstrations.

In 1964 we also saw telling arguments against any size increase. The Claremont Colleges were designed to be "small" because of the sense of community and common learning that occurs when the students and faculty all know each other. Their creation was inspired by the colleges of Oxford and Cambridge, which feel that one risks losing this sense of intimacy and identity when the size of a college exceeds, say, three hundred people. Even if one believes the limit may be three times that size, there comes a size at which students and faculty know each other in mutually exclusive groups. Granted that there are groups of ten people who can't abide each other, and Marine divisions of 50,000 with a strong sense of common purpose, size is something to watch when one expects every member of a group to learn from the others.

By any reasonable estimate we couldn't afford a size increase. We had just completed a bare minimum of buildings required to house, feed, and instruct students on our own campus. To increase to (say) 380 or 400 students would require a new dormitory, and additional laboratory buildings, more classroom space, and more faculty offices. We still had some indebtedness on our existing buildings! Our endowment was providing less than 2 percent of our operating income, and we were raising $680 in gift income per student to break even. It was not clear that we could raise, each year, another $68,000 for another one hundred students. This view prevailed among our Board of Trustees and our faculty, when they began examining these issues in the early 1960s. Later, when the decision came in 1965 following that year's Saddle Rock meeting, the discussion was not about whether, but when, we would increase in size.

Two events set the stage for the 1965 decision. The first one came in early 1964 when Norman and Caryll Sprague decided that one building on campus should carry the Sprague name, since Caryll Mudd Sprague and Norman F. Sprague, Jr., had for many years been an integral part of the Mudd family. A library building, which would be a centerpiece on campus, appealed to them. The Spragues had for some years been contributing to the Sprague Fund, and Norman informed the board in January, 1964, that they would like the fund to be used for library construction.

We promptly began negotiations with our sister colleges to agree that a library building belonging to Harvey Mudd College would house a collection of books, primarily about engineering and the sciences, belonging to all the Claremont Colleges. The collection, once established and housed, would be administered by the Libraries of the Claremont Colleges. These negotiations were concluded by 1965, and preliminary drawings for the library building were under study. The board endorsed the Spragues' suggestion that the library building be named for Norman's father, a distinguished physician and community leader.

In the mid-1950s the Ford Foundation began a notable program intended to increase the stability of higher education in the United States. A considerable number of universities and colleges, designated by the foundation as particularly significant to the nation, were offered grants of millions of dollars, subject to matching. The purpose of these grants was to increase endowments, reduce indebtedness, or take other steps to place the grantee institutions in a more secure financial position. Needless to say, the Claremont Colleges, individually and collectively, applied for consideration under this program.

We waited for a number of years. Our unusual form of organization did not readily fit the patterns that had served the foundation elsewhere. The Ford Foundation, not surprisingly, had many more applications than could be funded. We were, of course, independent corporations, but we constituted a planned group. It would have been awkward and disruptive to place the Claremont Colleges in competition, awarding grants, say, to two of the then five colleges.[1] On the other hand, if one were to make an award to the group, what would be the matching agreements? Would one college cheerfully raise funds that might be matched with Ford funds assigned to another college? We made a variety of proposals to the Ford Foundation, none of which gained approval.

In 1964 we were given hope that another proposal might succeed, and that officers of the foundation would work with us to explore mutually satisfactory arrangements. It was clear that if we were to receive a Ford grant, each of our five colleges would embark on a campaign to raise its share of the matching funds. We assured the foundation we would find equitable ways to distribute any funds it granted us. And, as it developed, we did.

In April, 1965, the Ford Foundation indeed announced a grant of $5,000,000 to the Claremont Colleges, subject to our raising three times

1. Pitzer College was incorporated on February 21, 1963, after negotiations with the Ford Foundation were initiated, but, of course, long before the grant was made.

this amount from other sources. There were restrictions on the funds to be counted as matching; these were in general to be gifts of cash or negotiable securities, not gifts in kind or gifts subject to life income reservation. Also, the Ford Foundation did not propose to match gifts it had made us outside of this grant. (This restriction ruled out $200,000 we had just received from the foundation to assist in establishing our Engineering Clinic.)

After considerable discussion between the boards of the colleges, we developed our ground rules for meeting the Ford Foundation challenge. We would conduct seven separate campaigns: one for each of the six colleges (Pitzer College had been founded in 1963), and a seventh to raise funds for such common purposes as the library or the chaplaincy. Each college would keep the others informed of its progress, and prospect lists would be exchanged with the understanding that the college with the most contact would be the first to approach a particular prospect, the next college having an opportunity to follow after a period of months if the first proposal had not succeeded. Each college would contribute trustee support to the campaign for common purposes. We appointed Richard Grant as the Harvey Mudd College trustee who also served on the central Challenge Committee. Funds, including Ford Foundation funds and others given to the group as a whole, were to be divided so that an agreed fraction went for common purposes. Other funds, if given for a particular purpose such as the library, would of course be used as designated; gifts for general support of faculty would be allocated to colleges in proportion to the number of faculty members, and so on. This scheme worked remarkably well. We had openness and mutual trust between development offices on the allocation of prospects, no squabbles I can recall about the division of funds for general purposes, and more success than we had dared hope.

Each college had its own choice of development counsel, and we agreed that the "seventh campaign" would use the Robert M. Johnston Company as counsel. Harvey Mudd College chose to use the Chicago firm of Gonser, Gerber, Tinker and Stuhr, which began a cordial and productive relationship for two decades.

The development council of Harvey Mudd College had concluded that we needed a campaign to raise the funds required to go to "full size," whether or not a Ford Foundation grant materialized, and had so advised the Board of Trustees. The news of the Ford grant forced us to establish our goals and timetable, recruit more volunteers and secure more staff, and get on with writing and publishing the supporting materials we would need. Our sister colleges also had these chores to do. We kept in close touch through the Challenge Committee, and concluded that we could match the Ford Foundation challenge within the three years the foundation had given us, but that the three years should be the first phase of a seven-year program. Accordingly we adopted the following seven-year goals:

Pomona College	$24.00 million
Harvey Mudd College	$18.75 million
Claremont Men's College	$13.00 million
Claremont University Center	$11.20 million
Pitzer College	$7.15 million
Scripps College	$6.93 million

Together with the $5 million of matching funds we hoped to secure from the Ford Foundation, the total for the Claremont Colleges came to $86 million. The net worth of Harvey Mudd College as of June 30, 1965, was $7.7 million. Our goal of $18.75 million looked challenging enough!

We decided to call our campaign Impact/72, to indicate that its purpose was to bring the college to its full size by 1972.

The summer of 1965 was a busy one. At the September meeting of our board, George Gose was able to report that sixty volunteers had been recruited to help us identify and solicit prospects: five hundred foundations, corporations, and individuals of means were under research; and over the first five months of our campaign (from April to September, 1965) we had secured $623,000 in gifts and another $540,000 in pledges. I reported that the board of directors of North American Aviation Corporation had voted to contribute $500,000 over seven years to establish the James Howard Kindleberger Professorship of Engineering. I recommended that Professor Jack Alford be appointed the first Kindleberger Professor. The board applauded the recommendation and voted accordingly.

At the December meeting of our board, we heard of both the progress Harvey Mudd College was making and the overall progress of the Challenge Campaign for all six colleges. Much of the HMC campaign literature was by then available; some was in final draft. The alumni had formed their own association; in the year ending the prior June, some 71 percent of our alums had contributed to the Alumni Fundd. Membership was flourishing in both the Founding Friends and the Galileo Society. The Futures Committee could report five meetings for trust officers, lawyers, accountants, and bankers within the preceding six months. And we had raised $1.4 million since the HMC campaign began on April 1, 1965, which counted toward Ford Foundation matching. The Claremont Colleges as a whole were even further along, with a total of $17 million toward the seven-year goal of $86 million, although not all of the $17 million qualified for Ford Foundation matching.

We were approaching the time to make a public announcement of the Claremont Colleges campaigns. A major "kickoff" dinner was held on March 3 for supporters of all the colleges, with President Robert Goheen of Princeton University and Chairman James F. Oates of Equi-

2. The trip to the ancient British Universities was most interesting. I had anticipated we might receive a hospitable and informative reception, but I was unprepared for the extent to which our British hosts wished to compare experiences. One of the issues that has arisen throughout the centuries in our host universities was the question of balance between the powers of the University and those of the individual colleges. The question had recently been reviewed by a Crown Commission, which had recommended some substantial changes; indeed, perhaps six times in the long histories of these universities an external group reporting to the British Crown had been used to readjust this balance.

3. The story of this remarkable person is told in *Fortune Favors the Brave: The Life and Times of Horace Bell, Pioneer Californian,* by Benjamin S. Harrison (The Ward Ritchie Press: Los Angeles 1953). Horace Bell was born in 1830 to a frontier family. In a colorful career he was a gold prospector, frontier peace officer, soldier of fortune, abolitionist, Union scout during the Civil War, and reformist newspaper editor. Perhaps the shortest description of him as a person is

table Life Assurance Society as the principal speakers. A three-week tour of Oxford and Cambridge Universities sponsored by the Friends of the Claremont Colleges, left in early April by charter aircraft. Supporters of the Claremont Colleges thus became acquainted with the successes and operating problems of the institutions that set the pattern we tried to follow.[2] At the June meeting of the Board of Trustees, Bob Hastings reported to his fellow trustees that both the kickoff dinner and the tour had been highly successful and well attended. Over the fourteen months of the campaign, Harvey Mudd College had acquired $4.3 million in gifts and pledges. Mrs. Virginia Kingston, mother of Mrs. Victoria Mudd and the donor for whose family Kingston Hall was named, had announced her intention to rebuild the structures around the swimming pool we had originally acquired from Scripps. The new pool complex would bear the name of her grandfather, Horace Bell, a California pioneer and a very colorful man.[3]

The September, 1966, meeting of our Board of Trustees was one of reporting on the "advanced," or "within the family," phase of Impact/72, and of preparing for the more public declaration of our intent to raise $18.75 million. Henry Mudd reviewed our progress to date. We had recruited two additional trustees who had agreed to development assignments: William T. Sesnon, a well-known investor, who had been elected at our March meeting, and Hugo Riemer, president of United States Borax and Chemical Corporation. We had recruited L.A.("Pat") Hyland, general manager of Hughes Aircraft Corporation, as our campaign chairman.[4] The full list of our campaign leaders follows.

Going Up in Size—Impact/72

General Chairman	L.A. Hyland
Vice Chairman	Philip S. Fogg
Major Gifts Chairman	Charles W. Lee
Vice Chairman	Robert P. Hastings
Special Gifts Chairman	Preston Hotchkis
Major Corporate Gifts Chairman	Hugo Riemer
Special Corporate Gifts Chairman	Kenneth F. Julin
Vice Chairman	W. Gifford Myers
Public Relations Chairman	T.W. Braun
Evaluation Chairman	Oliver C. Field
Pomona Valley Chairman	Gerald R. Case

In addition, Mr. Mudd reported that five campaign publications were now published: a "case statement" entitled *Make No Mistake,* largely written by Professor Davenport; a brochure, *Facts,* giving information about the college; a tax brochure, *Giving and Taxes;* a booklet describing gifts we needed, entitled *Opportunities;* and a book of suggestions for volunteers, called (unsurprisingly) *Committeeman's Handbook.*

Bob Hastings then called on me to review the educational goals of the college, which would be attained by the successful completion of Impact/72. My response follows:

The college was established to graduate engineers and scientists capable of undertaking responsible technical leadership. Every college with majors in engineering and science hopes to do the same. Our hopes are based on (1) We require first-rate academic performance of highly qualified students taught by a fine faculty. (2) To prepare students for a rapidly changing technology we teach them the unchanging laws of nature and how to apply them. (3) About one-third of the curriculum is committed to the humanities and

given in his citation on discharge from the Federal army: "His gallantry, resolution, intelligence and promptness have been marked and commended. He has rendered the U.S. Government great service."

4. "Pat" Hyland was a legendary figure in the aerospace industry. While he was nominally vice-president of Hughes Aircraft Corporation, the president was Howard Hughes, who was by 1960 effectively a recluse. Pat ran Hughes Aircraft. He had added to a going aircraft company a group of very able electronics engineers and others in high technology, who did much to bring into being what is now called the field of avionics. Pat, an indefatigable worker with a shrewd sense of getting at the core of things, had begun his career as a technician at the Naval Electronics Laboratory in Washington, where he had been codiscoverer of the reflection of shortwave radio waves from flying aircraft—the basic fact which makes radar possible. Hughes Aircraft, under his leadership, led the way into high electronic and optical technology for what became the aerospace industry.

The plaque (left) adorning the entrance to the Harvey Mudd pool (facing page).

DEDICATED APRIL 21, 1968

BY MRS. FREDERICK KINGSTON

IN MEMORY OF HER GRANDFATHER

MAJOR HORACE BELL

social sciences, more than any other accredited engineering curriculum, and more than most liberal arts colleges require of physics or chemistry majors. (4) A student learns to apply what he or she knows to new problems by tackling new problems, and to accept responsibility by taking responsibility. The college sees that he or she is able to do both.

The results of the program are becoming apparent. In June, 1966, Harvey Mudd College graduated more physics majors than the University of Southern California, and more chemistry majors than Stanford. Our graduates are earning advanced degrees from the nation's best graduate schools and are being employed in responsible positions by first-rate companies.

Harvey Mudd's graduates represent a little less than one in ten thousand of the nation's baccalaureate students, and less than one in a thousand of those who expect to become professional engineers, mathematicians, or physical scientists. We are becoming the undergraduate source of about one in three hundred of the nation's Ph.D.s in engineering, mathematics, physics, and chemistry. For this purpose we are about thirty times as big as our enrollment would indicate. If we can make a significant contribution with sixty graduates per year, we can make more with eighty-five.

The college would be better and its impact greater if it were somewhat bigger. We could use more variety and depth in our technical and nontechnical courses. To do this requires more students and more faculty, which is another reason to go up in size by one hundred students. We plan to add more research and more engineering design. We can treble these activities to the advantage of our students, without neglecting teaching. Research and design involving students are forms of teaching, and we plan to make the most of them. These things require more laboratory, library, and living space.

The whole purpose of Impact/72 is to provide the funds to accomplish these educational and national goals.[5]

5. Minutes of the Board of Trustees, September, 1966.

Dick Grant reported from the central Challenge Committee that the Claremont Colleges as a group had raised $33.1 million toward our overall seven-year goal of $86 million. Of this, Harvey Mudd had collected $4.6 million in gifts, grants, and pledges. Trustee Jim Davenport reported that the advanced-gifts phase of our campaign had brought in enough endowment so that our total endowment funds now exceeded $1 million. (This, to my mind, was a major milestone.)

In short, we were about to go to the larger community with our story, and we had prepared for the adventure. The next months would be busy ones for all of us concerned with fundraising.

When we reviewed our progress at the June, 1967, meeting of the board, there was much solid accomplishment to report, and enough apprehension to keep us on the edges of our seats. We had increased the membership of the Founding Friends, enlisted a number of new friends of the college who were capable of substantial financial help, and further strengthened both our Board of Trustees and our other volunteer fundraisers. We had consolidated the plans for our second laboratory building, the Sprague Library, the refurbishing of the initial laboratory building, and the construction of lecture auditoria into an overall design now named Project Libra; this consolidation gave the whole considerable architectural unity, and brought about substantial construction economies.

In another major step forward, our new trustee, David X. Marks, pledged $400,000 toward the cost of the fourth dormitory we would require at "full size." While the building had not yet been completely planned, nor its cost estimated, this gift clearly would meet the bulk of the costs, and the income on the dormitory should service any remaining debt. This pledge, announced by Bob Hastings at our December meeting, really added joy to our holiday season.

On the other hand, as of June, 1967, we were behind schedule on what we had planned, and hoped, to have as funds in hand. Our three-year goal was $8.4 million. With 72 percent of the time elapsed, we had raised 70 percent of the funds in gifts or pledges, or $5.9 million. Gratifying as this result was, we were by no means confident that we could raise the rest on schedule, or for the purposes we most urgently needed. Furthermore, time was running out. If we were to be at "full size" by 1972, we needed to admit a larger freshman class in September, 1968. We now knew we could house them and the successively larger classes that should follow. But where would we find laboratory space for them, or classroom space, or space for the added faculty we would then need?

Much of the summer and fall of 1967 was devoted to planning for contingencies, as well as to cultivating potential donors. At the September, 1967, meeting of the board, Bill Coberly reported that Edward Durell Stone, Inc. and Earl Heitschmidt and Associates would provide architectural services for Project Libra; and that the Heitschmidt firm and James H. Van Dyke and Associates would provide architectural services for the Marks Residence Hall. We could begin preliminary plans and make cost estimates for both projects. It had also developed that the college might be eligible for a federal grant, under the Higher Education Facilities Act, which could finance a portion of the costs of Libra; if we were to apply for the grant we would need to do so by December 1, 1967, with a credible plan for the matching requirement.

We also had planned to place the next laboratory building, which was a portion of Project Libra, on land which in fact belonged to Claremont University Center, a party to our planning. To apply for a

6. The agreement between Claremont University Center and Harvey Mudd College was adopted by both institutions, the Harvey Mudd Board acting on September 20, 1967. In the agreement, Claremont University Center stated its intention to use the area in question for laboratories and other facilities for science instruction serving all The Claremont Colleges, and transferred title to Harvey Mudd College for the land required for Project Libra. Harvey Mudd College agreed to construct a lecture auditorium, library building, and laboratory building on the land now deeded to it, to renovate the structures standing on the land to which Harvey Mudd College had previously had access and now gained title; and to secure funds for the purpose, provided that Harvey Mudd College not preclude financial contributions from other Claremont Colleges. HMC further agreed that the vacated portion of Columbia Avenue would be developed to guarantee continued pedestrian access from Foothill Boulevard to Twelfth Street and beyond; that the library would come under the Honnold Library Operating Agreement and that students and faculty of all The Claremont Colleges have access to the library on equal terms; that the lecture auditorium and classrooms and office space be available to the other Claremont Colleges for the teaching of mathematics, natural science and engineering, provided that Harvey Mudd College have first call on these facilities; and that HMC would grant to the other Claremont Colletges access to shops and other technical services in these buildings, subject to the conditions that HMC have first call on the services and that other Claremont colleges reimburse HMC for the actual cost of such supplied services. The two contracting Colleges agreed to establish an intercollegiate committee of faculty members in mathematics, engineering,

federal grant, we would need to show clear title to the land. The reader may recall that Claremont University Center had previously helped us acquire our first laboratory building through the gift of the land on which it stood, the use of bank credit extended to Claremont University Center, and the outright gift of some of the construction funds. Accordingly, a formal agreement was drawn between Harvey Mudd College and Claremont University Center, in which Claremont University Center designated the area between Dartmouth and Columbia Avenues, and between Twelfth Street and Foothill Boulevard, for "laboratories and other facilities for the teaching of mathematics, the natural sciences and engineering."[6] Both boards approved, and Harvey Mudd College was free to apply for federal support.

We also were greatly helped in this portion of our planning by Trustee Clair Peck, Jr., then executive vice president of C.L. Peck, Contractor, a major building firm in the Southern California area. Both Clair and the firm that bore his father's name had a reputation for excellent workmanship and management. At no time did the Peck firm bid on any of the college buildings, but Clair devoted many hours, and volunteered the service of some of his professional colleagues, to insure that we had made the most of the building dollars available to us, and that our specifications gave us buildings that would serve us well and long.

At a special meeting of our Board of Trustees called on November 1, 1967, on a motion made by Bill Sesnon and seconded by Pat Hyland, the officers of the college were instructed to increase the number of students admitted to reach the enrollment level of 400 by 1972, to take the necessary administrative and financial decisions to accomplish this objective, and to file applications for a federal grant, plus federal loans, which might be needed to finance necessary construction. The vote was unanimous.

We learned in May, 1968, that Harvey Mudd College would be awarded a $1 million federal grant toward the estimated $3.7 million costs of Project Libra. We had raised $400,000 toward the Libra project, and had a number of possible additional donors under cultivation.

Another complication, possibly an opportunity, had arisen. Immaculate Heart College, which had a campus in downtown Los Angeles, was considering a move to Claremont and had made a commitment on land across Foothill Boulevard from the Harvey Mudd campus. Immaculate Heart College would need laboratory space for science instruction now on its downtown campus and wanted to know if we could add sufficient laboratory space to Project Libra to accommodate their teaching needs in biology and chemistry. The board, at its April meeting, appointed Richard Grant its representative to explore with the Immaculate Heart College board what contractual arrangements would make this possible, and recommend to the Harvey Mudd board what action to take.

As of the June 9, 1968, meeting of our Board of Trustees, gifts and pledges to the Impact/72 campaign came to $8.85 million. We had met and exceeded our three-year goal of $8.4 million, but we still had much to do toward our seven-year goal of $18.75 million. Our sister Claremont Colleges had also done well as of the three-year mark with total gifts and pledges to the Claremont Colleges Challenge Campaign coming to $51 million, and more than $17 million of it was applicable to the Ford Foundation matching terms. We had succeeded in "earning" the Ford Foundation's $5 million! It was time to take a deep breath, smile briefly, and get back to raising more money.

A special meeting of the executive committee of our Board of Trustees was convened on October 8, 1968. Upon the recommendation of Richard Grant, Harvey Mudd agreed to build a wing on Project Libra for the benefit of Immaculate Heart College. Building costs were escalating rapidly in the late 1960s, and our architects, who had the plans for Project Libra nearly completed and out for bid, could still include this extra space if we hurried. We hurried. The wing would be built unfinished, with detailed room layouts, plumbing, wiring, and interior walls yet to be specified, and the costs of the added architectural effort and of construction would be borne by Immaculate Heart College. Either college could terminate the agreement on three years' notice, and Harvey Mudd would then buy out Immaculate Heart's interest over a period of years.

Alas, this joint venture was not to be. We did indeed instruct the architect to add the unfinished shell of the wing to the plans, and the added architectural cost was borne by Immaculate Heart College. When the plans were put to bid, the ten bidding contractors ranged from $4 million to $5 million, with the James I. Barnes Construction Co. the low bidder. The Immaculate Heart College portion of this cost came to about $300,000. That college was having financial difficulties (and eventually discontinued its post-secondary operations), and reported that it was unable to meet the terms of the proposed agreement. We then considered whether we should build the shell at our own cost. To redraft the plans, and put the building (less shell) again to bid, might well result in a cost that would be $300,000 higher than the bid we now had in hand. The board concluded we should instead build the shell of the wing, knowing that in time we would need the space and would probably never again have an opportunity to construct it at this price.

President Benezet of Claremont Graduate School and University Center then suggested that CGS might have use for the space, and be able to help with our funding. The Graduate School had an active and growing Master of Fine Arts program, with a faculty of practicing artists and some twenty or thirty degree candidates, and a studio building was high on the CGS gift list. Most of their existing studio space was provided in faculty garages, and the standing joke was that the Fine Arts faculty members were the only ones in Claremont that made house calls.

and the natural sciences to propose to HMC the most effective use of the laboratories, lecture hall, classrooms, and offices to be constructed or renovated. The two institutions agreed that one or more of the buildings should carry a plaque or plaques (subject to the consent of donors) indicating the common purposes for which the facilities had been provided.

The two Claremont colleges agreed that HMC would build the wing, and that CGS would provide three payments of $100,000 each, the first to be paid on June 30, 1970, and the remaining two at six-month intervals thereafter. CGS might undertake such additional construction within the shell as it chose, provided that no such construction should preclude the eventual conversion of the building to laboratory use. CGS was guaranteed the use of the space for ten years, unless an earlier date for transfer of use was mutually agreed upon, and the usage could be extended beyond ten years by mutual consent. HMC agreed to reimburse CGS for the depreciated value of any improvements it retained if it reclaimed the space.

Harvey Mudd College authorized the beginning of construction on Project Libra, wing and all, on December 9, 1969. Ground was broken for Project Libra on January 5, 1970. The agreement between colleges was concluded in February, 1970. The total project cost, including a minimum of landscaping and laboratory equipment, was $4.75 million. The funds available included $903,000 in hand, plus a federal grant of $1.186 million, plus a $300,000 commitment from Claremont Graduate School. We had a bank line of credit for $1.5 million, and a number of prospective donors for additional gifts in support of the building.

One of the companies that had made generous contributions toward the construction of the engineering building was the Ralph M. Parsons Corporation, one of the major construction firms on the West Coast. It had built airfields and industrial plants and major water projects, and much else, in many parts of the world. Ralph Parsons became interested in the college, and was elected to the board. He was faithful in attendance and read everything we sent him. No chatterbox he; I had little notion of his interest in Impact/72. After one board meeting in which I had been through admission schedules, timing of faculty appointments, charts of completion dates of buildings, and cash-flow projections to explain how we hoped to go to full size, he observed, as we walked away together, that there was more to running a college than he had realized. Some months later he pledged $1 million, in addition to his corporation's contribution, toward the engineering building. The board promptly voted to name the northern portion of the Libra complex the Ralph M. Parsons Engineering Building.

Meanwhile, as of June, 1970, our Impact/72 campaign had raised $13.7 million in gifts and pledges toward our seven-year goal of $18.75 million. We were on schedule, but just barely so. The Claremont Colleges as a whole were further ahead: their total came to $79.5 million toward a seven-year goal of $86 million.

Our building program was well along by June, 1971. The swimming pool renovation had been completed in 1969, and the new structure named for Horace Bell. Marks Hall, our fourth dormitory, had been completed in the fall semester of academic year 1969-1970, and had promptly won its loyal dorm members. The building, completely landscaped, was dedicated by David X. Marks on March 15, 1970. Most notably, ground had been broken for our major building adventure, Project Libra, in January 1969. In June, 1970, trustee Marian Garrett reported to the board that Project Libra was 87 percent complete and about on schedule. We had, or would shortly have, the buildings we needed to accommodate a student body of 400.

We did not as yet have the financial support we would need. In fact, things were even more challenging than that. The seven years of Impact/72 fell within the most rapid period of inflation the United States has experienced in this century. Accordingly, we built as promptly as we could in view of rising construction costs, and our operating costs were larger than we had initially thought. We were reaching our fundraising goals for Impact/72 in total, but too much was required for construction and for operations, and not enough was being raised for the endowment on which the future of the college would depend. Privately, we calculated that to accomplish what we had initially hoped to do with $18.75 million, we would now need $25 million.[7] The end of our Impact/72 campaign was in sight and would require substantial effort. When and if that was accomplished, we still needed to raise many millions of dollars in endowment.

Fortunately the development council of our Board of Trustees, under the trustee leadership of Hugo Riemer and the staff leadership of George McKelvey, had been building for more than a year the resources we would need for our "final over-the-top" effort. We had recruited several

7. $18.75 million in 1965 dollars came to nearly $25 million in 1972 dollars, and if we were to make the inflationary correction with the construction price index rather than the consumer price index, the 1972 figure would exceed $25 million.

David X. Marks with student at Marks Hall (a.k.a. South), fall 1969.

Project Libra: Sprague Library and Galileo Hall under construction.

able new trustees who were diligently cultivating new sources of gifts. I will report elsewhere on the overall changes in our board, but new and effective trustees on the development council included Alexander Hixon of Hixon and Co.; Ed L. Shannon, Jr., president of Santa Fe International Corporation; Trude Taylor, chairman and chief executive officer of Electronic Memories and Magnetics Corporation; Robert P. Miller, Jr., of the Sweco Corporation; and Mrs. Frederick E. Giersch, a lady with many friends and great energy. George McKelvey had strengthened the staff with the addition of Nichol Sandoe (formerly associate director of development at Dartmouth College) as our director of development, and Harvey G. Pawlick (formerly resource development officer, Union College) and Russell Medevic as assistant directors of development. Charles Kittleson also joined us, in 1971, as development officer.

With this structure, the development council decided in June, 1971, to launch an augmented "mini-campaign" to reach our goal of $18.75 million. Considerable thought was devoted to a possible challenge. Alec Hixon volunteered to join with other trustees in establishing a matching gift, to contribute a dollar for each other dollar raised. The group decided some exclusions would be needed: there was no point in matching grants from the federal government, and nobody would be enticed by funds from Henry T. Mudd or the Harvey S. and Mildred E. Mudd Foundation, because those who knew the college well knew that both would contribute as generously as possible, whether or not there were new funds to match. Ken Julin felt that our developing Engineering Clinic would offer a distinctive opportunity to raise additional industrial gifts from corporations that were already contributing to us on the same terms they did to other technical colleges. Jerry Case planned an approach to members of the Galileo Society—most of them living in or near Claremont—to fund the lecture hall area in Project Libra. Trude Taylor and Lotsie Giersch began plans to expand the membership of the Founding Friends of Harvey Mudd College and to approach some of the members of means who were not also college trustees for specific gifts. Both the Parents' Fund (Mr. Patkay, father of Pierre Patkay, as chair) and the Alumni Fundd planned additional solicitations. Hugo Riemer and Alec Hixon volunteered to approach a number of individual donors, including board members, about contributing gifts or adding to prior contributions.

An active and productive ten months followed. The challenge did help raise funds from both individuals and foundations. We did increase our corporate gifts and grants, and laid the foundation for the very considerable industrial support the Engineering and the Mathematics Clinics would later enjoy. Our trustees, and a number of other regular donors, went beyond their expected giving. The Galileo Society did indeed fund the lecture halls and the Case Foyer which serves as their entrance and as an informal meeting place for many college functions. Each of the committees of the development council had triumphs to report.

On April 1, 1972, at the conclusion of our Impact/72 Campaign, Pat Hyland, as campaign chairman, and Hugo Riemer, as chairman of the development council, were able to report that $18,964,609 had been raised, including pledges and letters of intent. Of this, gifts and pledges from trustees came to $6,875,991. We were, in fact, 1.14 percent over our goal!

For some ten months, under the skillful and imaginative hand of Lotsie Giersch, we had been planning a victory celebration. We had several reasons. First, we wanted to show our gratitude to the many donors who had made Impact/72 successful. Second, this seemed an important rite of passage for the entire college community, to rejoice in our success and look forward to our common future. Third, many new friends had joined us in making Impact/72 possible, and this seemed a good time to welcome them to the college family. We were concerned that our celebration be appropriate to its place in the brief history of the college, but also concerned that nobody thought we were squandering our hard won resources on riotous living. Accordingly, a number of trustees who had been involved in the work of Impact/72 agreed to share the costs of the celebration (Alec Hixon, in particular, volunteered to provide liquid refreshments) and we agreed to sell tables, as is the practice among charitable organizations, so that all individuals and organizations who chose to share the costs might have the opportunity.

The result was clearly the outstanding Celebration! we all enjoyed. Perhaps a thousand were there: donors, trustees, students, parents, faculty, groundskeepers, janitorial staff, the president—all of these people and their families were in attendance. Music was provided by the Air Force Band, brought from the Air Force Academy for the occasion. Hugo Riemer acted as master of ceremonies. Our featured speaker was the Honorable Daniel Patrick Moynihan, who made a masterly presentation of the importance of higher education to the nation, and noted our par-

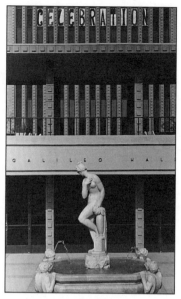

Student contribution to the victory celebration marking the success of the Impact/72 Campaign

ticular portion of this responsibility. Hugo Riemer, Henry Mudd, and I, not surprisingly, felt called upon to express our gratitude for the successful conclusion of Impact/72.

The day was not without incident. We were surprised, once we arrived on campus for the normal academic day, to discover paper letters, each some four feet high, across the fourth floor of the Norman F. Sprague Library. Although the library has sealed windows, these letters spelled out: CELEBRATION! across some sixty feet of the fourth floor level. It turned out that some nameless undergraduates, wishing to have their full part in the day's events, had prepared the letters and had sent rock climbers of their number in the night, to emblazon the message. During the day perhaps fifteen hundred small round glasses, containing votive candles, were placed on the campus walkways, to be lighted at dusk and illumine our way. Our guests started to arrive, and tour the campus, long before dusk. (We provided a shuttle service to the display of corporate jets at the Ontario Airport.) After tours of inspection, there was opportunity to visit and to enjoy a cocktail or soft drink. Then came dinner, and the formal program. In Hixon Court of Libra, and other venues, the Air Force Band provided very danceable music long into the night. We saw friends we had met in many different circumstances. Some of our guests left as early as 10:30 P.M., and, as far as I could tell, all were gone by 1 A.M.

Nevertheless, Jean and I felt obliged to make a final tour of campus, at two in the morning, to make sure all was well. It was, indeed. Our guests had not left any visible valuables, and the campus was reasonably ready for the next academic day. We did, at the end of our tour, discover a campus cat who had found a cache of shrimp discarded after the cocktail hour. The cat waddled across the campus to the center strip on Twelfth Street, rolled over on its back with all four feet in the air, burped, and went sound asleep. It had been a great CELEBRATION! for man and beast.

In retrospect, Impact/72 was even more important to Harvey Mudd College than we realized at the time. We doubled the total assets of the college, which was essential to our increase in size and a major accomplishment at any time, in any institution. Furthermore, we raised enough funds to support our ongoing operations while increasing in size, despite our shortfall in endowment. And we substantially broadened our constituency. We now belonged to the larger Southern California community, and were no longer exclusively the responsibility of our sister Claremont Colleges, nor of the Mudd family. We would continue to need all the help we could secure from our founders as well as from our more recent friends, but we were reaching fiscal adolescence.

CHAPTER II

Our Second Decade—An Overview

WHEN my family and I arrived in Claremont in September, 1956, Harvey Mudd College had no buildings, no faculty, and no students. The college had an idea, trustees, land for a campus, some funds, and a president. A decade later, in September, 1966, we had a campus with buildings, a faculty of forty-three (including our share of joint appointments), and a student body of 283 young men and women. The college had gained recognition, primarily because of the records our 257 graduates were establishing in industry or graduate schools; we were attracting able students and faculty.

What were our challenges for the second decade?

We shared a number of them with all of higher education. The national competition for faculty became intense in the 1960s. The "baby boom" nearly trebled the number of students seeking post-secondary education, while the pool of available faculty members remained almost constant. We had attracted a good faculty in our first decade. A number of these appointments had been for part-time teaching, with time released to develop our new curriculum with the help of generous funding from the Carnegie Corporation and the Sloan Foundation. These "extra hands" we had been able to appoint early became available for later full-time teaching assignments. But we too needed more faculty members in our second decade. Fortunately, we continued to attract outstanding recent Ph.D.s to our faculty, interested in both teaching and research. Also, we had met most of our subject matter needs by 1966; we had no fields in which we absolutely required a particular specialist. Accordingly this national shortage gave us less trouble than it did most institutions.

When Harvey Mudd College opened its doors in 1957, there was a national consensus on the need for well-educated scientists and engineers; President Eisenhower and others had emphasized this national priority. Ten years later, with 450,000 United States troops in Vietnam, there was less agreement on this and many other matters. We needed to make the case for educated technical leadership more strongly than ever.

Many young people of college age were distrustful of authority in general and of higher education in particular. The resultant "student unrest" disrupted many campuses and lost much public support for colleges and universities. Although we in Claremont were spared major disruption, money, both public and private, was less readily given. We needed, and developed, more volunteer friends to help us obtain gifts.

We were not spared the concerns of students about the mismanagement of world, national, and local affairs by their elders. Harvey Mudd's students, faculty, and trustees spent many hours developing a mutually agreed statement of student rights and responsibilities which would guide us.[1] This policy statement dealt with non-discriminatory admissions, freedom of classroom expression, protection against improper academic evaluation, release of student records, freedom of association including recognition of student organizations, student publications, standards of conduct and disciplinary proceedings, as well as rules and procedures governing disruptive conduct.

Since students from one Claremont college might engage in disruptive conduct (such as sit-ins) on the campus of another, all six colleges adopted resolutions giving the president of any of the Claremont Colleges the right of "summary suspension" with respect to any Claremont student disrupting the normal course of business on the campus of that president. The trustees of the Claremont Colleges authorized each president to use it each year from 1968 to 1976. The "summary suspension" (the withdrawal of the student's right to attend classes or continue in student status) would be upheld or canceled within a few days by the proper judiciary board, but during the interim the student was not entitled to be on campus or earning academic credit. This power was used by my fellow presidents; as it happened, I never needed to use this authority.

Finally, science and technology were changing. The "decoding" of the DNA molecule taught us the mechanism for transmission of information within living organisms and brought important new intellectual tools to biology. The increasing awareness of the fragility of our ecosphere brought urgency to the heeding of biological limits. Also, the growing utility and availability of computers remade the methods of retrieving and using information in all fields. A recurring set of questions, debated for several years at Saddle Rock meetings and in faculty meetings, dealt with how we best might develop instruction in these two new fields. Each of these advances continues to have a profound impact on our curriculum and our methods.

1. Minutes of the Board of Trustees of Harvey Mudd College, September 23, 1969.

We shared these challenges with many other institutions. We also had challenges of our very own.

When the college was new, all our students, faculty, and trustees were aware that we had a rare opportunity to find new and better ways to accomplish our mission. We were agreed that we were pioneering. We expected hard work, not much plant or equipment, and a need for ingenuity. We were in this together! What we did have was a strong sense of community and of common purpose to create a college. In the second decade, many of our ways were established, some arriving students assumed the college had always been here, and we had graduates to remind us that they liked the place as it had been. Nothing makes a person conservative more rapidly than having something to conserve, and we now had something. Would we continue to modify, to test, to improve our college? Were we all still in this together?

We had had our setbacks. As the reader has learned, we lost a much larger portion of our second class, the Class of 1962, than we had expected. As of 1966 we were still searching for ways to make the academic load bearable as well as sufficient for the goals inherent in the idea of the college. The retention of our students—the fraction of an entering class that would graduate in four or even five years—improved steadily through the 1960s and by 1976 was hovering around 65 percent—far better than the national average for colleges of engineering and science.

In Chapter 6 I have discussed some of the first changes we made in our effort to retain students. A great deal of faculty time and thought was given, during our second decade, to the "common core" of studies, which evolved substantially. As of 1966, we expected all our students, whatever their intended fields of study, to have most of their first two years in common: two years of literature, one of history, two years each of mathematics, physics, and chemistry, and an introduction to some engineering concepts. Not only was this a demanding academic load, but for many of our students, for whom things had come easily in high school and who had been at the top of their classes, the competition suddenly seemed brutal. They complained that it took all the fun out of life to work perpetually simply to survive.

Part of the answer, the faculty decided, was to eliminate freshman grades. We wanted our freshmen prepared for the work of the sophomore year, but it mattered not whether a particular student was number seven or number seventy in that class. Accordingly, the freshman grades became *pass, high pass,* and *no credit.* This indeed decreased the students' attention to the pecking order. We also found that we had been losing an undue proportion of the students who had planned to become engineers; two years of mathematics and science was a high price to pay for admission to one's first engineering course. The faculty reduced the time committed to physics and chemistry (by about 25 percent over the two years) and used that time not only to learn engineering concepts, but also to form teams to solve engineering problems. Time was also found to teach students the computing skills they would need throughout their professional lives, introducing them to an exciting new body of knowledge. These steps provided satisfactions some students had previously been missing.

In the late 1960s, our faculty moved again to reduce stress and to improve learning in the freshman year. The faculty at large delegated to an interdisciplinary group—the persons who were actually teaching freshmen—the responsibility for planning and managing freshman instruction. The person teaching introductory physics no longer would be responsible to his colleagues on the physics faculty, but to the other HMC faculty teaching freshmen, for the content and method of delivery of the freshman physics course. From the point of view of the student, this reduced the competition to see which department could demand the most study time; from the point of view of the instructors, they knew what else the students were learning at the time and could plan their presentations to use and reinforce other knowledge the student was currently mastering.

Still another concern about our initial "lock-step" common core was that not all students arrive with the same preparation. For example, as an increasing number of entering students came with some knowledge of calculus, they were allowed to "test out" of introductory calculus and to substitute other material.[2] Similar advanced placement later became possible in other fields. The consequence was to broaden the number of options available to freshmen; not all of them took the same courses, but by the end of the sophomore year each had mastered a common body of knowledge.

I will discuss in a later chapter another educational innovation we introduced (and, alas, later dropped): *The Quest for Commonwealth*, an ambitious introduction to the humanities and social sciences.

Faculty, trustees, and students were also much interested to learn what the college could do to promote personal growth of students in such areas as intellectual independence, willingness to accept the responsibilities of leadership, and understanding of the motivation of oneself and others. These themes recurred in the Saddle Rock meetings of the second decade. The development of the honor code, the contribution to personal motivation of the Clinic experience or the experience of independent research, self confidence gained through intercollegiate athletics, or the Bates aeronautical program, or through participation in student organizations were all reviewed in terms of these less quantifiable contributions.

Another interest that increased in the second decade was "faculty renewal"—how to help faculty members develop new interests, whether in research, administration, or scholarship. Sabbatical leaves are intended to accomplish this purpose, but so do leaves of absence, changes in

2. In 1986 the mathematics department recommmended, and the faculty voted, to require single-variable calculus of all entering students, with special "remedial" attention available for those unable to meet this entrance requirement. Hence, in something over a decade, the fraction of entering students with secondary school courses in calculus shifted from a minority to the substantial majority. (Personal communication from Mel Henriksen, May, 1992.)

assignment, or sometimes simply a vacation with time to think. In our first decade, Art Campbell had taken a partial leave of absence to direct the CHEM Study, much to the advantage of the college, and Al Focke had taken two years' leave to establish and direct the London branch of the United States' Office of Naval Research. In our second decade, Mack Gilkeson was on leave to participate in the development of new small industries in Brazil and later in India. Jim Monson spent a year as a Ford Foundation fellow with AT&T, helping to modernize a major switching center. Ted Waldman took two years' leave to participate in "the Tussman College experiment"—the establishment of an undergraduate, interdisciplinary college on the Berkeley campus of the University of California. The list of sabbaticals for the second decade is much too long to recite here, but each of these leaves, sabbaticals, or changes of activity served the purpose of giving the returning faculty member a new fund of experience to share with his students.

Our second decade also increased the outreach of Harvey Mudd College into the international scholarly community. Here again the beginnings were earlier. Bill Davenport and John Rae had been active in the liberal studies division of the American Society for Engineering Education. Dave Sanders became president of the division in our second decade.[3] John Rae was a founder and later president of the Society for the History of Technology. We had visitors from Canada, Yugoslavia, and England, plus a constant stream from the United States, many remaining for a year of the 1966-76 period, to learn our methods of teaching mathematics and the sciences, or the art and practice of engineering, or the humanities and social sciences. And our faculty published books—perhaps thirty books in our second decade, (at least ten of these in the humanities or social sciences) plus many more journal articles. Our students also were authors of journal articles. The college played host to conferences of secondary school administrators and teachers, and for two summers we provided (at the request of the Department of State, and with its support) a program for college principals invited from India to acquaint them with educational planning and management in the United States.[4] We were coming of age in the community of scholarly institutions.

Both students and faculty were concerned about the lack of diversity in our student body. Harvey Mudd had admitted women since it opened its doors for instruction, but in our early classes no more than perhaps 5 percent of the students were women. In the second decade this fraction increased to over 10 percent. We also began attracting more students of Latino, black, and, particularly, of Asian ancestry. We were still predominantly male and caucasian, but under the leadership of our Office of Admission, and with the help of such programs (to which Harvey Mudd played host) as Upward Bound[5], we made slow but regular gains in the heterogeneity of our student body.

3. At the time of his election, Dave Sanders was on the Clarkson faculty. His involvement with the Liberal Studies division had begun at Harvey Mudd College and would continue after his return.

4. We had many summer conferences, covering a wide range of subjects and groups. The IDEA conference, underwritten by the Kettering Foundation to improve secondary school teaching, continues to be held on our campus at the time of this writing. The programs for Indian college principals were planned and arranged by the late Raymond Iredell, then retired as dean of faculty of Pomona College. We still hear occasionally from one of these principals.

5. The Upward Bound program is explained and discussed in Chapter 14.

We grew in size, which after all was the purpose of our Impact/72 campaign. Our opening enrollment in September, 1966, was 283 students, and we had a faculty of forty-three, including our share of joint appointments and the appropriate faction of those who served part-time. The same figures for September, 1976, were 497 students (including four master's candidates in engineering) and fifty-four faculty members. Our student/faculty ratio had grown, over the decade, from 6.6 to 9.2. We had many more student research projects, or engineering design projects, actively under way.

We remained financially pinched, despite growth in enrollment and several tuition increases. The inflation of costs during our second decade had required more construction funds for Project Libra than we had anticipated at the beginning of Impact/72. Accordingly, while we had slightly exceeded our campaign goal, we had much less increase in endowment than we had expected. The academic year 1972-73 had in fact ended with a deficit of $320,000 in operating funds, which was balanced by a transfer of funds from quasi-endowment—the wrong way to

An aerial view of the campus.

build endowment! Substantial belt tightening and greater concentration on soliciting operating funds brought the college back into the black for 1973-74. The remainder of our second decade we were able to remain in the black for operating funds; as one might expect, every year showed growth in the net worth of the college.

It was a rewarding decade for students, faculty, and trustees. We had interest and advice from trustees on matters of curriculum or student life, help from the faculty in the solicitation of funds, and much student involvement in every aspect of the college. We knew and respected each other.

As of June, 1966, Harvey Mudd College had graduated 257 students. Ten years later the total had increased to 958 graduates. We were beginning to serve our purpose.

CHAPTER 12

Trustees of the Second Decade

I N Chapter 10, I reported on the major fundraising campaign of the second decade of Harvey Mudd College, and indeed without that fundraising there might have been no further decades. Members of the Board of Trustees took most of the leadership of Impact/72, and much of their work went beyond fundraising. Between 1966 and 1976 we added to our student body, built and equipped new buildings, developed a considerable body of faculty and student research as well as thriving clinics in engineering and mathematics, and graduated 701 students—444 more than in the prior decade. With Claremont Graduate School, we initiated a five-year program leading to the degree of master of engineering. We also were host to several significant programs for others than our own students. Together with our sister Claremont Colleges, we took steps to define the authority required to contain disruptive student unrest. In each of these major actions in the history of the college, the board made the final decisions—as noted in the last chapter, usually after extensive consultation with faculty and students.

The board grew modestly in size during its second decade. Thirty-four trustees were elected during that period, and nearly that number left the voting membership of the board by accepting honorary appointments, by resignation, or by death. In an earlier chapter the reader has met some of the decade's new trustees who were active in Impact/72; here I will present all other trustees who joined the board between 1966 and 1976.

The board elected Hugo Riemer, then president of U.S. Borax & Chemical Corporation, on September 21, 1966. Hugo, a Bucknell graduate who had then taken his law degree at Columbia, was the son of a professor of mathematics who had been a college president. Hugo shared his father's commitment to higher education. Hugo, who was at the time of his election national president of the Merchants and Manufacturer's Association, was widely respected in the business community. He first became interested in Harvey Mudd College as a corporate volunteer (recruited, I believe, by George Gose), and was an effective fundraiser before and after election to the board. When George Gose retired from business (as executive vice president of Pacific Mutual Life Insurance Co.) he also resigned as a trustee of the college, and Hugo succeeded him as chairman of the Development Council.

A.M. Zarem, who founded Electro-Optical Systems in 1956, was elected in December, 1966. Abe, a gifted electrical engineer, had earned his Ph.D. from Caltech magna cum laude, and had been designated "the nation's outstanding young electrical engineer" in 1948. He had served in the Manhattan District, and with the Stanford Research Institute, before founding his own company. Abe took a lively interest in the teaching at Harvey Mudd College, and had useful ideas for improvements—as well as an eye for where clinic projects might be secured. When he joined the board, he had sold Electro-Optical to the Xerox Corporation, but was still its operating manager. By 1973, as a director of Xerox, he was involved in bringing several new technologies into the research and development activities of the parent corporation. As he began spending much of his time on the East Coast, he resigned from the Harvey Mudd board. He and his wife, Esther, established a lecture fund at Harvey Mudd College that brought us a number of distinguished visiting scientists and engineers, with a particular emphasis on keeping our students and faculty current on emerging technologies.

Preston Hotchkis was elected to the board in December, 1966. Pres, who had captained the intercollegiate boxing team during his student days at Berkeley, was chairman of the Fred H. Bixby Ranch Company. A lawyer by training, Pres had also been a founding officer of Pacific Financial Corporation, and served as director of a number of corporations. Widely respected in the community and active in business associations plus any number of civic activities, he was in remarkable physical condition until he was nearly eighty, as I can testify from having hiked through hill country with him. He asked not to be re-elected in 1975, when he felt he was beginning to slow a bit; the board promptly voted him honorary membership.

Mrs. Robert E. Gross, the widow of the Lockheed board chairman, joined the Harvey Mudd board in June, 1967. A gracious and thoughtful lady, Mrs. Gross, who had served with Mrs. Harvey S. Mudd in various civic activities, took a generous and informed interest in the college which bore the name of Mildred Mudd's husband. Among many other charitable activities, Mrs. Gross was on the national board of the ARCS Foundation—a group of determined women who have been important to Harvey Mudd college students, and to students of many other colleges and universities.

Ralph M. Parsons was elected a trustee in June, 1969, and served until he resigned for reasons of health in 1974, only six months before his death. Ralph, a highly entrepreneurial builder, was born in a fishing town on Long Island, where his first job as a boy was hauling lobster pots. He entered the contracting business as a young man, and later was one of the team of contractors that built Hoover Dam. After World War II he founded his own business, which grew to become one of the major construction contractors in the United States, with projects in many nations. Ralph was a compact bundle of energy not much given to chatter. He studied and understood all the material that came to the board, and was a conscientious and generous trustee.

Seeley W. Mudd II, M.D., Henry Mudd's cousin, also joined the board in June, 1969. Seeley's father, a distinguished medical research man and civic leader, was Harvey Mudd's brother. Following his brother's death, the senior Seeley W. Mudd advised against the founding of what became Harvey Mudd College on the entirely reasonable grounds that the family did not have enough money to build a first-rate college, and should not be involved in something less than first-rate. When his advice was not heeded, he was friendly to those of us who were involved but remained aloof from any participation. His son, following his father's death, did choose to participate and did so with real warmth and effectiveness. The younger Dr. Seeley Mudd and his wife, Virginia, became good friends of Jean's and mine; we had happy evenings together at their cabin in Big Sur.

Two other new trustees were elected at the June, 1969, meeting of our board. One was Laurence A. Green, a Stanford alumnus then vice president of The Signal Companies, who introduced the college to a number of new corporate friends and was active in the Founding Friends and the work of the Bates Foundation. He resigned from The Signal Companies to enter his own business and left Southern California in 1971. The other was William Ballhaus, president of Beckman Instruments, who would become vice chairman of the board for business affairs, with oversight over our budget and fiscal planning, buildings and grounds, and investment committees. Bill, a Stanford graduate with his doctorate in mathematics from Caltech, had been an aeronautical engineer and vice president of Northrop Corporation prior to joining Beckman. (Bill impressed me as a strong advocate and a tireless worker. I once asked him what he did for recreation. He replied that his hobby was breaking quarter-horses to ride on his ranch.)

The academic years 1966-67 through 1968-69 saw losses from the voting membership of our board, including some resignations and a death. Phil Fogg, who by then had sold Consolidated Electrodynamics and was chairman of the executive committee of Lear Siegler, suffered a heart attack in 1966 and asked to resign. The board elected him an advisory trustee, and he did indeed advise us and kept in touch with our progress. In 1967, Dean Wooldridge retired from the chairmanship of the Thompson Ramo Wooldridge Corporation, and the Wooldridges moved to Santa Barbara; Dean also accepted reappointment as an advisory trustee. In 1968 Stuart O'Melveny declined to be re-elected because of his age. In June of that year the board adopted a memorial resolution for R.J. Wig, one of our founding trustees some of whose contributions are detailed in Chapter 3; R.J. had been in failing health for several years. Clifford Tweter resigned from the board when he retired as president of United California Bank (now First Interstate Bank). Raymond Hill, another founding trustee, resigned as a voting member in September, 1969 and was elected honorary trustee for life.

The academic year 1969-70 saw further notable additions to our board: Trude Taylor, then chairman and chief executive officer of Electronic Memories and Magnetics Corporation, joined the board that September. As of this writing, Trude has committed twenty-two years of very effective service to the college. Trude, himself a pilot, worked with the Bates Foundation as well as with the Founding Friends; he was a major source of strength in our Impact/72 campaign and our subsequent development activities, and he and his wife Joan have come to know all aspects of Harvey Mudd College with understanding and warm support.

Alexander Hixon, another pillar of strength in the life of the college, was elected in December, 1969. Alec, a successful manager and investor, and his wife, Adelaide, had accepted two major multi-year assignments for the United Nations Development Program; the first as a regional representative in West Africa, and the second in Western Samoa. (While Alec may have held the title, each assignment was clearly a two-person responsibility, as are some college presidencies.) Alec and Adelaide have taken a lively interest in the contribution the humanities and social sciences make to the personal development and the professional breadth of view of our students. The Hixon professorship at Harvey Mudd College is in the humanities.

The reader may recall that one board member, since the early history of the college, was a faculty member from a non-Claremont college or university. Dr. Frederick Lindvall, then chairman of the division of engineering and applied science at Caltech, had served with insight, great good humor, and much diligence until his retirement from Caltech in 1969. He then took a several-years appointment as vice president of John Deere, Inc., to help with the engineering development activities at that firm. When he left the area, the board elected him advisory trustee. In April, 1970, we had the good fortune to attract to the board Dr. George W. Brown, a Harvard graduate and Princeton Ph.D. in mathematics with substantial experience in high-technology industry, then as dean of the School of Management at the Irvine campus of the University of California. George brought his academic and industrial experience to bear on our developing curriculum, and our need to "join the emerging computer age." He brought balanced good judgment and many helpful suggestions to discussions of the academic work of the college with faculty and trustees.

Another academic board member, ex officio, was the president of Claremont University Center. Louis T. Benezet had held this position from Harvey Mudd's beginning. Louis resigned late in the academic year 1969-70, to become president of the Albany campus of the State University of New York. His successor was Howard R. Bowen, a social economist who had previously served as president of Grinnell College, and then of the University of Iowa. Over President Benezet's term of office, Claremont University Center had helped Harvey Mudd College greatly in making land available for and assisting in the financing of Project Libra. Under his leadership, Claremont Graduate School had joined with HMC in establishing a master's degree in engineering. We were sorry to lose Louis. But when Howard Bowen joined our board in July, 1970, we gained the wisdom and perspective of one of the major statesmen of American higher education.

At the June, 1970, meeting of our board we elected Edfred L. Shannon, Jr., then chief executive officer of Santa Fe International Company. Ed and his wife, Ruth, rapidly became participating members of the college family.

The academic year 1970-71 saw five additions to our board. Two, who were elected in December, 1970, would devote exceptional time and service to the college. The first was Robert P. Miller, Jr., then vice president of Southwest Engineering Company. Bob has been a pillar of our development effort during the succeeding two decades, and has chaired the board's Affairs Committee, which plans the activities and the recruiting of the board. Bob and his wife Louisa are, and have long been, informed and enthusiastic spokespersons for the college to the greater Los Angeles community. Their interest is exemplified by the Miller Professorship in the humanities. The second was E. Hubert Clark, Jr., president of Baker Oil Tools, Inc. (which, during Hubie's period as chief executive officer, became Baker Hughes International). Hubie, a Caltech graduate with his master's degree in mechanical engineering, served with diligence and quick understanding as chairman of the Education and Student Affairs Committee of the board, and would succeed Henry Mudd as chairman of the Board of Trustees. Active in many civic affairs, Hubie and his wife, Patti, are another husband and wife team.

Victor M. Carter, a civic leader and well-established businessman, joined the board in March, 1971. Born in Russia, he had been president of both Builder's Emporium and Republic Corporation. His list of community activities, too lengthy to list here, included his presidency of the Jewish Community Foundation and honorary life presidency of the City of Hope.

Marshall K. Evans was also elected at the same meeting, and his connection requires a bit of telling. Marshall took his first degree, in economics, from Penn State, and his M.B.A. from Harvard. Following military service, he joined Westinghouse. At the time of his election to our board, he was vice president of planning at Westinghouse Electric Company and lived in Pittsburgh. He regularly became acquainted with new professional employees at Westinghouse and followed their early careers. He found several "new hires" from Harvey Mudd College who impressed him, and Westinghouse thereafter annually recruited at the college. Marshall let us know he was impressed, and we invited him out to speak to parents' groups and faculty. He agreed to serve on our board, with the understanding that he would attend some but not all board meetings; he saw to it that the college was introduced to foundations in the Pittsburgh area. He was our first out-of-state trustee, and remained on the board until he retired from Westinghouse.

That same March meeting we elected Mrs. Frederick E. Giersch, Jr., whom the reader met in Chapter 10, managing the Libra celebration. "Lotsie," *née* Carlotta Busch, daughter of Augustus Busch of St. Louis, came from a long-established family of brewers. She was active in a variety of civic activities in the Los Angeles area, including the Los Angeles Zoo. Her range of acquaintanceship was remarkable, and she believed in getting things done. She was of great help to Harvey Mudd College in expanding the membership of our Founding Friends, in obtaining corporate support, and generally as an enthusiastic interpreter of the college.

The academic year 1971-72 saw one addition to our Board of Trustees: A.J. Field, then president of Global Marine Company. A.J., a Caltech graduate with his master's in science from Stanford, headed an organization that drilled the deepest man-made holes in the ocean bottom and had the cores from the Mohole project (a National Science Foundation project to explore the earth's mantle) to prove it. Global Marine also drilled offshore oil wells. The specialty of Global Marine was to position a ship with the stability and precision needed to serve as a drilling platform. A.J., the son of our former trustee Oliver C. Field, took a lively interest in planning and promoting our Engineering Clinic, and continued the family interest in the Bates Aeronautical Program; indeed, as befits a trustee, he keeps a good eye on all college activities.

In the academic year 1972-73, at its September meeting, the board elected to membership William M. Keck, president of Coalinga Corporation. Bill, a grandson of the William Keck who founded Superior Oil, promptly set about learning what the college does and what it aspires to do. At the December meeting the board elected Franklin Otis Booth, Jr., a Caltech alumnus and at that time vice president of the Times Mirror Corporation. His father had been an early supporter of the college, and the younger Otis Booth carried on the family tradition. In March of this academic year the board elected its first member from the alumni: Malcolm Lewis, '67, son of Pat and Claire Lewis. Malcolm, who by then had earned a master's degree in engineering from the Thayer School at Dartmouth College, was (and is) a consulting engineer in the Los Angeles area, active in alumni affairs. Malcolm helped to forge the understanding with the Harvey Mudd College Alumni Association whereby the trustees consult with the association to choose alumni members to serve a term as trustees. Trustees may also elect alumni who are not part of this rotating alumni succession. As of this writing, Malcolm has served for nineteen years, and has made many contributions to the life of the college.

I know of no other single meeting of our board (perhaps excluding the initial one) at which so many members were elected as that held in September, 1973. Gunnar B. Bergman, a practicing engineer and Caltech alumnus, had been interested in Harvey Mudd college since our early years, when I had tried (without success) to add him to our faculty. At that time Gunnar was technical director of Western Offshore Drilling Corporation, which was subsequently acquired by the Fluor Corporation, of which Gunnar became vice president. As our Engineering Clinic became established, he served most effectively as a member of its advisory group.

Henry A. Braun, vice president of CF Braun Engineering Co., was also elected at that meeting, and he and his wife, Ginnie, became active members of the group supporting HMC. CF Braun Engineering had the reputation of being "the Cadillac of engineering construction companies" on the West Coast, and Henry Braun's ability to find clients for the company kept that Cadillac moving.

Gordon L. Hough, then head of Pacific Coast operations for the Bell Telephone system, was also elected. Gordon had expected to move from San Francisco to Los Angeles, but the breakup of the Bell System, which gave rise to Pacific Bell, intervened; he remained in the Bay area and did an outstanding job of introducing Harvey Mudd College in the Bay area.

Dr. Joseph J. Jacobs, founder and board chairman of Jacobs Engineering Group, joined our board at that meeting. Joe and Vi Jacobs have become generous supporters of Harvey Mudd College and warm friends of the Platts. Joe, the son of Lebanese immigrants, earned his way through Brooklyn Polytechnic Institute (now Polytechnic Institute of New York) and stayed on after his baccalaureate to earn his doctorate in chemical engineering. (Joe points out that a graduate assistantship didn't pay much, but it was a job, which wasn't too bad for a chemical engineer in the mid-'30s.) He then went to work for a pharmaceutical company, where he made important contributions, but because he wanted his own company, he was off to the West Coast, where in due course he founded Jacobs Engineering Group.[1] Joe and Vi have been enthusiastic and significant supporters of his alma mater, as well as of Harvey Mudd College.

1. The complete story is told in Joe Jacobs's autobiography, *The Anatomy of an Entrepreneur* (San Francisco: ICS Press, 1991), which I found fascinating reading.

Kenneth A. Jonsson, a private investor and builder of television networks, also was elected at this meeting; he and his wife Diana have served with warm interest and loyalty. Ken is the son of Eric Jonsson, the co-founder of Texas Instrument Corporation, and Ken brought to our college long-range planning some of the clarity and discipline he had learned from that corporation.

Everett J. Long, an engineer who had founded a firm (Everett-Charles) manufacturing high-tech test equipment, also joined. Ev, a man of widely ranging interests and curiosity, had worked at Los Alamos National Laboratory during World War II, where he had learned to build sophisticated test equipment for such complicated devices as microchips. Years later he decided he and his family could build a company that built and sold such test equipment. They did!

Finally, John B. Merritt, a senior executive of the Borg-Warner Corporation, joined our board at that meeting.

Three other new members were elected later in this academic year. William C. Eldridge, a widely respected management consultant, was elected at the December meeting. Bill, who had earlier been of real help to the college by volunteering his services and helping us to reorganize our administrative staff, was a knowledgeable trustee who served us well as we grew by assuring us all that our business affairs were properly managed and understood by the board.

The June meeting of the board saw two additions. Fred Lindvall, his task at John Deere successfully accomplished, returned to Southern California and the board promptly returned him from advisory to voting status. Finally, at the June meeting we elected Clifford A. Miller, then president of Braun and Company. Cliff had known the college since our first year of teaching, when Ted Braun and his colleagues chose to help the college in our community relations. Cliff was one of the two staff members who had done research on the college before the Braun organization decided to advise us. As of this writing (1992), Cliff has been associated with the college as long as have any of our alumni, and he is currently chairman of the Board of Trustees.

The next two academic years brought two additions to our board. Edward M. ("Mo") Benson, Jr., then vice chairman of the Atlantic Richfield Corporation (ARCO), joined in December, 1974. Mo, a petroleum engineer, and his wife, Shirley, have been loyal and effective members of our trustee team, and Mo has taken particular interest in getting to know our students. William Barkan was elected in March, 1976.

Bill, a banker, was then responsible for the Southern California operations of Wells Fargo, and he saw to it that the college was introduced to a sector of the business community that we might not otherwise have met.

The academic years 1969 through 1976 saw losses from our board as well. Henry Duque, who had led in the formation of the Founding Friends of Harvey Mudd College, submitted his resignation in December, 1969. The board adopted a resolution of appreciation for his major service, and elected him a honorary trustee.

George Gose, who had been a real pillar of strength as chairman of our Development Council, retired in 1970 from his position as executive vice president of Pacific Mutual Company, and resigned at that time from our board. He left with our most heartfelt gratitude; he was a major builder of this college. George wished no resolution of appreciation (he hoped to vanish without a trace), and we reluctantly honored his wish.

The academic year 1971-72 saw several departures from the board. At its September meeting, the board accepted the resignation of Laurence Green, who was leaving Southern California. The board also accepted the resignation of Ernie Loebbecke, then recovering from a heart attack and under medical orders to reduce his load. The reader may remember that Ernie had been the trustee leader in establishing a Futures program at Harvey Mudd College. The board also remembered, and elected him an honorary trustee. At its March meeting the board accepted the resignation, also for reasons of health, of Bill Sesnon.

At the December meeting the board adopted a memorial resolution for our founding trustee, William W. Clary. Will Clary, who had also been chairman of the board of Claremont University Center and had served for a time as its president, was one of the small group of trustees who really advanced the Group Plan in Claremont by assisting in the founding of Claremont McKenna College, Harvey Mudd College, and Pitzer College.

In March of 1973 the board accepted the resignations of Abe Zarem and Ed Shannon, each of whom had business responsibilities that took them away from Southern California for much of their time. In June of that year, the board accepted the resignation of Hugh Clary, who was one of our early trustees, and elected him an honorary member. Hugh and his wife, Huldah, had been interested and faithful members of the college family.

The board accepted resignation in the academic year 1973-74 from Ted Braun, who had been the architect of the college's effort to become favorably known, at home and across the nation. He was promptly elected an honorary trustee. In the next academic year the board accepted the resignation of Ralph Parsons (September, 1974) and also designated him an honorary trustee. The board also accepted, with regret, the resignations of Everett Long and Preston Hotchkis (June,

1975). In the academic year 1975-76, the board accepted the resignation of Marshall Evans, then retiring from Westinghouse.

We lost a number of current or former trustees by death during the academic years 1972-76. The minutes of our board show memorial resolutions for our founding trustee, Garner Beckett (June, 1974), and for our early trustee, Stuart O'Melveny (also June, 1974). Ralph Parsons died in the following academic year, as did Franklin Otis Booth, Sr., an early and staunch supporter of the college and father of our trustee Franklin Otis Booth, Jr. The final memorial resolution the board adopted in our second decade (in December, 1975) noted the contributions of our early trustee Hugh Clary.

Harvey Mudd College has given few honorary degrees. We were quite self-conscious about wishing to honor only persons who represented the goals of the college and who knew the college. (I may have been a bit put off by an approach in our second year by a rising television

Honorary degree

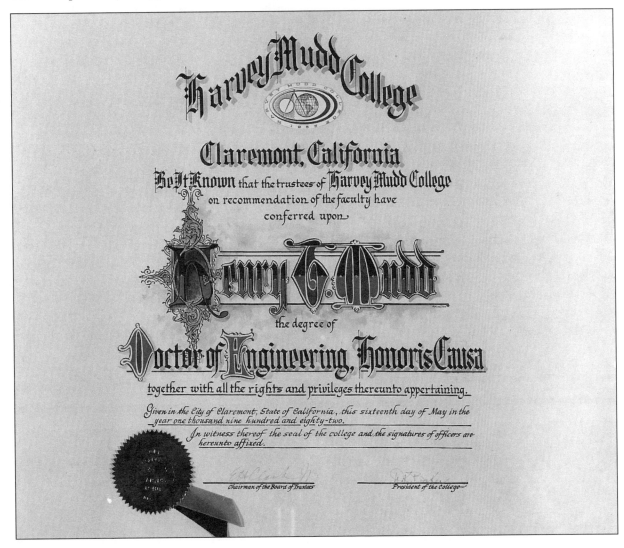

Ralph M. Parsons

comedian, who volunteered that if we gave him an honorary degree he could guarantee national visibility for the college.) Accordingly the criteria adopted by the board, on recommendation of the faculty, included demonstrated leadership in engineering, science, or a related field, with understanding of the impact of the leadership on the rest of the society; a record of public service; and a recognized connection with the college. (The board has also been cautious about granting honorary degrees to currently active trustees, faculty, or administrators to avoid the appearance of self dealing.)

The first such degree was awarded to Ralph Parsons, in June, 1971—the degree of Doctor of Engineering, Honoris Causa. Alas, at the time Ralph was hospitalized, and the degree was awarded, for him, to his proxy, a vice president of the Ralph M. Parsons Co., James Halferty. Our founding trustee, Raymond A. Hill, was also awarded the degree of Doctor of Engineering, Honoris Causa, and knew of the board action, but the degree was awarded posthumously. Both of these distinguished engineers, by then honorary trustees, more than met our criteria.

The trustees listed in this chapter, together with the fifteen who joined the board in its first decade and continued active membership through 1976, are the ones who held the legal responsibility for the affairs of the college for the decade from 1966 to 1976. Their active help made it possible for the college to grow and prosper over that period. We came to "full size" over those years. A larger fraction of our graduates were subsequently earning the doctorate than was true of any other institution in the nation, and many were rapidly gaining responsibility in industry and a wide range of other employment. These trustees served the college, our graduates, and our nation well.

CHAPTER 13

Faculty and Staff of the Second Decade

I N our second decade Harvey Mudd grew in size and breadth. At no
time during this ten-year period did the total faculty exceed fifty-
five persons, although more than 120 names appear on the faculty roster
for these years.[1] These were the years when the faculty initiated the Engineering Clinic, the freshman division, and Quest for Commonwealth
(all to be discussed in Chapter 15), sharply increased research and design
projects, and made important changes in the work of each department.

DEPARTMENT OF CHEMISTRY

In the academic year 1965-66, the Department of Chemistry consisted of
professors Art Campbell, Tad Beckman, Steve Filseth, Ken Harmon, Mits
Kubota, Phil Myhre, Bill Sly, and Roy Whiteker. A decade later we had
lost Roy Whiteker, who resigned in 1974 to become executive secretary of
the Fulbright Commission, and later dean of the faculty and then provost
of the University of the Pacific. Tad Beckman, who from his undergraduate years had a dual interest in philosophy and chemistry, began teaching
both; by 1970 he was on our humanities faculty as a fully credentialed
philosopher. Steve Filseth left in 1971 to head the undergraduate chemistry
program at York University in Toronto. Ken Harmon left in 1969 to head
a research program at the University of Washington, and subsequently
became professor of chemistry at Oakland University in Michigan.

The remaining four, happily, stayed at Harvey Mudd College. They
were joined in 1970 by Jerry Van Hecke, a member of Harvey Mudd
College's founding class. Ron Vaughan arrived in 1971, to serve for four
years before moving on to industry.[2] Paul van Eikeren came in 1972, to
remain for fourteen years before moving on to a research organization in
Bend, Oregon. Greg Kok came in 1974, to serve for six years. Mike
Flood and Jim Byrd each served one year.

1. This figure of 120 reflects joint
appointments, liaison engineers
appointed by our Clinic clients, and
visiting faculty members. All of these
people are listed, together with brief
professional vitae, in the Appendix.

2. I am sorry to report that Ron Vaughn
and his wife, Lee Hesse '65, were killed
in 1981 when their small personal
aircraft crashed in a snowstorm.

3. Art Breyer, then of Ohio Wesleyan University, began this pattern when he was with us in 1963-64 as visiting professor, moving on to become chairman of the department of chemistry at Beaver College. Pat Wegner taught for us in 1968-69 before going on to California State University at Fullerton. Daniel Blake spent the academic year 1970-71 with us as visiting assistant professor, and then went to the University of Texas at Arlington. Gerry Palino and Jim Robinson were also visiting assistant professors, in 1969-70 and 1970-71 respectively. Dave Philips of Wabash College spent his sabbatical year 1975-76 doing research with Mits Kubota here. Professor M.H. Pankhurst of the University of Otago, New Zealand, was with us for a semester, and Professor Keith Oldham of York University, Canada (who was on sabbatical at Claremont Graduate School) also taught a course for us.

The chemistry department was both larger and more fluid over the years 1966-76 than would appear from the roster cited above, due to skillful use of funds from the Sloan Foundation, the National Science Foundation, the Petroleum Research Fund, and the Research Corporation. Most of these funds were given to support research, but some were discretionary with the college, intended to advance both teaching and research. As sabbatical leaves began to occur for our own core faculty, visiting professors from other institutions came as temporary replacements. This arrangement gave us the benefit of the experience of other institutions, and it has over the years built bridges to departments of chemistry elsewhere.[3]

We also were helped by our own graduates who had earned doctorates elsewhere and returned for one or two years before moving on to longer-term academic appointments. Ken Stevens '61 taught with us in 1967-69, moving on to the University of the Puget Sound. He later changed fields, became a ceramicist of wide reputation, and as of 1992 is chairman of the Department of Fine Arts at that institution. Mike Beug returned in 1971-72, and then moved on to Evergreen State College in Olympia, Washington, where he is currently academic dean.

Others were attracted who were not our graduates. Graham Morrison joined us for the period 1976-78 before moving on to the National Institute for Standards and Technology. Cathy Koerntgen was a post-doctoral fellow with Mits Kubota before moving on to Chaffey College. Bruce McKay was with us on a NASA fellowship from 1969 to 1971. Per Martinson, of the University of Goteborg (Sweden) was visiting assistant professor of chemistry, working with Phil Myhre, for the year 1969-70. Terry Barr was with us for 1970-72 before joining Universal Oil Products Company. Bob Witters and Dave Barnhart were post-doctoral fellows with Bill Sly before moving on to the Colorado School of Mines and Eastern Montana College, respectively.

What did all these people do during this decade? They established a record in the graduation of chemists that most universities would envy: 138 in total, nearly all of whom went on to graduate work elsewhere. The faculty made it possible—indeed, mandatory—that each of these students graduate with experience in independent research, and in most cases with a record of professional publication. These graduates, in turn, have subsequently built the reputation of the college as a source of highly qualified professional chemists. Furthermore, at the end of the decade Harvey Mudd College had a number of research programs in chemistry that were active and thriving.

ENGINEERING

In September, 1966, the faculty in engineering consisted of Jack Alford, Mack Gilkeson, Jim Monson, Rich Phillips, Arnold Ruskin, Sedat

Serdengecti, Harry Williams, and Warren Wilson. A decade later we lost Warren Wilson, who had founded and staffed our engineering program, and Arnold Ruskin; both of these able engineers had moved on to the world of industry. We had added Ben Francis, John Molinder, Don Remer, Elliott Sigman, Wing Tam, and Tom Woodson.

The Engineering Clinic, which began the decade as an operation subsidized in considerable part by foundation grants, developed a solid industrial clientele under the industrious and outgoing leadership of Tom Woodson, who had earlier headed product development operations for General Electric Company. The clinic was helped in this transition by Rex Mack, who had had extensive development responsibility in the aerospace industry.

As the clinic grew and flourished, we had Al Fischler, Don McClung, Johan Selman, and Erich Valstyn as adjunct faculty members, whose primary employers were clinic clients. André Charette, professor of engineering at the Chicoutimi campus of the University of Quebec, visited for a semester to teach in the clinic and to learn what might be useful for his university. Patton Lewis, then director of research and product development of Lockheed Aircraft Service, and father of Malcolm Lewis, HMC '67, lent us his expertise as well.

We had other faculty members who both came and left in the decade: Don Ingels, a chemical engineer who had had industrial experience with Dow Chemical Corporation, came in 1970 to stay three years, and Amin Degani, in metallurgy, came in 1973 to stay two years before returning to his native India. Walter (Yeong-wen) Hwang, an electrical engineer, was with us for 1969-73, before returning to his native Taiwan.

We had leaves of absence. Mack Gilkeson spent three semesters (1966-67) in Brazil with a team that established small technical industries there, and later took a sabbatical (1971-72) in India, accomplishing the same purpose. Jim Monson spent a sabbatical year in Ireland as visiting professor at Trinity College, Dublin, followed by a month in Bulgaria on a visit sponsored by the U.S. National Academy of Sciences. Harry Williams spent a year in England, observing emerging European technologies for the U.S. Office of Naval Research.

The number of students graduating as engineering majors was ten in 1966 and thirty-eight in 1976; not only were there more students in total at Harvey Mudd College, but an increasing fraction of them wanted to be engineers. The concept of the clinic developed an enthusiastic following, both within our student body and among our industrial clients.

In addition, by 1976, with the support of the Claremont Graduate School, we had a number of years' experience with our joint master's degree program in engineering, complete with graduates who were doing well in industry.

HUMANITIES AND SOCIAL SCIENCES

The Department of Humanities and Social Sciences also grew during the decade. In 1966, the department included Bill Davenport, John Rae, Dave Sanders, Mike Seven, Ted Waldman, and George Wickes—three professors of literature, one of history, one of psychology, and a philosopher. Ten years later both Bill Davenport and John Rae had retired; fortunately for us, both continued to teach part-time and to write. George Wickes had left to become professor of English at the University of Oregon.

We had gained historians of science. Dick Olson, HMC '62, who had been teaching at the Santa Cruz campus of the University of California, joined us in the fall of 1976. John Blackmore joined us in 1972. Margaret Osler was with us from 1970 to 1974. We also had, as a joint appointment with Claremont Graduate School, our one Pulitzer Prize winner in history: Leonard W. Levy. In 1970 J'nan Sellery, now Louisa and Robert Miller Professor of Humanities, joined us as assistant professor of British and American literature; she later would teach media presentations, women's studies, and much else. Dave Sanders left in 1970 for a three-year tour as chairman of the program in humanities at Clarkson University, to return in 1973 as department chairman here. Bill Allen, who later would be the only member of our faculty to serve as chairman of the U.S. Civil Rights Commission or to run for the U.S. Senate, joined us in 1972 as a political scientist. Tad Beckman, earlier an HMC chemist, entered the department as a philosopher in 1970. Ron George, a professional engineer with a doctorate in psychology, became our second psychologist on full-time appointment in 1970, along with Mike Seven, who by now held joint appointments in psychology and engineering. Gary Pahl, an able Mesoamerican archeologist/anthropologist, taught for us in the years 1974-76 before returning to digging.

Accordingly, at the end of the decade, the department included three professors in literature, two in history, two in psychology, two in philosophy, and one in political science—plus distinguished part-time service in literature by Bill Davenport, and in history by John Rae and Leonard Levy. We were assisted in rhetoric by tutors George Crawford and Jim Viator.

The Claremont Colleges have great strength in the humanities and social sciences, and one might ask why we have required so many teachers in these fields on our own faculty. One reason was to provide instruction giving a common background to our students in these fields, as we also do in engineering and the natural sciences. Another was to have humanists and social scientists involved in the ongoing educational planning of the college. Our students could, and did, make use of the rich resources of the other Claremont Colleges in following their individual interests, but it was clear that Harvey Mudd College considered work in the humanities and social sciences to be essential to a rounded education, and had made a real faculty commitment.

Our alumni are generally grateful for the breadth of background the college provided—more outspokenly so as they grow older. Some have developed lifelong avocational interests in music, sculpture, or literature. Some have become professionals in fields one might not expect. Although most of the several hundred college or university faculty members among our graduates teach engineering, mathematics, or the natural sciences, some are professors of history, philosophy, art, drama, political science, economics, and literature. We would be disappointed if this had never happened!

We have regularly had students from our sister Claremont Colleges enrolled in courses in the humanities or social sciences taught by our faculty. Our humanists and social scientists have taught extensively at Claremont Graduate School. Our students have benefited substantially from the intercollegiate exchange program through courses taken on other campuses, and we attempt to repay in kind our share of this help.

Our humanists and social scientists published a sizable number of books in our second decade, and saw their full share of service on national scholarly societies. John Rae, for example, was a National Science Foundation senior post-doctoral fellow at Manchester University, and George Wickes, Dave Sanders, and others were Fulbright Scholars. John served on the NASA Historical Advisory Committee; Bill Davenport consulted with Oak Ridge National Laboratory on its public education activities. The engineers, mathematicians, and scientists had no monopoly on outreach!

MATHEMATICS

In 1966 our Department of Mathematics consisted of Bob Borrelli, Court Coleman, John Greever, Robin Ives, Bob James, Alden Pixley, and Al White. Bob James, who had planned and staffed our program in mathematics, resigned in 1967 to do these things all over for the graduate department of mathematics at the Albany campus of the State University of New York. His six colleagues, fortunately for us, were still teaching at Harvey Mudd College in 1976, and indeed in 1992. As of 1976, this core group had been joined in 1967 by George Orland (who came on a visiting appointment and stayed), by Stavros Busenberg[4] and Hank Krieger in 1968, and by Mel Henriksen in 1969. We also had mathematicians who came and left in our second decade: Ernie Fickas, from the University of Victoria; Barry Dayton, a Pomona College alumnus; Paul Palmquist; Tom Savage; Steve Bellenot; and Tom McCutcheon (the last two HMC graduates). Finally, Murray Projector, a consulting actuary living in Claremont, taught his specialty to interested students and attracted a goodly number of recruits to his profession.

4. I am sorry to add that Professor Busenberg, a victim of amyotrophic lateral sclerosis, died in April, 1993, after a distinguished twenty-five years of service to Harvey Mudd College as a teacher and as a research mathematician. He continued to teach until the week of his death.

5. The client was the Bell and Howell
Corporation, which manufactured
microfilm readers. Customers who
spent many hours using such readers
complained of eye fatigue. It turned out
that twinkling occurred out of the plane
of the image, which kept the reader's
eye constantly attempting to refocus.
The problem was due to the properties
of the light forming the image; it was
partially coherent (laser light *is* coherent;
incandescent lamplight usually isn't).
The mathematics for predicting the
behavior of coherent or incoherent light
was well known; the trick was to
develop the appropriate mathematical
tools for partially coherent light. When
these tools were developed, the
twinkling became understood, and it
became apparent how to reduce it.

6. This paragraph is copied verbatim
from a private communication from Mel
Henriksen, May, 1992.

Our mathematicians began speculating in 1969-70 on the possibility of a Mathematics Clinic, using students to solve problems in applied mathematics for industrial clients. In 1973 a puzzling mathematical problem showed up for an Engineering Clinic client, and Stavros Busenberg of our mathematics faculty helped a student team find an elegant solution.[5] The Harvey Mudd College mathematicians, with John Greever as initial director, promptly established their own clinic and sought other clients. By 1976 the Mathematics Clinic had completed a number of projects, and we also had been of help to the mathematicians of Claremont Graduate School in founding their clinic. Jointly, the two clinics secured a grant from the National Science Foundation in 1975, which speeded their establishment.

Any history of the mathematics program at HMC must take into account the cooperation between the mathematics programs at the several Claremont Colleges, most notably in graduate teaching. Our most capable majors in mathematics took most of their mathematics courses as seniors, and often as juniors, in courses taught cooperatively with Claremont Graduate School. Our upper division mathematics offerings have been strengthened over the years by sharing advanced courses with colleagues in the other Claremont Colleges.[6] We have enjoyed intercollegiate cooperation in other fields as well, but mathematics is the area that has had the most intercollegiate planning and staffing of those in which Harvey Mudd College has participated.

Over the decade 1966-76 Harvey Mudd College graduated 134 mathematics majors, including eleven who were "double majors"—having also completed the requirements for another field of concentration. Many of these graduates now hold the doctorate, and a substantial number are on faculties of other colleges and universities. Not surprisingly, the largest single number are employed in industry.

PHYSICS

The Department of Physics in 1966 consisted of Graydon Bell, Al Focke, John Goodman, Tom Helliwell, Ben Robertson, Ro Rojansky, Sandy Sandmann, Ted Stoddard, Eldred Tubbs, Jack Waggoner, Enos Wicher, and Bob Wolf. During the next decade Al Focke and Ro Rojansky retired, in neither case very perceptibly. Al, who had led the planning and staffing of the department, could regularly be found in the seismology laboratory he had built with the support of Guy Edwards, a retired exploration geologist and benefactor of the college. Ro was busily writing a text on electricity and magnetism. Enos Wicher, who had been a creator of the freshman year program, retired at the end of the decade. We also lost John Goodman, who left to establish a public physics teaching facility in Orange County modeled on Berkeley's Exploratorium. Ben Robertson left to accompany his wife to her native Guatemala, where her family's affairs needed his attention. We added Dan Peterson to the department in 1974, and John Townsend in 1975. Ellen Domb joined us in September, 1976.

A number of physicists both came and left during this decade. Art Cary joined us in 1969. He left in 1975 for California State Polytechnic University at San Luis Obispo, where he would later be department chairman. Ron Brown joined us in 1968, to leave in 1974. George Cooper came in 1969, also to leave in 1974. Lucian Carter held an appointment shared by Pomona and Harvey Mudd Colleges in 1974-75. Carol Webb, an astronomer, was with us from 1972 to 1974. Peter Smith, a Canadian national, taught with us for the academic year 1972-73. And finally (taking a leaf from the chemists' book), Ken Orloff, HMC '66, was with us as visiting assistant professor of physics for the year 1975-76, on leave from his engineering job with NASA.

One hundred ninety-six students graduated with concentrations in physics over those years, making physics second only to engineering in popularity. We entered the decade with research programs in theoretical physics, atomic spectroscopy and low temperature physics; at the end of the decade we also had active programs in astronomy, seismology, and solid state physics. The physics undergraduates had a record of independent research in which the faculty could take pride, and their subsequent careers have only increased that pride.

JOINT PROGRAMS

We had a variety of instructional programs through our second decade, which Harvey Mudd shared with our sister colleges. The largest was in physical education, a joint venture with Claremont McKenna College (then Claremont Men's College) and Scripps College. The physical education programs provided instruction in sports and regular exercise, and also offered those of our students who chose to do so an opportunity to compete in intercollegiate athletics. We also had programs of intramural athletics, usually involving more than one of the Claremont Colleges.

Scripps offered our women instruction in dance as well as in intercollegiate women's sports. There were, for our men and women, usually a range of intramural sports in progress. Since the size of our student body was in general about half that of CMC, and since practice time for team sports was apt to be in conflict with laboratories, we used less than a third of the available people and facilities. For quite a number of our students it was important to participate in intercollegiate sports; indeed the track, field, and swimming record books of the Stags for the decade carry their share of HMC names, and Steve Endemano (HMC '71) once beat Olympic medalist Bruce Jenner in an Olympic pentathlon tryout. (Jenner went on to win the decathlon at the '76 Olympics; Steve, alas, did not.)

As of 1966-67, the physical education group was headed by Bill

Arce, who had founded the program and was also baseball coach. Ted Ducey was the basketball coach, Dez Farnaday the swimming and water polo coach, Don Stalwick (assisted by Walt Klinker) the football coach, and Vince Reel the track coach. (These were the primary assignments; each of these coaches could and did coach a range of sports.) The program was supported by Frank Sacks, who doubled as trainer and equipment manager, and by the departmental secretary Mildred Standish.

As of 1976-77, Bill Arce continued as head of the physical education program. Ted Ducey, tragically, had died attempting to save others in a flash flood on the Colorado River. Dez Farnaday had moved on to his alternate career as a professional sculptor, Don Stalwick had entered private business, and Vince Reel was in the Republic of China, coaching the national track team for the Asian Games. Tom Grall was now swimming coach, and also president of the NAIA Swimming Coaches Association. Dave Wells (CMC) was basketball coach, returning to a team on which he had once been a star performer. John Zinda was football coach, and Gail Hopkins was track coach. Frank Sacks and Mildred Standish were still seeing to it that the whole program worked.

In addition, Bill Arce was in international demand to train competitive athletes (as had been Vince Reel before his departure), and he took any number of baseball players, including some from HMC, to teach and to demonstrate baseball (and from time to time to be beaten by their students) in European nations.

Music and drama were also important to many of our students. We shared with Scripps College the services of John Lilley, associate professor of music and director of the Concert Choir, and of Jesse Swan, professor of drama and speech. Our joint program with the Bates Foundation, very important indeed to the students enrolled in it, weathered some financial struggles and survived the decade under the skillful hands of Iris and Howard Critchell. (Bates graduates would include enthusiastic private pilots, aeronautical engineers, an airline pilot, and an astronaut.)

THE BEGINNINGS OF COMPUTER SCIENCE

Harvey Mudd had bought its first computer, an IBM 1620, in 1962. By 1966, our second decade, all of our students had some exposure to computing as freshmen, and it was clear to our faculty (if not yet to me) that we had barely scratched the surface. Jim Monson, Alden Pixley, and Sedat Serdengecti decided to plan and implement a program that would prepare those interested students in engineering or mathematics with the basic knowledge they would need for graduate study in computer science. Each of the three brought relevant experience to the task. Jim Monson had spent the year 1965-66 as a Ford Foundation resident in engineering practice at Western Electric Company, where he had gained a working knowledge of digital electronic switching systems. "Pix" (not everyone

Harvey Mudd College's first computer purchase.

calls him Alden) had worked for IBM for some years before returning to the teaching of mathematics. And Sedat had done his full share of teaching of computing. Together they developed a set of three courses, available to any students who wished to take them, and sufficient to give a basic comprehension of computing theory and practice. They were greatly helped by the growth in computing in all the Claremont Colleges. Fred Weingarten, who directed our Joint Computer Center over the years 1969-73, brought considerable professional experience to the group, and did some teaching. Walter Brainerd, a Purdue Ph.D. who came to us from the department of Information Statistics at Columbia University and who was a member of the mathematics faculty for 1972-73, was a valuable addition. Paul Nahin, who was on our engineering faculty for the period 1971-73, a Caltech Ph.D. who had been a digital design engineer with Beckman Instruments, also helped to develop our program.

We substantially increased the computing equipment available to students and faculty. Pomona College had acquired an IBM 360, a large computer by 1966 standards, and the other colleges shared in its use for administrative purposes. Harvey Mudd College found itself acquiring, by gift where possible and by discounted price if not, an increasing amount of equipment. Nearly all our faculty and much of the student body were interested in learning what help computers could be in teaching or in research. Accordingly, faculty in chemistry, physics, and the humanities were also involved in the cultivation and dissemination of "computer literacy," although it is fair to say that the initial impetus and most of the course development in computer science came from the individual engineers and mathematicians I have cited.

By 1973 there was enough student and faculty interest—nay, excitement—about computing that the faculty proposed we have a "computer science group" to advise the president and the dean on the adequacy of our offerings, the emerging needs for additional faculty staffing in computer science, and the best ways of coordinating the new techniques computers made available with our existing curriculum. Accordingly, at faculty request, I appointed such a group: professors Brainerd, Monson, Nahin, Pixley, and Serdengecti, with Sedat Serdengecti as chairman. The conclusion was that we *did* need to expand and regularly update our offerings in computer science, that for the time being the faculty members involved in teaching computer science could be included in the existing departments of engineering and mathematics, but that some additional appointments in these departments would be needed. The possibility should be kept open that in time a separate department of computer science would be appropriate, and the college might in time consider offering a computer science major.[7]

7. I am indebted to Sedat Serdengecti for the use of his excellent records on our evolving computer science program.

AN EMERGING NEED: BIOLOGY

The reader will have discovered that Harvey Mudd College had few departments: chemistry, engineering, a variety of faculty appointments in the humanities and social sciences gathered for administrative and planning purposes in one department, mathematics, and physics. The initial faculty, the trustees, and I had agreed in 1957 that we would concentrate our attention and faculty appointments in these five areas and attempt to present these fields well, rather than divide our effort among more fields of study. Fortunately for our students excellent instruction was available in our sister colleges in such other fields of interest as biology, the earth sciences, foreign languages, music, and the graphic arts.

Biology, a much longer established field, was the next to concern our faculty after computer science. From the early days of the college several of our students had planned to enter biological research or the practice of medicine, and the biology departments of our sister colleges had served these students well. Our concern was that with new developments (such as the study of the DNA molecule) and the growing importance of understanding the biological limits to responsible human activity, *all* our students should become acquainted with the basic facts of biology. We expected many to become interested in entering the "bridge fields" of biochemistry, bioengineering, biomathematics, and biophysics; we also anticipated growing interest in biotechnology and biological research. We would need instruction in biology which made use of the backgrounds of our students in engineering, the physical sciences, and mathematics to make the most of these opportunities. Fortunately for us, the same idea had occurred to the family of Stuart Mudd, a distinguished microbiologist on the faculty of the University of Pennsylvania.[8] Accordingly, the family established a professorship at Harvey Mudd College, and we

8. One can assess the range of Stuart Mudd's interests from a book he edited for the World Academy of Art and

searched for the Stuart Mudd Professor in 1976. In 1977, with the appointment of William L. Purves, (then head of the Biological Sciences Group of the University of Connecticut) we began instruction in biology on our own campus, with our own faculty.

CHANGES IN ADMINISTRATION IN THE SECOND DECADE

As of September, 1966, the administrative officers of the colleges included me, Joseph B. Platt, as president, Eugene Hotchkiss III as dean of the college, George I. McKelvey III as director of development, and William C. Radley as assistant to the president. (Bill Radley had replaced Edward F. Little a year earlier, when Spif had returned to studying and teaching. In both cases the "assistant to the president" was in fact the business and personnel manager.) In addition, we shared with CMC our dean of admission, Emery R. Walker, Jr., and his colleagues of the Office of Admission. We shared John W. Hartley as treasurer and Richard C. Hill as controller with all the Claremont Colleges.

George McKelvey was ably assisted (as of 1966) by Mike Kearney, associate secretary of development, and by assistant secretaries Jack Charleville, Bill Cole, and Dorothy Harris. George's secretary, Doris Cederlind, saw to it that everyone knew what needed doing. The Development Office required a good deal of correspondence, as the staff roster shows. Zaner Faust presided over the Office of Public Information, assisted by David Arnold, Mary Post, and Marian Gabler.

The college had substantially more in buildings and grounds by 1966 than we had had in the earlier years. Bill Radley and his secretary Edith Davies kept track of the grounds staff, which was headed by Oskar Soolepp and his deputy Josef Lorincz; and our residence hall custodians and housekeepers, headed by Irene Levy and Charles Gregory. John Thompson took care of our offices and classrooms, and Rudolph Messier of our laboratories. By this time we also needed technicians to build and maintain apparatus: Ed Newton in engineering, Bill Hoesen in physics, George Glonka in chemistry, and Bill Schaufelberger, our machinist.

No accounting of our staff would be complete without the department secretaries: Marcia Myers in chemistry, Norma Kruger in engineering, Margaret Thompson in humanities, Marion Snyder in mathematics, and Evelyn ("Aunt Evvie") Lee in physics. And finally, any faculty member can tell you who runs the college: the registrar. In 1966 our registrar was Evelyn Town, assisted by Venus Martinez.

In 1968 Gene Hotchkiss ("Keen Dean Gene," according to the student yearbook) resigned to become executive dean of Chatham College, Pennsylvania. He remained in that position for two years, leaving to become president of Lake Forest College, Illinois. We found he would require *two* successors. During Gene's final semester at HMC, we instituted searches for a dean of faculty and a dean of students.

Science: *The Population Crisis and the Use of World Resources* (copyright 1964 by Uitgeverij Dr. W. Junk, The Hague, Holland). Dr. Stuart Mudd and Harvey S. Mudd were cousins; Stuart and his wife Emily (herself a social scientist and past president of the American Association of Marriage Counselors) followed the founding of Harvey Mudd College with interest and sympathy. Following Stuart's death, his family established the Stuart Mudd Professorship in Biology at Harvey Mudd College.

Our new dean of faculty was Jacob P. Frankel, who had been professor of engineering and associate dean at the Thayer School of Engineering, Dartmouth College. An able and forthright engineer with a wide range of interests, Jack stayed at HMC until 1974, when he left to become president of California State University at Bakersfield. We persuaded Art Campbell to act as dean of the faculty for the interim year 1974-75, while we searched for our next dean. He is Samuel B. Tanenbaum, then professor of electrical engineering and director of the minority engineers' industrial opportunity program at Case Western University. Sam finally gave up this position in 1993 to return to teaching.

We were also fortunate in our search for a dean of students. William L. Swartzbaugh, then associate dean of the college at Amherst, agreed to come for a period of years. Bill and his wife, Jean, both ardent and able sailors, became well known and liked by our students, many of whom were either guests in their home or with them afloat. They remained for three years, finally succumbing to the lure of managing a yacht brokerage firm in their native New England. We instituted another national search, appointing in 1971 William R. Gann. Bill, a University of Missouri undergraduate with experience as a high school teacher and counselor, we found at home: he had been chairman of collegiate relations of the California Scholarship Federation, and then director of the Program of Special Directed Studies for the Claremont Colleges. Bill Gann remained as dean of students throughout my presidency, and for years thereafter.

The 1966-76 decade saw many changes in the administrative staff, both through turnover and through changes in responsibilities of many continuing staff members. A roster, as complete as we can make it, is in the Appendix. (I have attempted to use descriptive titles, not always the formally correct ones.) Three comments occur to me on this roster. The first has to do with development. Impact/72 did require a substantial staff, but much of the turnover came because "alumni" of George McKelvey's training moved on to become heads of development programs elsewhere: the universities of Iowa, Oregon, and Colgate, among other institutions.

My second comment is that I personally was very fortunate in the presidential secretaries who ordered my life and managed much of the college: Phyllis Colclough until 1967, then Phyllis Heesch until 1973, and finally Doris Cederlind.

Lastly, the "administrative assistants to the president" were graduate students, employed on a part-time basis, who did a great many useful things for me. They planned and organized Saddle Rock meetings, worked with faculty in developing new programs, helped plan accreditation preparations and meetings, organized public functions, and found accommodations for visiting scholars—to mention a few of their chores. They also contributed to my education. I looked in once on Ellie

Johnston to find her studying Ugaritic, of which I had not then heard. It turns out that Ugaritic was the Semitic language of the prebiblical city of Ugarit, in what is now Syria. Ellie is now (1992) Eleanor Beach, professor of religion, Gustavus Adolphus College.

I was also forever riding airplanes, and the assistants to the presidents either drove me to and from airports or found students to do so. Part of my responsibilities included the recruiting of senior faculty or staff, and calling on foundations, both of which involved travel.

I also served a number of other organizations, which in total probably amounted to an extra half day's work per week; in many cases these contacts were of use to the college, and in any event I believe that as a college president who depends on volunteers I should volunteer some community service myself.[9] More often than not, when in some distant place, I managed to find some college business as well. It was a comfort to meet a familiar car and driver on returning to Southern California. It was also a comfort, in 1969-71 amidst student unrest, to have the help of Dan Sisson, who understood the issues better than I.

The academic year 1975-76 was my final one as president of Harvey Mudd College. I was offered, and accepted, the presidency of Claremont Graduate School and University Center, and I spent the next five years ending, June, 1981, in that responsibility. Jean and I take real satisfaction from our years with Claremont Graduate School and University Center, as we had with our years at Harvey Mudd College. However, the decision to make the change was not an easy one.

Claremont Graduate School and University Center has few analogues in American higher education. Along with its sister Claremont colleges, it has its own board, is financially independent of the other colleges, grants its own degrees, and appoints its own faculty and staff. Most graduate schools, as colleges of a university, can draw both financial and faculty support from undergraduate colleges under common management. CGS does indeed enjoy faculty support volunteered from the undergraduate colleges, and it shares with them economies of scale in central services, but it cannot command such support. In its University Center responsibility, CGS & UC has two added duties other graduate schools do not. The University Center operates most of the services jointly supported by all Claremont colleges, and also acts as agent for the group in its common planning. In this last responsibility, it planned, organized and founded Scripps College, Claremont McKenna College, Harvey Mudd College, and Pitzer College.

Accordingly both Harvey Mudd College and the Platts have deep loyalties to Claremont Graduate School and University Center. Harvey Seeley Mudd had been chairman of that board when CMC was founded, and had been a supportive member of that board when the idea of an engineering college was first proposed. Many of HMC's initial trustees—

9. Over the 1966-76 period I was a trustee of two federally funded research corporations, the Aerospace Corporation (architect-engineer for military space systems) and ANSER (Analytic Services Inc.) of which I was Board chairman. ANSER does system and operations analyses for a variety of agencies, including in particular the Air Force. I also was a trustee of the Carnegie Foundation for the Advancement of Teaching, which was engaged in policy studies for higher education. I served as member, vice chairman and chairman of the National Science Foundation's Advisory Committee on Science Education. I also was a member of two panels of the President's Science Advisory Committee.

The National Academy of Sciences had me on its list of willing volunteers for international scientific activities, and I had served twice as a member of the United States' delegation to the biennial meetings of UNESCO—my assignment being international science programs. In 1964 I was asked to explore the possibility of a cooperative program between the United States' Academy and the Academia Sinica of the Republic of China. In 1964 the per capita income in Taiwan was US $180, and that government was eager to develop its technical industry and the university and research infrastructure it would require. For the next fourteen years I served as chair of the United States' Committee on Sino-American Science Cooperation, and a very rewarding experience it has been. Both university science and technical industry now flourish in the Republic of China because of Chinese initiative and drive, but I believe we may have helped.

In May, 1971 the California Coordinating Council for Higher Education appointed a Select

Committee of seventeen citizens to review the California Master Plan for Higher Education, and to recommend to the legislature and governor any desirable changes. The committee elected me its chair, and we put in a strenuous fifteen months of public hearings, study and discussion. We coordinated our efforts with a similar committee of the California Legislature. Our primary conclusion was that the citizens and the economy of California had been well served by the Master Plan, and that it should be continued with no radical changes. We also made recommendations for what we believed would be improvements, a number of which were adopted by the State.

In these "extracurricular" ventures—many of which did turn out to be useful to the college—my wife Jean Platt was supportive and often a participant. She has travelled with me to Taiwan many times, has met trustees and staff and families of research organizations, has entertained colleagues in Paris with UNESCO, in Guadalajara with the Carnegie group, and in Claremont whenever my colleagues in any of these ventures came by. I'm grateful to say she shares my satisfaction in the outcomes of many of these activities.

10. More correctly, Claremont Graduate School and University Center had been drawing down its quasi-endowment, which are funds given to the institution for unrestricted use but designated by the board for endowment purposes. (Funds specified by the donor explicitly for endowment are always held for that purpose.) At the discretion of the board, quasi-endowment can be invaded if necessary. However, the total of funds serving as endowment (including quasi-endowment) for CGS & UC stood at about $30 million in 1975, and nearly half of these were committed by terms of the gifts to the support of group enterprises, not graduate study.

11. The history of this period is given in Chapter 8 of Howard Bowen's gracious and thoughtful book *Academic Recollections,* published with the support of the American Association for Higher Education and the American Council on Education by Macmillan Publishing Co. (1988). Both Howard Bowen and Barnaby Keeney had major national accomplishments as academic administrators before coming to Claremont. Howard had held, among other responsibilities, the presidencies of Grinnell College and the University of

Robert J. Bernard, Garner A. Beckett, William W. Clary, Ford J. Twaits, Van Renssalaer G. Wilbur, and R. J. Wig—were members of the board of CGS & UC. Jean and I had first heard of Harvey Mudd College from George C.S. Benson, then president of CMC acting as emissary of this group. We had our campus because CUC, as agent for the group of colleges, had preserved the land for future colleges. The laboratories of HMC stood on land given us by CUC, and we had been able to finance their construction with the help of CUC—later, in President Benezet's time, we had acquired a wing to the first laboratory building at no net cost to HMC through the good offices of CUC. Furthermore, I remember with gratitude commitment of many senior members of the CUC board to the progress of Harvey Mudd College in my early years as president.

As of 1975, Claremont Graduate School was in severe financial difficulty. Graduate enrollment had increased nearly tenfold since World War II, supported in part by federal grants and loans to graduate students under the National Defense Education Act. Over a four-year period, the number of such graduate full-tuition fellowships (with their associated institutional grants) had gone from fifty-five to zero. This had happened concurrently with other problems of decreasing income and rising costs. CGS had had to draw down substantially on its limited endowment to meet its annual operating expenses.[10]

It was clearly important to our fifth-year students and to all the Claremont Colleges that CGS & UC remain in good health. With the help of CGS, the undergraduate colleges could attract faculty members who also had interest in graduate-level research and teaching, and those upperclassmen who chose could have access to courses at the graduate level. CGS had prepared faculty and academic administrators for many other school systems, colleges, and universities, and was important to the academic reputation of the group. When the Board of Fellows of CGS & UC decided to approach me about the presidency, I was urged by my fellow presidents of the Claremont Colleges and their board chairmen to accept. The provost, who would, I hoped, continue in office, also urged me to accept. The Board of Fellows of CGS & UC had experimented with an unusual organizational structure over the years 1970-75.[11] Howard Bowen, who had agreed in 1970 to become interim president after Louis Benezet resigned, had been succeeded in 1971 by a "troika" in which Howard (designated, against his recommendation, as chancellor) became the principal planning officer of the group, Barnaby Keeney became president of Claremont Graduate School, and E. Howard Brooks became provost, responsible for administering the central services of the Claremont Colleges. This change had required modification of the constitution of the Claremont Colleges, voted by all six boards of trustees. Now, with the resignations of Howard Bowen and Barnaby, the constitution would again need to be modified by the several boards of trustees to appoint a single president.

After consultation with my two principal advisors, Jean Platt and Henry Mudd (both of whom told me it was my decision), I agreed to serve if elected, subject to these conditions first having been met:[12]

1. Adoption of the revised constitution of the Claremont Colleges by the six boards of trustees.
2. Appointment of the two central officers (vice presidents for finance and for development) required by any probable reorganization plan.
3. Agreement on a financial plan to assure Claremont University Center's solvency.
4. Resolution of a specific legal controversy between colleges.[13]
5. Strengthening of common planning for the colleges.

The Harvey Mudd board, at its meeting of December 17, 1975, appointed a presidential search committee with two trustees, Frederick Lindvall (chairman) and Hugo Riemer; two faculty, Bob Borrelli and John Rae; one student, Steve Woods '76; and one alumnus, Dave Howell '61.

At the June meeting of the Harvey Mudd board, our chairman Henry Mudd was authorized to offer appointment as president of HMC to D. Kenneth Baker, then vice president, dean, and acting president of St. Lawrence University. Ken, a physicist and co-author of a widely respected book on modern physics, holds his doctorate from the University of Pennsylvania, had taught at Union College, served as director of university relations for the General Electric Company, and had been program leader for a USAID project in India. As for me, I was able to report that CGS and UC had met my first three conditions for accepting their presidency, and that the fourth appeared well on its way to resolution. Each board had expressed its intent to cooperate in the fifth condition; by the nature of the Claremont Colleges, one cannot guarantee common planning.

I am happy to note that Ken and Vivian Baker accepted appointment, and served Harvey Mudd College very well indeed for the next twelve years. My fourth condition was also completely met in the summer of 1976, and Jean and I entered on a fulfilling five-year period of service at Claremont Graduate School and University Center.

Iowa; Barnaby had been president of Brown University and Director of the National Endowment for Humanities. After years of effort as administrators in Claremont, Howard Bowen returned to research and teaching in 1974 (in which he made more national contributions over the next several years) and Barnaby Keeney resigned in 1975. Howard Brooks, fortunately for me, remained as provost, and his urging and support were essential to my decision to accept the responsibility I was offered.

12. Minutes of the Board of Trustees, Harvey Mudd College, December 17, 1975.

13. The controversy was between Claremont McKenna College and CGS & UC, each of which claimed to be the "Claremont College" named in a substantial bequest. An intercollegiate group of trustees negotiated an appropriate allocation of these funds if received, and the Court returned a stipulated judgment accepting this agreement.

Kenneth Baker

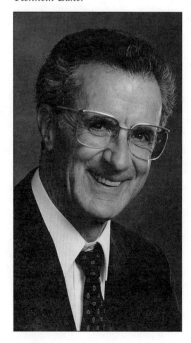

CHAPTER 14

Students of the Second Decade—1966-76

WE expected changes in the student body over the second decade of Harvey Mudd College. Many of these changes were in accordance with our hopes. We had more students. From the eight graduations of our first ten years we counted 257 graduates; the ten such ceremonies of our second decade added 701 baccalaureates. By 1976 we enrolled 493 students; in 1966 we had enrolled 283. Sixty-two percent of the entering Class of '66 graduated; for the Class of 1976 the figure was 70 percent. We had an increasing number of women students, but women still made up only 10 percent of our student body in 1976. An increasing fraction of our student body, both men and women, chose to study engineering.

Our students had their share of triumphs, both academically and in extracurricular activities. We continued to have a high proportion of our graduates earning advanced degrees elsewhere after leaving Harvey Mudd College, and these graduates also earned many National Science Foundation predoctoral fellowships, Marshall scholarships, and other highly competitive national awards. Harvey Mudd students were represented on athletic teams that were invited to compete in regional and national post-seasonal competitions. The records of the student council of the Associated Students of Harvey Mudd College show that hardly a week went by without a dance, a rock concert, or some other major social activity. In short, our students made excellent academic progress, and life was more than study.

However, the decade 1966-1976 was an uneasy one for the United States, for higher education, for the Claremont Colleges, and even for Harvey Mudd College. "Each year, more and better" would be an inaccurate view of student life at HMC in those years. The cloistered colleges of the past could not stand under the pressure of world events and domestic reaction to those events.

In 1966, Lyndon Johnson was president, and 385,000 United States troops were in Vietnam with others offshore or in Thailand. These numbers grew, partly in response to the Tet offensive of early 1968. Neither military pressure by Vietnam or by the United States nor continuing peace talks seemed to promise an end to this war. President Johnson decided not to stand for reelection; Richard Nixon was elected, taking office in 1969. The Vietnam War grew in unpopularity. In November, 1969, 250,000 antiwar demonstrators marched in Washington. In early May, 1970, U.S. troops entered Cambodia (the "Parrot's Beak") in an attempt to cut Viet Cong supply lines. In the resulting nationwide protests, four students were killed by national guardsmen at Kent State University. In response to the claim that a person old enough to be drafted was old enough to vote, the Twenty-sixth Amendment, enfranchising eighteen year olds, was enacted in 1971. The Vietnam War ended, as did the drafting of young men, in 1973. Richard Nixon resigned the presidency in August, 1974, to be succeeded by President Gerald Ford.

The United States was swept by its full share of racial unrest. The Watts riots of 1965, in Los Angeles, were followed in 1967 by riots in Newark, New Jersey, and in Detroit, Michigan. In each case, dozens of people were killed and hundreds of million dollars worth of property was destroyed. The growing civil rights movement was sharply accelerated by outrage following the assassination of Martin Luther King in April, 1968. Other segments of our society, including in particular the Mexican-Americans, joined in demanding equality of opportunity. Many were also concerned about the injustice of apartheid in South Africa.

We had our national successes as well as our troubles: Neil Armstrong set foot on the moon in July, 1969. President Nixon visited China in 1972, reestablishing contact with the world's most populous nation. Progress was made in arms limitation agreements with Russia. But, on balance, the growth in interracial and intergenerational divisiveness was a major characteristic of the decade.

There were about 3,300 universities, colleges, and community colleges in the United States in 1970. Not surprisingly, each institution responded to these national events in its own individual way. However, each did respond. The riots in major cities, and the civil rights movement, had sensitized many institutions to the need to admit students more representative of the ethnic composition of the society at large than had been traditional. Although some of this interest in admission and retention of "minorities" (we are becoming a society in which there is no ethnic majority) dates from the 1950s, nearly every institution readdressed itself to these issues after the King assassination, and on many campuses Black and Chicano students became more militantly insistent that their numbers increase through additional financial support, recruiting, and "relevant" teaching. The Berkeley Free Speech Movement in 1964 was initially concerned with providing facilities for personal and political expression for all students or faculty who had something they wanted to express. The Students for a Democratic Society began to appear on major university campuses in the early 1960s. Tactics of class disruptions, sit-ins, teach-outs, peace marches, mass meetings and moratoria from usual academic pursuits occurred in many institutions. Both students and faculty committed time and attention to understanding the Vietnam War and to promoting whatever point of view came from this understanding. In a number of instances, buildings were bombed, and there were many threats and acts of violence.[1]

THE ANTIWAR PROTEST MOVEMENT

I do not remember the Claremont Colleges as an island of calm repose during this period, although happily we were not as much in the public eye as some major universities. Of the six colleges, Harvey Mudd was perhaps the least unsettled (we were the smallest, and most of our students were more concerned with changing than abolishing the social structures they expected to enter) but much of our local student unrest cut across campus boundaries. Mass meetings, peace marches, and sit-ins recruited students from any campus. We had many such demonstrations, initially tolerant of differences of opinion but increasingly strident as unrest continued and grew. Accordingly, the boards of the six colleges adopted regulations permitting the president of any one college to suspend ("summary suspension") students of any Claremont College disrupting the operation of that president's college. The suspension would later be revoked or upheld by the judiciary procedures of the student's home college, but in the interim the student became a trespasser against whom civil penalties could be directed if necessary. (To the best of my knowledge no such penalties were used.)

The Council, which consisted of the six college presidents, regularly met to deal with intercollegiate issues (which now included student unrest), as did the academic deans and the deans of students. (The deans of students, in fact, had the primary responsibility for all student affairs, including unrest.) The spokesperson for the Council of Presidents was known at that time as the provost, a responsibility which rotated annually from one president to the next. Because four of the six colleges changed presidents over that period, and a new president had a year of grace before becoming provost, I was provost in 1965-66, when unrest was beginning, and again in 1969-70. President Atherton of Pitzer College was provost in 1966-67, President Lyon of Pomona College in 1967-68, and President Curtis of Scripps College in 1968-69. (President Alexander

1. An excellent overview of this period in higher education is given in *Academic Transformation*, assembled and edited by David Riesman and Verne A. Stadtman (McGraw Hill,1973.) Commissioned reports are presented on seventeen institutions, including Antioch, Berkeley, City College (New York), Federal City College, Harvard, MIT, Michigan, Old Westbury, Pennsylvania, Princeton, Rutgers, San Francisco State, Stanford, Swarthmore, Wesleyan and Wisconsin. The external pressures of the late '60s changed each of these institutions, several of them dramatically.

of Pomona College was the final presidential "provost" in 1970-71.
Thereafter a full-time administrator was appointed to manage the central
services, and took the title of provost.[2] The title of the chairman of the
Council of Presidents then became—unimaginatively—chairman of the
Council.)

I was involved with disruptive student unrest primarily as provost. As
we shall see, we of Harvey Mudd College did re-examine our goals and
our common life over these years. So did the members of each
Claremont college. But the mass meetings, sit-ins, and other events drawing media attention were largely on other campuses.

Considerable faculty and student concern about the Vietnam War had
been evident in the academic year 1964-65, leading to campus meetings
to learn more about the issues involved in that war. There were knowledgeable faculty members on each of our campuses who felt the United
States should withdraw promptly from Southeast Asia. On the Harvey
Mudd faculty Robin Ives, Bob James, Enos Wicher, George Wickes, and
Alvin White appeared in student-faculty discussion meetings in opposition
to the war, and similar numbers of faculty members were involved in each
of our sister colleges. There was general faculty interest in sponsoring a
series of debates on the war, with invited speakers, in the fall of 1965.

Events overran this scholarly scheme. The first antiwar protest march
came on October 14, 1965, one of the first of many such demonstrations
held nationally that week. I was asked for permission to hold a peace
march of faculty and students, to conclude with a rally on Pomona's
Alumni Field. Shortly thereafter I was asked for permission to hold a second march, organized by the Committee to Support American Fighting
Men. Both groups were granted permission, and both worked with the
student deans, the director of campus security, and Robert Cooper, then
assistant to the provost, to ensure that no serious verbal or physical abuse
befell either group. All went well. The two groups had agreed to use a
common line of march, and did, separated by some fifteen minutes from
each other. Initially the peace march was to have gone first, but it took
that group longer to get organized, and, accordingly, the "supporters of
fighting men" led. Both groups had subsequent rallies, the pro-war group
meeting on Parents' Field, Claremont McKenna College. In both cases
about one thousand persons attended the rally. The college personnel in
attendance estimated about twice as many marched for the "fighting
men" as did for the antiwar group, despite the fact that the latter group
had many more off-campus supporters marching.

The marches were covered by mobile units from KNBC, a regional
television station. Very little of the footage was in fact used, as I recall.
The television crew had been concerned that not enough placards would
be in evidence in the antiwar march, and had brought along several
dozen with antiwar sentiments, which were passed out to student

2. We had the great good fortune to
attract Dr. E. Howard Brooks to this
position in the summer of 1971, and we
rapidly came to appreciate what an
improvement in central services we
were enjoying compared to the period
when a president gave this key
responsibility whatever part-time
attention he could spare.

marchers. The students had prepared their own placards, and a number were enraged at this manipulation; new placards reappeared in minutes with anti-KNBC messages.

Over the next several years peace marches and teach-ins (on campus) or teach-outs (off campus, intended for the public) became regular occurrences. If the proposed activity were legal and nonviolent the colleges did not object. We did our best, in fact, to maintain good communications with all student groups of whatever persuasion. There were, to be sure, threats of violence, but graffiti or perhaps a broken window were about the extent of property damage.

Jean and I remember one winter's meeting during my 1969-70 tour as provost with some regret. A group of students had sought, and been given, permission to camp around the main flagpole of the Claremont Colleges, in front of the Honnold Library. They had demanded to fly the flag at half mast and read each day the most recent list of the war dead. I had denied their request to fly the flag at half mast, since no official mourning had been declared by national, state, or local government, but had agreed to have them read the casualty list at any time of their choosing—which turned out to be at the lowering of the flag. They sought one more audience in which to convince me of my wrongheadedness, and I had invited them to our home in the evening. In came perhaps a dozen who had clearly been camping out, and after half an hour or so Jean appeared with hot chocolate and homemade cookies, as she might with any student group, aggrieved or not. For most of the group these refreshments were clearly welcome, but one student simply refused by pulling his stocking cap further over his ears and sinking deeper in his chair. Twenty minutes later one of the other students explained that the young man in the stocking cap was also fasting in protest. We would not knowingly have tormented him.

Students of the Claremont Colleges were not alone in protesting the Vietnam War on our campuses. Townspeople joined in from time to time, and there were experienced student organizers from northern California who also became familiar to us. During the 1969-70 academic year I went to most protest meetings, which dwindled in size as the year wore on and the novelty wore off. By March we were down to less than a hundred attendees, including those I have mentioned as well as college administrators, campus security officers, local police, and military intelligence personnel. There were few surprises, either for protesters or for the authorities.

This relative calm was shattered in early May by the Cambodian incursion, followed by the Kent State killings. Mass meeting attendance increased tenfold. Proposals were made to sit-in on the freeways, burn ROTC, hold protest marches and teach-outs, to insist that the colleges abolish ROTC, to call emergency meetings of all boards of trustees, and to send a delegation to Washington to protest directly to officers of our national government. A sit-in blocked President Neville's office at CMC most of May 4 until the organizers ended it late that evening.

There were clashes at the ROTC headquarters between students intent on "trashing" the building and other students joining campus security officers in opposing such action; we had much discussion, but no damage to persons or property. A major antiwar parade was held in Claremont on May 7, a day on which most colleges and universities in California, including most of the Claremont Colleges (but not HMC) had declared a moratorium from classes. At one mass meeting, when there was a demand to hear from the administration, I had told the meeting that those sitting-in on the freeways or destroying property could expect the penalties of civil law; that all were free to discuss, hold meetings, demonstrate, and persuade others; and that if students wished to send a delegation to Washington they might not use college funds, but were free to go at their own cost—if they decided to underwrite such a venture, I would go along at my cost.

The Washington delegation was soon chosen and comprised two students each from Pomona, Claremont McKenna, and Pitzer Colleges; two from Claremont Graduate School; one each from Scripps and Harvey Mudd Colleges. Professors Gordon Douglass of Pomona and Edward Haley of CMC volunteered to go at their own cost, and so did our Claremont Colleges chaplain, James Joseph. One trustee, Mrs. Sallie Seaver of Scripps College, also volunteered.[3] Jim Johnson, the 1970-71 president of the Associated Students of Harvey Mudd College, was our student representative. It soon developed that many other colleges and universities were also sending delegations to Washington.

I had two immediate problems. The first was to find what, if any, message we might bring on which the delegation could agree. The second was to find out whom we might see in Washington other than the airport porters.

The second problem was well and promptly solved. I remembered that Cliff Miller, (as of 1990 chairman of the Harvey Mudd Board of Trustees) was an advisor to President Nixon, and I asked if he and his colleagues of Braun & Co. might gain us any official entrée. Cliff promised they'd try. We arrived in Washington to find we had appointments set up with Mr. Herbert Klein, White House director of communications; Mr. Macomber, deputy undersecretary of state for administration; Dr. Daniel Moynihan, special assistant to the president for urban affairs; Mr. Robert Finch, secretary of health, education and welfare, and his associate commissioner of education, Allen; and Secretary of the Interior Walter Hickel. In addition, several of the students had studied the voting records of members of Congress to determine possible "swing votes" and had telegraphed ahead for appointments.

3. I am happy to report that Mrs. Seaver (now Mrs. John L. Reynolds) continues as a Scripps College trustee in 1992.

4. The Claremont Colleges Communique (Claremont University Center Public Information Office) July 13, 1970. In brief summary (the statement is six pages long) we discussed the causes of the then prevalent uncertainty and violence, methods of restoring and strengthening communication between the higher education community and the Federal government, the primary issues to be clarified in discussions on dissent by non-violent methods, methods of making possible greater student involvement in the normal political processes, the importance of action on the eighteen-year-old vote, and the extent to which the Internal Revenue Service might more clearly define legitimate political activity of students and faculty of tax-exempt educational institutions.

By the time we had arrived in Washington (we stayed at the Pick Hotel, near the airline transport terminal in downtown Washington) we had agreed on a statement to which we could all subscribe, albeit with varying degrees of enthusiasm. We had a very busy two and a half days of Washington visits, and we compared notes in the evenings. We learned a good deal, and I think we may also have done some useful teaching. We were urged by Secretary Finch and Dr. Moynihan to report our findings to them, and we did so; I made a preliminary report to Secretary Finch on a subsequent visit to Washington on June 25, 1970, and we submitted a formal statement which appeared on July 13, 1970.[4]

My view of the subsequent year, in which President Alexander of Pomona College was provost, is no doubt colored by the fact that I no longer needed to be involved in every communal Claremont College crisis. However, a dispassionate reading of the news indicates that the major antiwar actions on campuses were simmering down, not only in Claremont but nationwide.

Harvey Mudd may have been the quietest of the Claremont Colleges, but we were not comatose. As of September, 1965, students and faculty organized and presented a series of discussions entitled "Value Dilemmas on Campus." Later that year, the minutes of the Student Council also show both financial support and support by participation in a meeting on "South Africa: A Week of Concern." A year later the Student Council (among many other actions) approved the Claremont Colleges chapter of Students for a Democratic Society as a recognized activity for HMC students. As of 1967, the board agreed that the forthcoming Saddle Rock conferences should discuss "the contemporary student generation"; we had a lively student group preparing for months for this discussion. There was also increasing attention to draft counseling. In addition to a Claremont Colleges draft counseling service, several HMC study groups were developing on-campus expertise.

A substantial amount of student, faculty, and trustee time was used over a period of eighteen months to draft a statement of student rights and responsibilities. The final version, endorsed by faculty and the Associated Students of Harvey Mudd College, was adopted by the trustees on September 23, 1969. The statement guaranteed freedom of expression to all members of the academic community; provided an appeals mechanism for grades that the student thought were biased because of personal opinion; dealt with confidentiality of student records, including records of disciplinary action or of political activity; established standards of independence for student publications and student government, and much else. I am very grateful to trustees Gerald Kelly and Robert P. Hastings, both well-established attorneys, for the many hours of (unbilled!) time that went into the drafting of this document and the legal education of all of us.

There were many faculty-student discussions on the Vietnam War and its consequences. We were helped in particular by George Wickes, professor of English, who had spent a portion of World War II as an intelligence officer in what was then French Indochina. We had students who felt strongly on both sides of the question about the U.S. involvement in Vietnam, and the same was true of our faculty; I am happy to report that our discussions in general took place with considerable mutual respect, however divergent and unreconciled the views. We had many students involved in teach-ins and teach-outs; we had our full share of students over those years who chose to join the Peace Corps as well as those who entered military service. Harvey Mudd students were involved in the prevention of violence at ROTC headquarters (Steve Endemano organized a 4 A.M. soccer game outside Bauer Hall, much to the surprise of a group intent on a predawn "trashing" of ROTC) and were very helpful in maintaining communication between aggrieved student groups and the administrations of the Claremont Colleges.[5]

In addition, the antiwar movement, plus the "trust nobody over thirty" syndrome that was endemic among students throughout the nation, spelled an effective end to the remnant of the *in loco parentis* tradition on our campus. Thereafter, neither students nor parents nor trustees expected the college to protect students from the penalties of civil law, and students expected more than ever to set and enforce their own social rules and regulations. Parents were not surprised when coeducational dormitories came into being in the 1970s, and the dormitory social regulations have been responsibly managed, primarily by students, from that time to the present.[6] Off-campus housing was another lively issue of the late 1960s. A significant number of students chose to live off campus, whether or not the college dormitories had been built and were budgeted on the premise they would be occupied. The demand for off-campus housing vanished about 1972. In the last three years of my administration, after the student body had grown in accordance with our Impact/72 planning, nearly every student hoped to live on campus, and we did not have enough dormitory rooms. Approximately half the sophomore class each year was housed in dormitories of other Claremont Colleges or else in town; the college required first-year students to live on campus, and the student body had given seniors and juniors preference in the lottery ("room draw") for available dormitory space. It remained for my successor, President Ken Baker, to find the means to build and authorize the construction of additional student housing on our own campus.

ETHNIC PROGRAMS AND ETHNIC CENTERS

In my account, I have lumped together several student discontents, primarily the Vietnam War, but also disenchantment with authority in gen-

5. President Jack Stark of Claremont McKenna College recalls (private communication) that not all such defenses were successful. Some "trashing" did occur from time to time, and in one occupation an ROTC classroom was essentially destroyed.

6. "Women Hours" (the times when women students are permitted to visit in male dormitories) were a sore point for HMC women over the years they were housed at Scripps College. Under the Harvey Mudd College Honor Code, students are permitted to study together unless a specific assignment is to be done alone. When we had relatively few women students, and they lived in separate dormitories, the advantage of cooperative study was effectively denied many of them. Students everywhere chafed about the social regulation implied in "women hours"; for our women these hours also constituted an educational disadvantage .

eral, concern about the environment, chafing about college social regulations, and unhappiness about housing. The remaining major issue that concerned students, faculty, and trustees over the second decade led in the 1970s to the establishment of ethnic programs and centers as features of the Claremont Colleges. Here is the history of that development.

Admission to any one of the Claremont Colleges has been open to applicants of any ethnic background since the founding of each college. As of 1967-68, however, the Claremont Colleges had only fifty-five black students, who constituted slightly over 1 percent of our total student enrollment. Blacks constituted more than 10 percent of the population of Southern California. Mexican-Americans composed an even smaller fraction of our students, despite their ever greater proportion of the total population of Southern California. Even these figures, modest as they were, had resulted from a number of years of special attention to the recruiting of minority applicants.[7] In particular, under the initiative of Chaplain Edgar C. ("Pete") Reckard of the Claremont Colleges, a grant of $750,000 had been secured in 1967 from the Rockefeller Foundation, with the expectation that other funds would be secured to total $2 million, to establish a program of studies to assist able but underprepared students from disadvantaged backgrounds to enter one or another of the colleges on equal footing with more conventionally prepared applicants. A group of forty students came to Claremont in September, 1968, under this Program of Special Directed Studies for Transition to College. Sufficient minority students were on our campuses to lead to the establishment of a Black Students Union and of United Mexican-American Students, a similar social group. Each group was interested in recruiting more Black or Chicano students, and in having its ethnic heritage more fully dealt with in the curricula of the colleges.

The assassination of Martin Luther King on April 4, 1968, triggered militancy among Black students on many campuses in the United States, including ours. The Claremont chapter of the Black Students Union was recognized as a student activity by early May, and its leaders presented a series of demands to the presidents of the Claremont Colleges. These included "increased minority student admissions, larger minority representation in faculty and staff, and more attention in curricula and library holdings to minority contributions to the American heritage and to contemporary social problems."[8] Student sympathizers disrupted classes to emphasize these demands. Occasional minor acts of arson, for which no culprits were found, added to the tension.

Many hours of negotiation followed between administrators (in particular, Provost Lyon) and the leaders of the Black Students Union. It was agreed that the undergraduate colleges would seek to increase to 10 percent the fraction who were Black of the students offered admission to the undergraduate colleges in September, 1969; the Black Students Union

7. President E. Wilson Lyon gives an excellent account of the involvement of faculty and students of The Claremont Colleges (and particularly of Pomona College) in the Civil Rights movement throughout the 1960s in his book *The History of Pomona College, 1887-1969* pp. 555-576 (printed by Pomona College, 1977). I recall that in 1964 a group of students and faculty of The Claremont Colleges, under the leadership of Prof. Robert Meyners of CMC (then acting chaplain) spent the summer in a small Mississippi town, registering voters, building a swimming pool available to blacks, and improving public health. Art and Dottie Campbell and Tom Helliwell of the HMC faculty were involved.

8. Quoted from my newsletter to the trustees of Harvey Mudd College, dated June 1, 1968. The newsletter also states "I should add that the demands of the Black Students' Union represented actions The Claremont Colleges have been trying to take for some years; we welcome and have been seeking more qualified minority students, faculty, and staff. We differ in the priority we assign to these efforts and in the success we believe it is reasonable to expect. In this the help of our black students—and students from other minority groups—may enable us to make significantly more progress than we have yet thought possible. . . . We plan to use all the help they can give us."

agreed to assist in this recruitment effort. The colleges agreed to hire a full-time black admissions officer to assist in this effort; they also agreed to seek additional financial aid for needy students. The colleges, as equal opportunity employers, agreed to seek aggressively additional minority applicants for faculty and staff positions as they became available. Faculty committees agreed to design and introduce additional courses giving attention to the contribution of minority groups to American civilization, and to the sources of racial problems in the nation. A statement of intent on these matters was issued by the Council of Presidents on May 29, 1968.

The academic year 1968-69 saw a great deal of attention given to implementing these promises. A Black admissions officer, Dr. Bert Hammond, was appointed to work with the several offices of admission of the colleges. President Mark Curtis of Scripps College, who succeeded President Lyon as provost, had the responsibility to ensure that progress was made in the planning of curricular offerings, in securing the necessary staff, and in the recruiting and admission of minority students. Mass meetings regularly reported the progress, or lack thereof, to date. A committee, chaired by Alden Pixley of HMC and made up of administrators, faculty, and students, reviewed procedures for the appointment of faculty and the approval of new courses which would give both programs of ethnic studies the tools they needed while guaranteeing faculty the freedom of inquiry and teaching traditional in higher education. The Black Students Union, in particular, was insistent upon "autonomy" for the director and staff of a Black Studies Center, in which Black studies would be taught and counseling made available to those Black students who chose it. The boards of trustees of the colleges were equally insistent that they could not divest themselves of final authority over an operation for which they were legally and fiscally responsible. An intercollegiate committee of trustees, faculty and students was set up to explore the maximum latitude necessary and desirable under the legal and fiduciary constraints.

On February 25, pipe bombs exploded in a Scripps College lavatory and in the foyer of the Carnegie Building at Pomona College. Mrs. Mary Ann Keatly, a secretary at Pomona College, lost two fingers and suffered eye damage. No one was injured at Scripps. Despite extensive police investigation, we have never learned who planted these bombs. The investigation indicated that the culprit or culprits used bombs of manufacture familiar to the police, which were very unlikely to have been made or used by persons from the student bodies, staffs, or faculties of the Claremont Colleges.

The Council of Presidents had scheduled a meeting that evening with the officers of the Black Students Union. We held the meeting, with a different agenda than initially proposed, and the meeting is engraved in my mind. A rumor was abroad that a group of white students, expert in the use of hunting rifles, had concluded that the BSU members were responsible for the bombings, and were determined upon vengeance. At the request of the BSU officers we pulled the shades of the meeting room before they entered the room. The presidents sat at the meeting table while the BSU officers sat on the floor in corners invisible from the outside with or without shades. We worked out a plan to get all Black students in our colleges off campus and in faculty homes overnight. There was in fact no violence that night nor in the succeeding days and nights. After these tense days, progress resumed on the design of a possible Black Studies Center.

The outcome of this period of alternate cooperation and confrontation was the establishment of a Human Resources Institute, inaugurated in the fall term of 1969-70, to contain a Black Studies Center, a Program of Mexican-American Studies (which evolved into a Chicano Studies Center), and a Center for Urban Studies (which didn't evolve). It was agreed that study at the centers and the program would be open to all students without regard to race or color. The institute was to be administered by Claremont University Center on behalf of the Claremont Colleges, and the colleges assented to share in the support of its budget, to the extent that gifts designated for that budget did not suffice.[9]

In 1974-75, when President Curtis of Scripps was chairman of the Council, both the Black Studies Center and the Chicano Studies Center were in regular operation. The early years were, as one might expect, uneasy ones for the directors of these new centers and for the Council of Presidents alike. The presidents needed adequate control over the budget and the program of each Center to guarantee its educational effectiveness and fiscal stability, and each director needed to convince the Black Students Union (or La Raza) that he was not the administration's lackey. In the spring of 1975 the Black Studies Center director chose to emphasize his demands by leading a sit-in of Pendleton Hall, the common business office of the Claremont Colleges; the director of Black admissions was also a participant. Mark Curtis informed the director of the center and the director of Black admissions that they were relieved of their responsibilities; they could not both be employees of Claremont University Center and indefinitely delay the payroll processing of each college. Both were informed of their right to appeal this decision in accordance with staff or faculty practice. Some two weeks time would be required before a panel of independently chosen faculty and staff could be convened.

The faculty committee upheld the termination.[10] When the director's desk was cleared, we learned that he had used the delay to issue letters of appointment to five part-time lecturers in Black studies. Any such appointment had to be subject to approval by the provost, and no such

9. Minutes of the Board of Trustees of Harvey Mudd College, June 8, 1969.

10. This action was again appealed, this time to a special committee of the Board of Fellows of Claremont University Center. The dismissals were again upheld in August, 1975.

approval had been granted; however, we were promptly advised by counsel that a court would probably hold that the lecturers, to the best of their knowledge, had bona fide offers of appointment. Accordingly Claremont University Center appointed all five for the agreed part-time, one-semester lectureships. One of the five was Ms. Angela Davis, academically well qualified, but best known publicly primarily because she had been indicted, but not convicted, of conspiracy in a Black Panther jailbreak in which police had been killed. Ms. Davis faithfully discharged the teaching duties she had engaged to perform.

Harvey Mudd College in 1969 had few black or Mexican-American students, and those we had were not active in the groups demanding ethnic centers.[11] Whether because of these low numbers or in spite of them, faculty, trustees, and white students of Harvey Mudd College were quite involved in the search for means more equitably to recruit and educate our students for a multicultural society. As noted above, both Alden Pixley, professor of mathematics, and George Wickes, professor of English, chaired or served on intercollegiate committees that planned the program finally adopted. Dr. Seeley Mudd was the Harvey Mudd College trustee who served (with George Wickes) on the intercollegiate committee on possible administrative arrangements for the Institute. Dave Sanders was the HMC faculty member of the group that organized the Chicano Studies Center. Trustees Robert P. Hastings, Preston Hotchkis, Gerald G. Kelly, and Hugo Riemer drafted the agreement approved by our board.

Jim Davenport, then executive vice president of Southern California Edison Corporation, was the trustee who headed the Budget Committee of the HMC board. He was a great help to me in that capacity. He was an able engineer with a reputation for careful probing and meticulous accuracy, combined with an instinct for what might go wrong. I found he had earned that reputation. Accordingly, when he did recommend a budget to the full board, there were no further questions. One particular day in 1969 after we disposed of the budget with somewhat less scrutiny than usual, Jim said, "Joe, I see you've been having some trouble in Claremont." I thought I would shortly hear of the virtues of a firm hand, and of tolerating no nonsense. Not so. Jim went on "I went through some of the labor troubles of the early 1930s, not too long after I joined this company. That's where I first learned about non-negotiable demands, violence and the threat of violence, walk-outs, sit-ins, picketing, and all that. The way Edison handled it was that we had a professional negotiator who met with the labor negotiator. Our representative got his guidelines from our board of directors. The only person authorized to speak for the company was the chairman of the board, and if anyone else volunteered any comments he was no longer a director, or else no longer an Edison employee. That system worked. In your case you may be president, but you have to do the negotiating, and any trustee, faculty member, student, or donor who dis-

11. As of 1990, with a total enrollment of 568 undergraduates, Harvey Mudd College had 6 Black and 27 Hispanic students. By far our largest "minority" group was made up of students of Asian ancestry.

12. Pete Reckard also employed Bill Gann, at that time a high school counsellor who had worked with disadvantaged students. Years later, when Bill Swartzbaugh resigned as our Dean of Students, Harvey Mudd College conducted a national search for his successor. We found that successor, Bill Gann, already in Claremont with the Program for Special Directed Studies.

13. In 1978, under the leadership of Professor Tom Woodson, Harvey Mudd College also started the MESA program to enrich the academic experience of underprivileged youngsters. While not a part of *The First Twenty Years,* the MESA program is another impressive contribution to equal educational opportunity. In 1992, fifty-eight graduates from the HMC MESA program entered colleges or universities. Another forty-one entrants graduated from Octavio Bubion's Upward Bound program. Very few of these ninety-nine would have entered university or college without the help of these programs. Of these graduates of 1992, six entered one or another Claremont College. (Ironically, none chose HMC.)

agrees with you is free to publish his views. I just want you to know I feel for you, and if I can be of any help, please let me know."

One legacy of that second decade that remains today (1992) at Harvey Mudd College is the Upward Bound program, in which we have cause for real satisfaction. At the time the Program for Special Directed Studies (PSDS) was established in 1968, Chaplain Pete Reckard employed Octávio Bubión, experienced in working with underprivileged young people.[12] The two sought and secured a grant from the Office of Economic Opportunity to give added academic work to promising high school students, particularly from minority families, who were not yet adequately prepared for college entrance. The Upward Bound program moved to Harvey Mudd College in 1976, as other portions of PSDS became assimilated into the ethnic centers. As of 1992, well over 2,000 students have completed the Upward Bound program based at HMC, and over 1,800 of them have been admitted to colleges and universities in the United States. We have many success stories among these "alumni." Of the Upward Bound programs in the United States, the one which Mr. Bubión directs has pioneered in placing student interns in government or industrial laboratories and other preprofessional experiences; in most cases the students have done well, and occasionally they have clearly found their careers.[13]

Whether or not because of these events, we have a number of Harvey Mudd graduates who have chosen careers that seek to better the lot of underprivileged peoples. I am pleased that a number have chosen secondary school teaching of such students over more lucrative jobs they might have had. Ken Frank '68 and his wife, Betty (Scripps '69), spent a number of years in a mission school in central Africa, and now hold similar positions in Turkey. Mahesh Kotecha '70 (who came to us from Uganda before Idi Amin exiled his family to England) is now a financier, and volunteers part of his time as a financial advisor to African governments. Frank Cummings '62, after earning his Harvard doctorate in chemistry, joined the faculty of Clark Atlanta University, a group of historically Black colleges, where he is now project director of the Child Survival Project. The Peace Corps has attracted Harvey Mudd graduates who have later returned to more conventional careers.

While this period of student unrest was not easy, we can identify some clear gains that would not have been made, or made so rapidly, had it not happened. At the Claremont Colleges, and at Harvey Mudd College, we have more students from non-white or underprivileged backgrounds than we had previously attracted. I hope and expect these young people will contribute their full share of the leadership, professional and social, that we need to become a stable multicultural society. Furthermore, students learn from each other, and the increasing variety of backgrounds in our student bodies better prepares all students for their responsibilities in that stable multicultural society. I for one do not lament the passing of much of the *in loco parentis* tradition of former years. Part of growing up is to learn to be responsible for one's own actions.

We were accustomed to dialogue that included trustees, faculty, and students, treating each other with mutual respect but with candor. Awareness of their new responsibilities is reflected in the students' continued commitment to such open and amicable discussion, particularly during a time of great social divisiveness. I am grateful to Mr. Wig and the practice he early insisted on: the annual Harvey Mudd College Saddle Rock meetings. I am particularly grateful to Vicki and Henry Mudd, who made these meetings possible, and for the solid trustee support each such retreat had. That tradition of trust served us well.

I conclude this chapter, much of which has dealt with student unrest, as I began it. The life of the students at Harvey Mudd College, although obviously changed in some respects, seems to have thrived during our second decade. The Harvey Mudd College alumni office keeps good records, so I looked up the present occupations of the sixty-two graduates of the Class of 1970, who were seniors at the peak of the unrest. It turns out that twenty-five of them now hold the Ph.D. degree, three the J.D. degree, and two hold medical doctorates; twenty-two earned masters as their terminal degrees, and thirteen the baccalaureate. The largest single group, thirty-three students, are now employed in a wide range of industries, from General Electric and DuPont to the Blue Heron Construction in Port Townsend, Washington, and to a one-person software company. Fifteen are employed in colleges, universities, or university research organizations. Of these, eight hold professorial (teaching) appointments, and seven research appointments; geographically this group is scattered from the University of Calgary in Alberta to the University of Florida, and from the Massachusetts Institute of Technology to Loyola Marymount University, Los Angeles. Two are secondary school teachers. Four are employed in government laboratories. Ten are self-employed; this group includes three lawyers, a medical doctor, a doctor of osteopathy, and a number who are consultants. While most are employed as scientists or engineers, the class includes a psychologist, two economists, a financier, and any number of administrators. (These numbers do not add up to sixty-two because a few graduates have more than one doctorate, or list more than one occupation.) All seem to me to be in intellectually challenging jobs, and seem to have done well with them. As I compare the present occupations of the Class of '70 with those of all HMC graduates of our first two decades, the Class of '70 looks remarkably typical.

Octávio Bubión

CHAPTER 15

Educational Innovation

What has been is what will be, and what has been done is what will be done, and there is nothing new under the sun. (Ecclesiastes 1:9)

I APPROACH this chapter with diffidence because any educational innovation has roots in earlier teaching and learning. But there have been changes in higher education; before the Civil War there were in this nation no institutions that we would now recognize as universities.[1] Chapter 2 described the major changes that were developing in engineering education after World War II. I believe that Harvey Mudd College has initiated its share of successful educational change. This chapter will attempt to substantiate that claim.

The most dramatic change in higher education is to found an institution which is different in kind from others then existing. Thus, Rensselaer Polytechnic Institute, founded in 1824, was the first institution in the United States to offer engineering instruction to civilian students. The more common change is within the form and content of instruction, as when Columbia in 1919 introduced a general education course designed to give an overview of the development of Western civilization.[2] We at Harvey Mudd have innovated in both ways; we began with a unique commitment to breadth of education, we had developed new methods of teaching engineering by the time our first class graduated, and we have subsequently found better ways to teach than those with which we began.

BREADTH OF EDUCATION

We were fully aware that we were the first privately supported college of engineering and science to be founded *de novo* since Carnegie Institute of Technology (now Carnegie-Mellon University) was founded in 1900. Our trustees, as we have seen, had in mind a new blend of a technical institute and a liberal arts college, and those of us who joined the initial

1. See *The American College and University* by Frederick Rudolph (Alfred A. Knopf, New York, 1962), Chapter 13.

2. Ibid., pp. 455 et seq.

faculty subscribed to the concept. We became then, and are now, a national leader in the commitment to breadth of education for engineers and scientists. We went even beyond the noteworthy attention given to the humanities and social sciences by Caltech and M.I.T.

Our trustees began by recalling engineers they had known and admired; men like Herbert Hoover or Harvey S. Mudd, who combined professional and management talents with a humane understanding of what they might do for others. The trustees believed our nation and our world would always need such technical leadership. We of the initial faculty attempted to translate this ideal into fields of knowledge and methods of learning. We fully understood that it is not possible, in four years or even a lifetime, to learn all that one might hope to bring to such a task. One can hope to learn within four years, in aesthetics as in science, in politics as in technology, the characteristic questions and methods of inquiry of several general fields of knowledge. Later on, when the graduate needs to know more of psychology or of regional history or of hydrodynamics, the tools are at hand for further learning and the practitioner, now a self-directed student, can recognize the need for the learning.

This point of departure led us to the "common core," a series of courses and experiences which would introduce all Harvey Mudd students to a variety of fields of learning while providing an adequate base for the professional careers they hoped to pursue. Clearly this core should include a good deal of reading and discussing literature chosen to broaden the student's understanding of varying points of view on such universal human experiences as one's own identity and place in the universe, how people organize to live and work together, and the establishment of personal and group hopes and goals. With this should come substantial practice in writing and verbal discussion, since skill in communication is essential to effective work with others. Mathematics is the language of science, as well as a powerful tool of analysis in its own right. We decided as well on the chemistry and physics all our students should know. From continued faculty discussion we evolved the initial portion of the "common core" and then, as we had more experience and more points of view, we developed the rest.

An essential part of this dialogue was to have on our early faculty not only engineers, scientists, and mathematicians, but also humanists and social scientists in the group deciding what we should teach. All had taught for years before deciding to come to Harvey Mudd College, and understood the art of teaching. Our humanists and social scientists required some self-denying qualities—there would be no department of history, no students majoring in philosophy; they would not enjoy some of the perquisites of their engineering and scientific colleagues. As we have seen in Chapter 5, we were fortunate in the humanists and social scientists who had joined us.

When the college opened its doors in 1957, we had agreed on the program for the freshman year, and we had the faculty and course of studies ready. We had broad agreement as well on the program for the following three years, but the details were yet to be worked out. During the summer of 1958, with the help of the Fund for the Advancement of Education, we explored these "details." All our initial faculty were involved, plus a number of knowledgeable visitors from other institutions, particularly in engineering, the social sciences, and the humanities.[3]

We made basic decisions about engineering instruction. Since the "core" would provide a strong foundation in mathematics, chemistry, and physics, we could reduce somewhat the time required for such "engineering sciences" as mechanics, thermodynamics, electrical devices, or energy and mass transfer. The "systems approach"—the emphasis on looking at all portions of a task before tackling the details of any portion of it, to make sure the final design would meet the needs—seemed to give a comprehensive method of teaching design. We decided it would take a new approach, and considerable ingenuity, to build the material an engineer needs in the "art and practice" of engineering. Traditional courses in surveying, foundry practice, or bridge design, dear to the memory of many engineers, would not adequately prepare our students to deal with a rapidly changing technology. All our engineering visitors were agreed that it would be a noble experiment to commit a third of the engineering student's effort to the humanities and social sciences, although several were convinced that it was not possible to spare that much time from professional material each engineer needs to know.

The actual engineering curriculum we first taught was developed by our initial engineering faculty. It was a program of studies in which engineering students take a minimum of 33 percent of their studies in the humanities and social sciences. At the time our first engineers made this decision, only a few other institutions had reached the 25 percent mark; now, in the 1990s, 25 percent is nearer the norm. As of 1976, the figure was still 33 percent at Harvey Mudd College.[4]

The 1958 summer study was important to us. We had visitors of long experience in teaching engineers who reviewed and criticized our proposed curriculum. We continued to believe that an unspecialized program introducing the student to all of engineering was the path we should take; that a "systems approach," in which the student is encouraged to concentrate on the overall solution of an engineering problem, is a sound integrative concept; and that design of a solution is the characteristic function of an engineer, not simply diagnosing a need or a problem. We also found many ways in which "fuzzy boundaries" between disciplines could be used to reinforce teaching in one field with that in another. Our mathematicians could help students to find engineering applications of mathematics; an economist could help define the social

3. We had some impressive visiting participants in this summer study. They included, in engineering, professors from Berkeley, UCLA, the University of Michigan, and the head of the engineering program of the Ford Foundation; senior humanists or social scientists (familiar with teaching engineers) from the University of Washington, MIT, and Clarkson College of Technology; the chairman of the Department of Philosophy of the University of Alabama, the director and another member of the Center for Advanced study in the Behavioral Sciences; and a musician, an artist, and an economist from our sister Claremont Colleges. We also had the help of three directors of engineering research, from the Ramo-Wooldridge Corporation, the Autonetics Division of North American Aviation Co., and American Potash and Chemical Corporation.

4. As of 1992, the figure is 29%. Both biology and computer science have been added to the possible fields of concentration at Harvey Mudd College, and the amount of both new fields included in the common core required of all our students has increased. Part of this time came from chemistry and physics, and part from the humanities and social sciences. Our students continue to have a "common core" of uncommon breadth, but somewhat less of that breadth is contributed by the humanities and social sciences. The present 29% is, to the best of my knowledge, still the national maximum for accredited four-year engineering curricula.

and economic boundaries within which a design solution must operate, and so on. We sought, and found, many cross-disciplinary ways in which to help our students and each other. We also found ways in which the engineers could help the science students, who also need to be able to design apparatus, communicate with graphic methods as well as with words or mathematics, and think in terms of a complete system. We will see later in this chapter how the engineering design program has evolved.

The entire group of faculty and visitors concerned itself, through this summer study, with how best to use whatever time might be available for the humanities and social sciences. We subscribed to the goals stated by the American Society for Engineering Education. These are to help the student to:

1. Understand our social organization and the influence of technology on its development;
2. Analyze intelligently problems involving social and economic elements;
3. Express thoughts logically and lucidly;
4. Understand the nature and significance of literature and the fine arts;
5. Develop moral, professional, and social concepts essential to a satisfying personal philosophy;
6. Develop an inquiring mind and a creative spirit, and
7. Find lasting interest and pleasure in these pursuits.

Not one, but four possible programs in the humanities and social sciences were put forth, again recognizing that the choice would be made by the faculty who taught the material. All programs had these elements in common:

1. A substantial portion of the material, both in the humanities and in the social sciences, should be in the "common core" required of all students, although the core material might allow the student some options on sampling areas of study.
2. In the elective portion of the work in the humanities and social sciences that would follow the core, the student should agree with a faculty advisor on an area of concentration, and group several courses together to learn in some depth a field such as history, economics, the fine arts, or literature.
3. Finally, each area should be taught from the viewpoint of its own field—history from an historian's perspective, sculpture from a sculptor's, and so on.

I have been asked from time to time why Harvey Mudd College has its own faculty in the humanities and social sciences when our sister Claremont Colleges have many able teachers from whom our students can learn these subjects. Many areas, including music, the graphic arts, and Japanese literature, are still available only through sister colleges, and our students are fortunate to have these opportunities. We have needed our own faculty to design our courses and participate in planning the entire curriculum, to illustrate by their presence that the college considers the humanities and social sciences essential portions of the education of each student, and to advise students on how to make the most of the time they do commit to these studies. I hope we have made these studies an integral part of the education of our students, not an appendage.

How has this experiment worked out? Impoverished as our engineering students may be in the time allotted to technical subjects in their four undergraduate years, they seem to have done well as professional engineers, and the many who have gone directly to graduate school have earned their next degrees promptly and often with distinction. They regularly report, some months after entering graduate study elsewhere, that their fellow students from more traditional institutions are better prepared than they in the details of specific engineering subjects—say, the variety of Fourier transforms used in electrical engineering, or specifics of machine design in mechanical engineering. But by the second year of graduate study these differences have evened out. Employers give similar reports on the performance of engineering graduates who go directly into employment. The breadth of education that should serve them well in the longer run does not cause them to stumble in the first year or two after graduation.

We are periodically visited by an inspection team from the Accreditation Board for Engineering and Technology. (Any accredited engineering curriculum in the United States undergoes such periodic inspections.) To date we have regularly been accredited, with misgivings or with enthusiasm depending on the composition of the particular accreditation team. We are, admittedly, at about the lower limit of the accreditable programs in the amount of the engineering sciences or the art and practice of engineering we require of all our engineering students. We remain a national "test case." As we have seen above, we attempt to make full use of the available time for the engineering sciences by careful interdepartmental planning, and we will see below how our engineering faculty has made full use of the time available to teach the art and practice of engineering.

I have dwelt on the engineering curriculum because it is the one demanding the most pre-professional time among the four undergraduate majors Harvey Mudd College offered in our first twenty years. Many liberal arts colleges regularly grant the Bachelor of Arts degree to students concentrating in chemistry, mathematics, or physics who have spent not more than 25 percent of their available time studying the humanities and social sciences, although the formal degree requirements would permit

35 percent (sometimes more) of the student's time or effort to be "outside the program of concentration." We, and most other baccalaureate institutions, have substantial latitude in mathematics and the sciences. It is in engineering that we are unique. As other engineering institutions increase their commitment to the humanities and social sciences, we may lose our singular position. We welcome them.

The Art and Practice of Engineering

The Engineering Clinic is the solution our faculty developed to teach the art and practice of engineering. It is a solution that evolved over a period of years, with the help of generous foundation support. The Carnegie Corporation gave us the first "seed money" in 1958 as part of their grant to develop new curricular material. The Fund for the Advancement of Education subsidized our opening years of clinic operation. Finally, the Sloan Foundation made the first grant explicitly for the clinic, which funded its operation until it became self-sustaining.

What characterizes engineers is their ability to develop solutions to real problems. Typically, they solve these problems for their clients, and their task is not completed until the client agrees that the solution is in hand, whether it be a working model or a package of software. Understanding the problem—the bailiwick of the scientist—is not sufficient for the engineer or the client. We began, in 1960, to pose problems for groups of freshmen to solve, and we found this provided important motivation for our prospective engineers. In 1960-61 our freshman class was organized into three teams, each of which was given the same problem. They were to assume that the surface of the earth would become uninhabitable for about a century, forcing them to design a survival colony for at least one hundred persons, with sufficient means to ensure continuity of human culture. (This problem was promptly dubbed "Project Noah.") The students had a semester's time to organize the design effort, decide who would be the "project engineer" directing the team, who the food specialist, the oxygen specialist, the radioactivity expert, and so on; set up timetables and coordinate their work so that a final report was in hand some weeks before semester's end. A team of staff members from the RAND Corporation agreed to judge the reports. We found that this competition generated enough excitement that we needed to caution students against neglecting their other studies. We also found that our students taught themselves a prodigious amount of biology, chemistry, and engineering practice, while they wrestled with the question of what constitutes a culture and how it may be preserved. Our friends from RAND found the final reports of professional quality. Furthermore, we had fewer dropouts from that freshman class than we had experienced with its predecessors. We have made the "freshman design experience" a continuing part of the "core." The problems change each year, but the challenge remains. We learned that, even at the freshman level, a design project is a powerful learning tool.

The junior-senior design laboratory for engineering students, developed by Jack Alford and Mack Gilkeson, followed the same approach. Our upperclass engineering students brought with them substantially more background in engineering and the sciences, were better able to communicate, and therefore could work problems in substantially greater depth than they could as freshmen, but the approach was much the same. We soon found that the experience of doing real engineering problems, with real clients, developed independence and the ability to learn new technology. Accordingly the "art and practice of engineering" learned in the junior and senior year (and later, including the fifth year for master's candidates) has continued in the same mold. That's how our Engineering Clinic was born.

Mack Gilkeson, when he was on the faculty of Tulane University, had developed and supervised a "practice school" in which engineering students worked in an industrial setting under faculty supervision. We were familiar also with work that Dean Llewellyn Boelter had encouraged at UCLA, where engineering students were given problems in which real clients had an interest, and with work at the graduate level of the same sort at Dartmouth's Thayer School. From such experiences emerged our pattern: a group of three to five engineering students negotiates with a client, most often an industrial corporation, to define and to agree to solve an engineering problem within a specified time and budget. The result may be a working model, a paper design, a package of software, or a feasibility study. The client contributes financial support on the order of tens of thousands of dollars, plus a day's service per month of a liaison engineer who answers questions and ensures that the client's real concerns are being dealt with. A faculty member acts as resource person for the team, helping them find information or equipment they need, but the faculty member does not direct the project. The result may be that the corporate client learns some commercially significant engineering method, or (more usually) that a method which looked promising really isn't; in either case, the cost of learning the answer is less than an industrial laboratory would normally require. By 1976 the bulk of our corporate clients were "repeat customers," most of whom had their own engineering development staffs, which testifies to the usefulness of the clinic to our clients.

The early years of teaching juniors and seniors the art and practice of engineering by doing real work for real clients were not easy ones.[5] The first problem was to find the real clients. We began with in-house projects such as solar heating of the college swimming pool, or public service projects such as designing a chamber for medical research on the biological effects of components of smog. Foundation grants supported the con-

5. Most of the succeeding material on the Engineering Clinic is copied from a paper I was invited to give at the 1989 Annual Meeting of Sigma Xi, the scientific honor society, held in Denver, Colorado. A major portion of that meeting was devoted to reports on new

siderable incremental costs of doing these projects, as contrasted with "standard laboratory experiments." One of our first real breakthroughs was a project brought to us from Fluor Engineering Corporation by Gunnar Bergmann, then vice president for research of that corporation, dealing with securely mooring an oil drilling platform. Another very successful initial project, sponsored by the IBM laboratories at San Jose, was to explore how densely information may be packed on a magnetic recording; this work has continued for decades. Over the next years we interested a dozen, then two dozen, corporate clients, and the performance of our students made most of them "repeat customers."

We had skeptics on our faculty opposed to granting academic credit for work the standards of which could not be guaranteed in advance. A few academic credits perhaps, but the equivalent of total credit for four or five semester courses for what might be routine industrial testing? The faculty voted a trial year in which a committee from the faculty at large would evaluate the educational merit of the clinic, followed by subsequent evaluations, and skepticism disappeared.

These early troubles were balanced by early successes: student performance of which we could all be proud, clients ready and eager for more clinic contact, and student enthusiasm that sometimes required us to point out that they were taking other courses as well. We were very fortunate in the optimism, persistence, know-how and drive of Tom Woodson, our clinic director as this educational transformation took place. Tom, who had decades of industrial design experience (see his vita in the Appendix), set out to find substantial client funding for every clinic project, which, he pointed out, guaranteed the attention of students, faculty, and client.[6] The time came when the number of clinic projects we had was limited by the number of students, not by the number of clients.

As of 1976 the Engineering Clinic had completed nearly two hundred projects for some seventy clients. Most clients had supported several projects. The range of projects covered many types of engineering: electrical, mechanical, chemical, thermal, or properties of materials. Other disciplines were also involved, as clinic projects had required economics, knowledge of ecology, or techniques of marketing.

With such a range of projects, it is not easy to select a "typical" one. A manufacturer of paper diapers had a problem with the thin plastic liner that waterproofs the product. These liners are produced in great sheets that move through the processing plant about the way newsprint moves through a large rotary printing press. But the plastic sheets are somewhat elastic. If the speed between rollers becomes too great, the plastic sags and gets tangled; if too little, it rips. In either case the result is a roomful of crumpled plastic. The need was for a device that measures the linear speed of the plastic to 0.1 percent without touching the plastic or requir-

and effective methods of teaching pure and applied science, including engineering.

6. When the clinic was well established, several faculty members suggested we should have an endowment so that some of the clinic projects could be college-supported for topics chosen by faculty. Our trustee Fred Lindvall, himself an able engineer and teacher, thought a moment and then commented: "An endowed cat catches no mice."

ing marks on it. The clinic team developed a hand-held optical device meeting these specifications.

Other examples included designing and building a prototype "weather station" for the Navy Civil Engineering Laboratory to measure wind speed and direction and measure the solar flux at remote tropical locations. The device needed to be capable of operating unattended for four months. Rancho Los Amigos, a rehabilitation hospital, needed a miniature device to measure pressure at several places on the foot as a handicapped patient took a series of steps. This information permitted diagnosis of the patient's medical problem. The essential portion of the solution was to invent a pressure transducer appropriate for the task; the ones commercially available could not fill the bill. Still another project was for a manufacturer of nuclear reactors, and was to determine the stability under earthquake conditions of the graphite blocks from which the reactor moderator was made.[7]

We found the clinic was a first-rate teaching mechanism which required skillful academic management. Placing students in charge of a project requires more faculty time (to advise them when they seek advice) than would be needed to direct them what to do. A faculty member who is advisor to two projects finds they take as much time as teaching one standard course. We needed to employ at least three more faculty members than we would have had we used more traditional course materials, and we needed more staff support. We needed to set up twenty to thirty meetings per month with corporate liaison engineers. Written reports required letter-perfect text and good graphics. All of this took money. By 1976 the charge per project to the client was $12,500, which at that time nearly covered the incremental cost to the college of the clinic, as contrasted to more traditional "art and practice" courses.[8] Our clients share the teaching, the management, and the financing of the clinic.

It falls to the clinic director, a faculty member, to match up each client with a particular clinic team. As proposals are made, the suggested problems are screened on pedagogical grounds: What will the students learn from completing the problem? Can the problem be completed within the available academic year? Is there a balance among problems that are basically chemical engineering, electrical engineering, mechanical engineering, or system design, so that there are choices for students of varying interests, and so that all students learn from their fellows a broader range of methods? The clinic director referees the selection process, in which the students would like a wide range of projects among which to choose, and each client would like to submit only the corporation's highest priority project.

We believe the clinic is worth the trouble. In 1974 a visiting team from the American Society for Engineering Education examined us, as they did a number of other institutions using such "experiential educa-

7. Two of these examples, and several others, are given in an article published in the September 1979 issue of *IEEE Spectrum,* the monthly magazine of the Institute of Electrical and Electronics Engineers. The article, written by Thomas T. Woodson, is entitled *Accelerating the Practice of Engineering.*

8. As of 1993-94, the cost per clinic project is $33,000.

A plaque listing the clinic sponsors for Projects Day 1993.

tion" methods as work-study programs, practice schools, and assigned engineering projects. The ASEE team interviewed students and graduates. The team concluded that the clinic had taught (1) "a problem orientation as opposed to a disciplinary orientation," (2) the open-ended complexity of real problems, and (3) the responsibility of solving the problem, with its attendant satisfaction. Moving up the hierarchy of skills, students reported they had been challenged to "grow in new ways, to lead, to cooperate, to manage, and to establish new kinds of relationships with their professors." Students ranked the clinic below classroom instruction as a mechanism for learning engineering fundamentals and computational skills, but found the clinic had taught these things also.

The ASEE team found that alumni rate the clinic experience even more highly than do students. We agree. Alums now in corporate technical responsibility bring in about a third of current (1989) clinic problems, persuaded they help both their employers and their college. Employers have told us they find our graduates are "self-starters." Neither students nor employers report valuing the clinic primarily as a recruiting tool, although a number of graduates have been hired by the corporations on whose problems they worked. What brings us corporate clients is the clinic performance in solving technical problems; we have not had a decline in projects even when recruiting fell off.

The clinic has been widely copied, both within and without the Claremont Colleges. I have reported on the early history of the Mathematics Clinics at HMC and at Claremont Graduate School; Professor Janet Myhre has also instituted a mathematics clinic at Claremont McKenna College. At this writing (1992) the Claremont Colleges have a

McKenna College. At this writing (1992) the Claremont Colleges have a Liberal Arts Clinic, funded by the Sloan Foundation, to teach the essentials of problem solving—and perhaps promote quantitative approaches to learning—among non-science students.

The University of Utah, Seattle University, the University of Cincinnati, the University of West Virginia, and several campuses of California State University now use this method of teaching the art and practice of engineering, and there may be other institutions that do. Many visiting faculty from other institutions in the United States and abroad have taken our approaches home, where they have been used, and copied or modified, by engineering faculties, including ones in Quebec, England (Cambridge University), Venezuela, and Brazil. We are no longer alone.

We are pleased with the clinic as a method of involving students in the art and practice of engineering.[9]

Another venture that our engineering and science faculty members initiated was not a national innovation, but was clearly an innovation for the Claremont Colleges. We developed and taught technical courses for non-technical students in our sister institutions. Rich Phillips of our engineering department taught non-technical students about computers in the late 1960s. As the demand for computer literacy spread in the 1970s each college developed its own computer course or courses, and Rich's pioneering effort was no longer needed. However, both nationally and in Claremont there was also student interest in becoming "technically literate," of learning enough of the concepts and methods of technology to become informed citizens on a planet of finite resources with rapidly changing human control of our environment. John Truxal, dean of engineering at the Stony Brook campus of the State University of New York, with W. A. Lynch, professor of elecrical engineering at the Polytechnic Institute of Brooklyn, had developed a course for non-engineers entitled *The Man Made World*, which was made available through the support of the National Science Foundation and was being widely used. It occurred to Rich Phillips, Sedat Serdengecti, and Arnold Ruskin that students of Claremont McKenna, Pitzer, Pomona, and Scripps Colleges might also welcome such instruction.

Our three engineers were encouraged and supported in this venture by our trustee Abe Zarem, himself a very effective entrepreneur, electrical engineer, and teacher. Abe explored with them the content and methods of instruction of three possible courses, two of which were developed, and supported the summer's work that developed the teaching materials. Rich developed a semester's course on the sources of energy on which our civilization depends, the methods of utilization and control, and the economics of energy. He taught the course for perhaps seven years, under the auspices of the Joint Science Center of CMC, Pitzer, and Scripps. The course is still being taught in the 1990s, usually

9. This sentence was also the conclusion of my 1989 Sigma Xi paper.

with an HMC engineer or scientist instructing. Sedat Serdengecti built and taught a semester's course on information, the descendant of which is still offered. Dean Gillette, former executive officer of the Bell Laboratories, later accepted a joint appointment with Claremont McKenna College and Claremont Graduate School, and taught the same subject until his retirement.

It was, and continues to be, a pleasure to introduce students of our sister colleges to the art and practice of engineering.

THE FRESHMAN DIVISION

On January 27, 1970, the faculty of Harvey Mudd College took an action which is, as far as I know, unique in American higher education. The faculty as a whole delegated to about one-sixth of its membership the full responsibility for designing, teaching, altering at its discretion, and grading the academic work of all first-year students. The faculty as a whole reserved to itself an annual review of the accomplishment of the Freshman Division, and could continue or abandon the experiment, but for the intervening year the members of the Freshman Division had full control of subject matter, workload, grading, academic advising, and would do all the freshman year teaching. More than twenty years later, the "experiment" is still in force, and an accepted part of the academic life of the college.

Six of the faculty members of the Freshman Division were to devote full time to this assignment, the faculty members needed to meet the remaining half of the freshman teaching load on a part-time basis, continuing with some teaching beyond the first college year. It was planned that the membership of the Freshman Division would change at the end of each year, with a portion returning to upper-division teaching and others volunteering for the subsequent year. The director of the division was appointed by the president of the college (advised by many) the first year; thereafter, the director would be selected from those teaching in the division the prior year. It was clearly the faculty expectation that the members of the Freshman Division would consider freshman teaching their primary responsibility during their tours of duty.

What were the reasons for adopting this unusual arrangement? Prior to this time the freshman physics course was taught by a physicist assigned by the Department of Physics, the mathematics by a member of the Department of Mathematics, English by a member of the Department of Humanities and Social Sciences, just as would happen in any self-respecting university or college. Why transfer the loyalty and accountability of the teacher to this newly invented entity?

The reader may recall that we lost a much larger fraction of the Class of '62 than we had expected, and that the faculty had made a number of changes in methods of instruction which had resulted in substantially better retention of students in the later 1960s. In 1970, we were retaining more freshmen than we had over our opening years, but we had learned from our students that further improvement was quite possible. The students reported that the workload of the first year was formidable, that departments seemed to be competing to see which could demand the most of the student's time, and that the work in one subject was sometimes out of step with the needs of other subjects. For example, calculus was needed in physics or chemistry before the mathematicians had taught it. Furthermore, there was the heartless practice of scheduling more than one midterm examination or term paper on the same day. Better timing of presentations and assignments might make it possible to level out the workload and to bring subject matter into more supportive sequence.

The faculty established in 1968 a committee, which also included a student member, to propose a restructuring of the work of the freshman year.[10] The committee found that better coordination should indeed be possible, but that it was far more important to decide what the freshman year should accomplish, and find the best way to do it. They recommended guidelines the faculty later adopted. One-third of the program should be devoted to the humanities and social sciences, and two-thirds to a technical core. The technical core should, wherever possible, be an integrated, multidisciplinary approach to science and mathematics. No freshman should be required to have more than three areas of preparation per week. A portion of the technical core should be devoted to special projects (such as engineering projects) or short courses (such as an introduction to computing) in the choice of which the students should have a voice. The Freshman Division should be able to adjust the academic program appropriately for students arriving with advanced placement in particular subject areas.

Having six members of the faculty whose full-time assignment was to teach freshmen meant that presentations, academic advising, and familiarity with students could have much increased attention from these committed volunteers. Annual rotation of about one-third of the Freshman Division faculty meant that this experience, over years, would involve most of the total faculty.

I was well advised on the appointment of the first director, and Enos Wicher agreed to serve for the academic year 1970-71. He then recruited the other teachers. Once appointed, the initial faculty members of the Freshman Division went briskly to work. They inquired of their colleagues in engineering and science the minimum preparation required for entrance to the core courses of the sophomore year and designed the work of the freshman year to ensure that students would be well prepared. The same questions were addressed in the humanities and social sciences, where more options are available but where, as we have seen, a substantial range and depth of learning was expected during the college

10. The committee included Professors Courtney Coleman (Chair), Bob Borelli, Enos Wicher, and a student member, Henry Brady '69. (Our most recent information places Henry on the faculty in political science of the University of Chicago in 1991.) The work of the committee included a summer study, made possible by the support of the Sloan Foundation, which examined a number of possible improvements in teaching, and recommended to the faculty as a whole the Freshman Division.

years. It did appear possible to design a sequence in chemistry and physics in which the student at any particular time was learning one, but not both; and to arrange the subject matter for timely provision of physics that would be helpful in the understanding of chemistry, and conversely.[11] The mechanics of leveling out the workload, and avoiding "double jeopardy" on major assignments did fall into place, with concerned student help about what constituted jeopardy.

11. The combined course in physics and chemistry was given the good nineteenth century title of "Natural Philosophy."

The Freshman Division has been continued, and its contents and methods of instruction have continued to evolve. As of 1976, it was clear that the autonomy granted the division, and the undivided attention some faculty could give to freshmen, was reducing the fraction of our students who dropped out in that year. This trend has continued since 1976, and we now (1992) have a remarkably high retention rate from entrance to graduation. This alone is ample cause to be grateful for the Freshman Division. Furthermore, having a subsection of the faculty devoted to making the most effective use of that year has, I suspect, helped us improve our teaching throughout the college.

THE QUEST FOR COMMONWEALTH

We expected that freshmen would devote about one-third of their class and study time—perhaps eighteen hours per week—to the humanities and social sciences. This amount of time made possible learning in some depth an important aspect of our common life, and doing so with substantial practice in effective verbal and written communication. In 1970 the Freshman Division decided to offer a course that would concentrate on "man's attempt through political institutions to form a community in which human needs, interests and aspirations may be satisfied or fulfilled." Problems explored in this course included war and peace, freedom and order, law and obligation, and individual and public rights. The rise of science and the effects of technology upon these problems would be examined. The course title (The Quest for Commonwealth) came from the search for the ideal community. The reading list for the first month included Thucydides' *The Peloponnesian War,* Aristophanes' *Lysistrata,* and other Greek authors, concluding with Plato's *Republic*; the second month's list contained readings from the Old and New Testaments of the Christian Bible; the first semester also included readings from Gibbons's *Decline and Fall of the Roman Empire,* readings from Hall's *The Scientific Revolution, 1500-1800,* Machiavelli's *The Prince,* Shakespeare's *King Lear,* and Hobbes's *Leviathan.* There is little doubt in my mind that this first semester of Quest left the student acquainted with much of the evolution of the Western concept of the good life, and how it might be attained. The second semester carried the student through the continuing evolution of this concept in the nineteenth and twentieth centuries.

The method of instruction was also ambitious. At the beginning of a topic (for example, Thucydides) the entire freshman class met with the eight faculty members teaching Quest, and one or more of the faculty would present a Thucydides work within an overview of the times. A second hour was devoted to discussion at which students and faculty participated. The class met next in some ten seminars of twelve students, each with a faculty tutor, and discussed the readings and lectures. A second seminar, without the faculty tutor, followed some days later, with a designated student presiding and another keeping a record of the discussion. Every week each student wrote a paper perhaps five pages long, and then had an individual meeting in which the student read the paper and the tutor commented on it. Students also kept journals in which they entered, day by day, comments on what they had read. After eight weeks each student changed tutors, and the program continued as before; over the year, each student had studied under four tutors. Not all of the tutors were humanists or social scientists. A number were from the faculties in engineering, mathematics, or the sciences. One of our most learned tutors was Daniel Rosenthal of our faculty in engineering, emeritus from UCLA. Dan, an expert in properties of materials, was also very well versed in literature and music. Each freshman student had ample experience in verbal and written communication.

The primary architect of Quest was Ted Waldman, professor of philosophy. Ted had spent the two academic years 1967-69 on leave from Harvey Mudd College, teaching in an experimental college at the Berkeley campus of the University of California with his earlier doctoral advisor Joseph Tussman. "Tussman College" was open to students intending to major in the humanities who had demonstrated good writing skills. The pattern of instruction was similar to that in Quest, except that the students spent full time (as contrasted to one-third time) in a curriculum in which one major work at a time was studied in depth. Since the Tussman College student had no other obligations, writing and tutorial assignments were more frequent and extensive. One hundred and twenty students spent two years in Tussman College before moving to upper-division status in a humanities major at the University of California. On his return to Harvey Mudd College, Ted designed Quest, a similar program, scaled to the time allotted to humanities within our newly established Freshman Division.

Student reaction to Quest was mixed. Quite a few found it a liberating intellectual adventure, and for some it changed the way they viewed the world and their place in it. Alumni occasionally comment on the personal growth they attribute to the course. For many, however, it was an introduction to literature they did not yet choose to study, and a formidable amount of work.

Tussman College existed for four years at Berkeley; its teaching placed on the faculty heavy demands that conflicted with other forms of professional growth. Instruction was labor intensive and hence costly. Quest also lasted four years at Harvey Mudd College; a faculty summer study in 1974 led to a reconstruction of the portion of the freshman year devoted to the humanities and social sciences. We had the Berkeley problems plus some of our own: this large a commitment to the humanities in the freshman year left less available time for the student in the junior or senior years, when she or he might be intellectually more ready for nontechnical study. And, while the engineers and mathematicians and scientists who taught in Quest became important role models for their students, they also had, as teachers, a great deal of unfamiliar subject matter to master.

I have dealt at some length with Quest because it was, to me, a notable example of commitment to the humanities and social sciences, involving most of our faculty. It also set standards of excellence which we have striven to maintain. We learn from experiments, including those which do not prove permanently sustainable.

UPPER DIVISION INSTRUCTION

The careful review of how best to combine teaching of various fields was extended, in each technical department, to the material of the junior and senior years. Perhaps the most notable of these reformulations was that of the Department of Chemistry. Phil Myhre, Mits Kubota, Steve Filseth, and (on Steve's departure) Jerry Van Hecke developed an "integrated junior laboratory" that combined the laboratories normally associated with four separate semester courses into a single, more extensive laboratory program in which the subdisciplinary boundaries disappeared.[12] Harvey Mudd College was one of the first, if not the first, institution to attempt what is now a rather widespread method of teaching.

RESEARCH AND TEACHING

I have been told by visiting faculty members that Harvey Mudd College has a remarkable amount of research for an undergraduate college. A common perception of the division of labor in American higher education is that colleges emphasize teaching, and research universities emphasize research. These visitors consider us a hybrid between the two models. In fact, many research universities do expect and reward good undergraduate teaching, and many colleges expect their faculty members to do research and publish their findings.

Many faculty members find teaching and research reinforce each other. Involvement in research is one way to remain excited by a field of knowledge, and that enthusiasm can then be transmitted to students. Furthermore, it is easier to remain current in a field if one is also active in exploring its boundaries. Teaching can also stimulate research; having to return to first principles to explain a field to newcomers forces a research

12. The semester courses which at that time were usually given with separate laboratory practice were analytical chemistry, organic synthetic chemistry, inorganic synthetic chemistry, and advanced instrumental chemical analysis. (Private communication from Professor Van Hecke.)

scientist to see his own research problems in a more general context. Furthermore, an undergraduate involved in research may get excited about discovery, learn a great deal, and explore the risks and rewards of a research career.

But no one has yet found a way to spend forty hours a week in teaching, and another forty hours a week doing research, without putting in an eighty-hour week. (My own experience is that a few such weeks in succession can ruin a month, and take the fun out of both teaching and research.) The conflict between research and teaching is a problem of time allocation. In this conflict the research universities favor research, and colleges favor teaching.

The initial faculty members of Harvey Mudd College were determined to carry on some research and scholarship, whether or not there was time or funding. Graydon Bell in physics, and Bill Sly in chemistry, and Bob James in mathematics, all found some time each week to plan and begin research that would be feasible for them; from the beginning our humanists were working on possible publications. We borrowed equipment and were given surplus equipment by industrial friends; in the early years of the college the Saddle Rock meetings often discussed how we might find a few dollars to start some research. Once we had a beginning, it became possible to obtain funding from the Research Corporation, the Petroleum Research Fund, and other foundations. In time we found we were visible to the National Science Foundation, the National Institute of Health, and other sources more familiar to research universities. These early faculty members are responsible for establishing our research tradition, and a number of our trustees saw to it that some modest college funding was on hand for "pump priming."

In the first ten years of our history it became apparent that research that involves students is a magnificent teaching tool. Just as engineering students become excited about solving someone's engineering problem in the clinic, students of science and mathematics often get very excited about finding some new knowledge that wouldn't be known without their help. They learn that science is dynamic, and that all sorts of significant things are not yet known or understood. They learn how far to trust their own initiative in developing procedures no one else has yet used. Many of our students have thanked us, on returning from graduate school, for getting them over the psychological hurdle of taking a research risk; as a consequence they have doctoral research well begun while contemporaries from other institutions are still trying to make up their minds.

At the end of our second decade we had well-established research programs in chemistry, mathematics, and physics; there was a substantial record of publication in history and literature. Our students were involved in these research activities, as they were with the clinics. Each student was required, and is now, to have completed some original research, or to have helped solve a clinic problem, as a condition for graduation. Not all faculty research involves students (depending on the field) but research experience is part of the lives of our seniors majoring in the sciences. It is also part of the lives of our faculty members.

Alden Pixley's *Annual Report of Scholarly Activity at HMC* for the academic year 1971-72 (the last one I can locate prior to 1977) lists twelve research projects in progress in chemistry, plus a book in preparation and a graduate student from Afghanistan working on the preparation of demonstration experiments for secondary schools in Kabul. The work was supported by HMC, plus W.H. Freeman Co., the Petroleum Research Foundation, the National Science Foundation, the National Institute of Health, a Swiss university (ETH, Zurich) and the government of Afghanistan. The Department of Engineering reported ten research or development programs, supported by California Tomorrow, Xerox, the NSF Cooperative Program with India, Trinity College (Dublin, Ireland) and the Jet Propulsion Laboratory. Members of the faculty in humanities and social sciences reported fifteen ongoing studies, including three books nearing publication, and four articles published. Support came from the National Science Foundation, NASA, Encyclopedia Britannica, and the University of California Press. The Department of Mathematics reported one book under preparation (supported by Prentice Hall) plus two sets of course notes that might become textbooks. There were also ten research projects, supported in part by the National Science Foundation, the National Research Council of Italy, and the Spencer Foundation. The Department of Physics listed fifteen research projects plus three books in preparation; support came in part from the National Science Foundation, NASA, and the Office of Naval Research. Perhaps fifty students were involved with faculty in these various projects. Research and publication were alive and well at Harvey Mudd College.

Research that involves students is not a unique Harvey Mudd College invention. Many colleges and some universities have well-established programs of student research participation. Our claim to distinction, in the opinion of our visitors, is that every student who graduates has had research or design experience.

THE CHEM STUDY

The innovations reported above were developed by the Harvey Mudd faculty for the benefit of our students. Some have been copied by other institutions. I conclude this chapter with an innovation in which the college was involved that was intended entirely for off-campus use.

In the 1950s there was concern, both in academia and in industry, about high school teaching in the sciences. Many of the scientific developments of the century had not yet found their way into high school courses, which too often dwelt on rote memory of facts rather than on the excitement of discovery. The result was that fewer and fewer students were choosing to study science in high school unless they needed the course for college entrance, and perhaps of those who did take such courses, more were dissuaded from scientific careers than attracted to them. Accordingly the National Science Foundation underwrote a number of course development programs, involving high school teachers and scientists at the forefront of current research, to update high school science teaching and make it more attractive. Biology, chemistry, mathematics, and physics were among these initiatives, and the courses developed under NSF sponsorship really did change the teaching of science in the schools.

13. The Chemical Bond Approach program was based at Earlham College, in Richmond, Indiana. It had been in operation two years at the time the CHEM Study was initiated.

As of 1959, the one such activity in chemistry was the Chemical Bond Approach (CBA).[13] A group from the American Chemical Society and the National Science Foundation approached Glenn Seaborg, Nobel laureate in chemistry and then chancellor of the Berkeley campus of the University of California, urging him to establish and chair a second high school curriculum development program in chemistry, to increase the options available to school systems. Glenn Seaborg agreed, provided "my long term friend and a master teacher, J. Arthur Campbell of Harvey Mudd College, Claremont, California," would serve as director. Art also agreed, which is how we became joint venturers with the University of California in producing the CHEM Study.[14]

14. A detailed account of this project is given in *The CHEM Study Story,* copyrighted in 1969 by the Regents of the University of California, and published by W. H. Freeman Co., San Francisco. I am much indebted to David W. Ridgeway, coauthor of this book and Executive Director since 1966 of the CHEM Study, for use of one of the few remaining copies, plus his own first-hand recollections.

A group of distinguished chemists, high school teachers, and scientific administrators agreed to serve on the Steering Committee of the Chemical Education Materials Study, universally known as the CHEM Study. The first four-day meeting of the group was held on the Harvey Mudd campus in April, 1960. At the conclusion of the meeting there was general agreement on the approach to be taken, and on next steps. A writing conference, to involve both college or university chemists and high school teachers, would occupy the forepart of the summer of 1960, and the latter half would teach volunteer high school teachers these new materials. Enough would be in hand by the end of the summer so that the course could be test taught by these trained teachers in the school year 1960-61. With this experience in hand, the text could be rewritten, more teachers taught, and more supplementary materials prepared in the summer of 1961.

Amazingly, this plan was realized as set out in that meeting. Heroic efforts on the part of the chemists and teachers who prepared these materials were required, and were supplied. In the first summer the Harvey Mudd campus was full of people writing, teaching, preparing laboratory experiments, planning short films to illustrate particular chemical concepts, deciding upon teachers' guides, developing testing materials, and coordinating all these things. Enough was in hand by summer's end to offer a high school chemistry course, including laboratory and reference materials, text and tests.

In the summer of 1961 two summer institutes were held, one at Cornell University and the other at Harvey Mudd, in which a total of roughly one hundred high school teachers were introduced to the material, which by that time was revised on the basis of the first year's teaching experience. In the summer of 1962 eight such institutes were held, involving seven hundred high school teachers. By the latter years of the 1960s, over half the students taking high school chemistry in the U.S. were using CHEM Study materials. Here is one teacher's endorsement: "I base my reactions on almost two years of trial experience with CHEM Study superimposed on a total experience of twenty years in teaching high school chemistry. Never have I witnessed such sustained interest on the part of my students. Never have I observed on the part of my students a more sincere and serious desire to learn. . . . a tribute to CHEM Study—its philosophy, its approach, its materials of instruction."[15]

By 1963, the output of the CHEM Study included the text *Chemistry, An Experimental Science* (W. H. Freeman & Co., San Francisco), plus a laboratory manual, a series of laboratory experiments, a teacher's guide, a series of representative examinations, and four ancillary publications. It also included some thirty (ten- to twelve-minute) single-concept films to illustrate chemical topics, plus seventeen more for teacher training.

These materials were made available to school systems at costs comparable to commercial texts; the materials not in commercial competition the school system bought at the cost of production. Both the University of California and Harvey Mudd College were reimbursed for all actual costs, and participants were paid stipends comparable to those they normally received. Royalties, beyond those needed for costs of reprinting, were returned to the National Science Foundation. Glenn Seaborg points out that the funds returned to the federal government were in excess of its support.[16]

Through December, 1968, the CHEM Study had authorized translations of its teaching materials into Chinese, French, Gujarati, Hebrew, Hindi, Italian, Japanese, Korean, Portuguese, Thai, and Turkish; an unauthorized version had appeared in Russian.[17] The influence of the project clearly did not stop at our national boundaries.

The activities of the CHEM Study were consolidated at Berkeley in 1963. By that time the initial development was completed, and there was a substantial management, warehousing, and customer service operation, which Berkeley was equipped to handle and Harvey Mudd College was not. (In the 1961-62 academic year, the portion of the CHEM Study budget administered at HMC essentially doubled our budget.) It is true

15. Ibid, p. 155. Quoted from Saul L. Geffner, Chairman, Department of Physical Science, Forest Hills High School, Forest Hills, New York.

16. Ibid, p. vii. *Chemistry, An Experimental Science* has sold well. David Ridgeway informs me (private communication) that the Regents of the University of California, in connection with the University's 125th Anniversary Celebration in February 1993, will receive from the publisher the one millionth copy of the English version of this text.

17. Ibid., p. 53. Unauthorized or not (we understand that some royalties were eventually agreed upon) the preface to the Russian edition contains the following ringing endorsement: "The book is distinguished for its teachability, rigor, and orderly presentation. It is the

first time in the history of scientific
literature that difficult concepts of
genetics and thermodynamics are
presented so simply and so clearly,
thanks to the excellent examples and
illustrations."

that we undertook our portion of the CHEM Study simply because we
shared Glenn Seaborg's confidence in Art Campbell, and because the
outcome could be expected to benefit the nation. We were right on both
counts. We did benefit as a college in one major way. When we undertook our participation we had been teaching for three years, and Harvey
Mudd College was not known to most high school science teachers. By
1963, every high school chemistry teacher in the nation had heard of us
and many thought well of us.

I selected the educational innovations reported in this chapter; colleagues of mine may differ on the choices and on the relative importance
I have attached to those selected. Those who differ may well be right!
Innovations provide means to better teaching; they are not ends in themselves. I do believe a faculty constantly searching for better ways to teach
is apt to improve the learning which students actually do.

CHAPTER 16

An Evaluation

Was it worth it and how would you know?

HARVEY MUDD College is a much-evaluated institution. We have evaluated ourselves. Every Saddle Rock meeting we have taken stock of where we were and where we hoped to be. Between these meetings faculty and trustee committees have kept track of our plans and our progress.

Regional and national groups have evaluated us. As a college, we have been formally reviewed at least every five years by the Western Association of Schools and Colleges. The Accreditation Board for Engineering and Technology has examined our engineering program equally often. The program in chemistry has been reviewed for approval, also every five years, by the American Chemical Society.

Foundations and corporations to whom we turned for support formed judgments of our probable accomplishment if we were given help. Students, parents, faculty, and those we hoped would become trustees made decisions that suggested to us their evaluations. Finally, we could find our ratings in national publications that regularly evaluate and categorize universities and colleges.

While all these opinions have been instructive—and some quite flattering—our most useful evaluations have come from our graduates. After all, we existed to educate these graduates so they would become productive members of the society at large, good citizens, and people able to establish for themselves personally satisfying lives. At Harvey Mudd College, we invested more effort and money in each student, and we expected more of each student, than did most universities and colleges. Are our graduates more productive, happier, or more responsible than they might have been had they been educated elsewhere? How would we know? Our alumni keep Harvey Mudd College well informed of their whereabouts, and I have some information on all but perhaps two dozen of the 958 graduates of our first twenty years. In many cases we know them well. I will report later on their postgraduate histories; these give the most telling evidence of the success, or lack of success, of the college. Of course, we have sought their opinions about our work. Fortunately, most are quite loyal to HMC, as they might well have been to another alma mater. We can ask, and have asked, employers of our graduates. Trying to assess the effectiveness of the college from these measures is a more difficult task than reciting national ratings, and a more meaningful one.

I have no doubt that establishing Harvey Mudd College was a very worthwhile task. Our national welfare depends on our educational system, and any addition of good quality is worthwhile. This chapter wrestles with the more awkward question of how well we have done with the considerable human and financial resources entrusted to us.

What have we learned about our first twenty years from these many examinations? Let us begin with the 1977 reaffirmation of accreditation by the Western Association of Schools and Colleges. The team that visited Harvey Mudd College consisted of six knowledgeable deans and professors from other institutions, who read the materials the college had submitted in the fall of 1976, and then interviewed administrators, faculty, students and trustees during a three-day visit in early 1977. Some team members attended classes, and others met with faculty committees. The college gave the visitors any information they requested, and they in turn made themselves available to anyone who wished to speak to them.

Although the team found Harvey Mudd College to be an exceptionally good institution, with more strengths than weaknesses,[1] more planning and more effort would be required of faculty and trustees. Because of the progress of science and technology, we needed to include in our curriculum more attention to computer science and to biology for all our students; this raised the problem of whether to institute majors in these fields, and also what content would be omitted in the core program to make room for the new material. The team also found the faculty to be unusually qualified, but overworked and underpaid; the college was advised to improve this situation. The college's greatest asset, they stated, was its student body, of remarkably high potential, with many responsible contributors to the welfare of the institution. The student services overseen by our dean of students were of good quality but insufficient to meet our needs; we had less academic and personal counseling available per student than our sister Claremont Colleges. Lastly, we were underfinanced; 43 percent of our income came from tuition, 50 percent from gifts and grants, and only 5 percent from endowment earnings. We clearly needed to increase our endowment.

This seems to me a very fair summary of the state of Harvey Mudd College in 1976. Happily, we were reaccredited.

1. This paragraph is paraphased from the accreditation report. I am not permitted to quote such a report verbatim, but a paraphrase is acceptable. I have attempted not to color the findings of the report.

We were early in establishing a reputation for academic rigor. One standard reference book for young people choosing a college, Cass and Birnbaum's *Comparative Guide to American Colleges,* stated in its 1968-69 edition: "Founded to produce annually a small crop of highly educated engineers and scientists who had devoted at least one-third of their study to the humanities and social sciences, Harvey Mudd has, within a dozen years, become one of the most selective colleges in the country. . . . Pressures for academic achievement are very intense. Only students with strong aptitude and background in mathematics and physical sciences will feel at home. Verbal ability of students is also greater than usual among science and engineering students." I believe this was another fair summary of the college, if forbidding to some prospective applicants.

In November, 1986, *Change,* a magazine dealing with higher education, published an article by Carol H. Fuller entitled "Ph.D. Recipients: Where did they go to college?" Dr. Fuller's research calculated the number of alumni who had earned the Ph.D. degree per year over the years 1951-1980, divided by the average number of bachelor's degrees conferred by a college per year over the years 1946-1976. As she pointed out, this technique allowed comparisons to include recently founded institutions. Harvey Mudd College was the leading national institution as an undergraduate source of Ph.D.s in all fields, adjusted for institutional size. The first ten in the nation included Caltech (which we happened to lead by a statistically insignificant margin), followed by Reed, Chicago, M.I.T., Swarthmore, Haverford, Oberlin, Harvard, and New College of the University of South Florida.

Preparation for graduate study is not our primary purpose. Harvey Mudd College was founded "to educate engineers, scientists and mathematicians well versed in all of these areas and in the humanities and social sciences so they may assume leadership in their fields with a clear understanding of the impact of their work on society."[2] However, leaders in the sciences, mathematics, and (increasingly) in engineering more often than not hold earned doctorates. We are gratified that so many of our graduates have reached this important milestone in their careers.

2. Harvey Mudd College Catalogue, 1992-94, p. 6.

WHAT HAVE OUR GRADUATES DONE?

The real contribution Harvey Mudd College makes to the society at large comes through the lives of its graduates. This book covers only the first twenty years of our history. The most recent of the graduates of that period have now been gone from the college for seventeen years, and the first two graduates for thirty-four years.

Who were these people when they graduated, and what have they done since?

As of June, 1976, Harvey Mudd College had graduated 958 women and men with the degree of bachelor of science; 33 had also earned the

3. These total 974 rather than 958. The
difference comes in the number of
"double majors," the students who
satisfied more than one set of degree
requirements.

degree of master of engineering (conferred jointly with Claremont
Graduate School), and three the newly offered master's degree in applied
mathematics, also jointly conferred. Of our baccalaureate graduates, 181
had satisfied the degree requirements in chemistry, 288 in engineering,
194 in mathematics, and 270 in physics; 41 had persuaded the faculty to
let them construct their own degree requirements.[3]

We do not know the subsequent history of all 958; perhaps 20 of
them have not kept in touch with the college. Another 14 have died,
most frequently through accidents. We also know the history of another
40 who earned their baccalaureates elsewhere after transferring from
HMC, but choose to consider themselves our alumni. We welcome them
and take pride in their accomplishments, but to keep the numerator and
the denominator referring to the same group, I will not include our non-
graduates in percentages that follow. Here is what we know of the 924:

The largest single group of graduates went on to graduate work.
Most went immediately after graduation. As we have learned, many
earned the Ph.D. degree; of the entire 958, 34 percent, or 328 of them,
now have earned that degree. If we include the other earned doctorates,
of which the M.D. (35 individuals) and the J.D. (another 29) are the
larger ones, but also include doctorates in education, osteopathy, den-
tistry, and management, the percentage rises to 41 percent. I will not
attempt a breakdown of the many kinds of master's degrees our graduates
earned; the total is 530, or 55 percent. Clearly our graduates are in the
habit of going to school! (One of our graduates holds earned doctorates
in philosophy, medicine, and jurisprudence. He primarily practices as an
M.D., but he also does some work as an oceanographer.)

It is not easy to summarize where these graduate students studied,
since they attended at least fifty graduate institutions at home and abroad.
The largest single group attended one or another of the campuses of the
University of California system, but other popular West Coast institutions
have been Stanford, Caltech, and the University of Washington. As one
might expect, HMC graduates have been drawn to M.I.T., Carnegie-
Mellon University, Case-Western Reserve University, Purdue, and Rice.
They have studied at each of the Ivy League institutions, most of the Big
Ten, and universities from Hawaii to Maryland. A few have earned
advanced degrees in other nations.

There comes a time when one must go to work. Indeed a good
number of our graduates go directly into employment, in some cases
returning later for further study. How are they now employed?

As of 1992, the largest single group is in industry—487, or 53 percent of the 924 of whom we have record. The industries are varied.
Westinghouse, IBM, DuPont, Eastman Kodak and General Electric are
employers, as are aerospace companies such as Boeing, TRW, Hughes,
and Northrop. Our graduates bear such titles in larger corporations as

member of the technical staff; systems engineer; senior research chemist, Shell Oil; director/member technical staff, Bell Laboratories; manager, international sales, Coors Ceramic; vice president, materials management, McKesson Corp; design engineer, Tektronix (where a classmate is listed as senior software engineer); senior vice president, Bechtel Corporation; vice president, Science Applications International (SAI also includes alumni who are program managers); and many others. I gather we have graduates well-scattered in the upper reaches of major corporate hierarchies.

More surprising to me is the number of our graduates who list themselves as presidents or owner-presidents of smaller corporations, ranging from a few hundred employees to single-person consultancies. About one in ten of them—or one in five of the industrially employed group—fits this category. Their companies make aircraft ignition systems, scientific instruments, computer peripherals, and dialysis machines. The smaller ones design and sometimes build machines for specific applications, or design the appropriate computer software for a particular business. In addition to presidents, one alumnus is chief financial officer of a sizable biotechnical (genetics) start-up firm. Another alumna lists herself as captain-vice president & treasurer-director, Bold American Shipping and Chartering Corporation.

One alumnus is executive producer of Warfield Productions, responsible among other things for the "007 movies." Another has his own winery. A third is president of Walt Disney Company/Hollywood Records. No doubt there are still more surprises, unknown to me.

We have a smaller, but considerable, group that I would categorize as in business rather than industry. Two of our graduates, both actuaries, are vice presidents of insurance companies. One graduate is a venture capitalist, and there may be others. Another is marketing director, Capital Markets Assurance Corporation. Several are brokers. Three are publishers. One deals in real estate. I estimate that this group comes altogether to 98 persons, or 11 percent of our total.

We have a larger group in teaching. Colleges and universities employ 117 of them, or 13 percent of our total. They teach in universities as far north as the University of Alaska and as far south as the Universidade Federal de Minas, Brazil, as far west as the University of Hawaii and as far east as University College, London. We have several graduates on the faculties of Canadian universities. At least one hundred of them are employed in colleges and universities in the United States. One alumnus, as of 1992, was professor of ocean engineering and elected chair of the faculty at M.I.T. Another, a former astronaut, is assistant provost and associate professor of astrophysics at the University of Washington. Still another is dean of the faculty at Evergreen State College, Washington. An alumnus who has been chairman of the department of chemistry at

Clark Atlanta University, an historically Black institution in Atlanta, Georgia, is now manager of that university's Child Survival Project. Another alumnus is assistant provost at Stanford. However, most of these graduates have successfully avoided administration (except for some department chair positions), and are teaching in scientific or technical fields in colleges and universities in the United States. Fifteen are teaching in community colleges. In addition to our college and university faculty members, I am very pleased to say that we have about a dozen who are teaching mathematics and science in secondary schools.

Not all our post-secondary faculty are teaching in technical fields. Two are chairs of university art departments: one at the University of Alaska, and another at the University of Puget Sound. Two are professors of philosophy at the universities of Montana and Pittsburgh. One is professor of drama at San Diego State University. We have professors of English, economics, and psychology among our graduates. Harvey Mudd College has on its faculty two graduates of classes prior to 1976. One is professor of chemistry, and the other of humanities.

We also have among our graduates another twenty who hold research, rather than teaching, positions in colleges and universities. They work at such places as the Stanford linear accelerator and the Smithsonian Astronomical Observatory at Harvard, and in medical research projects.

A larger group are employed by non-profit research organizations, including RAND, the Aerospace Corporation, Analytic Services, Inc., Lawrence Livermore Laboratory, Los Alamos National Laboratory, the Canadian National Research Council, and the Imperial Cancer Research Fund (London, England) as examples. I count fifty-two, or 5.6 percent, in this category.

I know of seventeen who are in government service, other than NASA and military laboratories. At the local level, these include the director of the chemistry laboratory, Los Angeles Department of Water and Power. At state level, an alumnus is chemist for the State of California Health Services. More are at the federal level. An alumnus is research oceanographer for the National Marine Fisheries Service, and in 1992 was scientific director of the fourteen-nation, 140-scientist team that assessed the biological damage to the Persian Gulf from oil spills. Staying with that portion of the globe, another alumnus was then director of Israeli and Arab affairs at the U.S. Department of State. An alumnus is lead scientist, Western Regional Research Center, United States Department of Agriculture. Another is project engineer for the U.S. Forest Service. An alumnus is chief, parthenogenesis branch, National Institutes of Health. An alumna is assistant U.S. attorney general, and an alumnus is assistant U.S. attorney, Department of Justice.

While we have had a number of our graduates of 1976 and earlier who have served in the armed forces, the Peace Corps, or VISTA, I know of none still in these services. We do have among our graduates federal civil servants who work for such organizations as NASA, the United States Naval Systems Center, the Pacific Missile Test Center, the United States Army Materiel and Chemical Command, and the United States Navy Electronics Laboratory. These add another twenty to our total of federal employees; we thus have thirty-seven, or 4.0 percent, in government service.

The remaining large, if varied, group is made up of self-employed professionals. Twenty-three graduates practice law; forty-three are medical doctors, two are dentists, and one is a doctor of osteopathy; six are members of the clergy (including one teaching missionary); one is a practicing psychologist, and there may be others of whom I have not learned. (We have fewer practicing law than have law degrees; I have listed a corporate counsel as industrially employed, another who holds a J.D. degree is a corporate president, and a third is an anesthesiologist.) Together these self-employed professionals come to 4 percent of our graduates of the first twenty years.

Two percent of these graduates keep in touch with the college but have not told us what they do for a living! Adding them in, we have now accounted for all the living graduates of our first twenty years of whom we have record.

What do I make of this?

I'm pleased. It seems to me that, as a group, these graduates thoroughly justify the commitments many people made to their collegiate education.

There are, of course, caveats to this anecdotal research. I have no similar group, educated elsewhere, with which to compare our graduates. If such a group were produced, I should not be the one to make the comparison! Every university and college has graduates of whom it is justly proud. It seems to me that we have an unusual number from our first 958 alumni and alumnae who are carrying and apparently enjoying unusual responsibility, but I agree this is a subjective judgment. I do believe the college has done a creditable job in "seeking to educate engineers, scientists and mathematicians well versed in all these areas and in the humanities and social sciences so that they may assume leadership in their fields with clear understanding of the impact of their work in society." As I review the individual records of these graduates, it regularly appears that they are regarded by their peers in their occupations as leaders, whether of a small or a large group.

We have also educated some practicing artists, philosophers, lawyers, economists, airline pilots, a ship captain, and other unexpected contributors. If that never happened, I would be concerned about the breadth of education available to our students.

A second caveat, which applies to us as to every institution, is whether the college, or the student, is entitled to the credit for subsequent performance. Clearly both played a part. We have, from the day Harvey Mudd College opened its doors, attracted very able students who might have been expected to do well anywhere else. What value did the college add?

According to our graduates, most are very pleased with the breadth of education available to them at Harvey Mudd College, and many are grateful for the demanding work habits they found necessary here and useful thereafter. Time and again we have heard that graduate school was no more demanding, and sometimes less so, than their undergraduate preparation. One graduate told me, "I discovered at Harvey Mudd that I could learn anything I needed in just six weeks." (He apparently never needed to speak and read Chinese.) When the alumni office asked what went well and what poorly with a Harvey Mudd education, a recurring response was of gratitude for a particular professor—different professors for different graduates—who had given attention to the student freely, and had set demanding standards. We share this "value added" characteristic with many other institutions; our graduates, who by now are experienced with many other institutions, often tell us we have done well in "adding value."

With all due respect to "demanding work habits," most of our graduates look back on their HMC days with pleasure, and seem to be enjoying what they are doing now. We have no doubt graduated some industrious drudges, but we certainly have graduated our full share of imaginative and venturesome engineers and scientists.

We also can report a modest amount of non-anecdotal research. Sam Tanenbaum, as our dean of faculty, questioned a random sample of 325 HMC graduates in 1984, asking how well their undergraduate college experience had prepared them for their subsequent professional lives. One hundred and eight responded, many at some length; the responses were divided into fifty-seven from those who graduated in 1975 or earlier, and fifty-one from graduates of 1976 and later. No significant differences were found between the two groups. On a scale assigning 1 to a very unsatisfactory preparation, 2 to an unsatisfactory one, 3 to an adequate one, 4 to a satisfactory one, and 5 to very satisfactory, the earlier graduates had a mean response of 4.37 for preparation for graduate study, 4.01 for employment, and 4.0 for interest in continuing to learn in nontechnical areas. (Interest in keeping up to date in one's own field rated merely 3.98.) In comparing their preparation with that of professional colleagues educated elsewhere, they gave graduate school preparation a mean rating of 4.54, preparation for employment 4.22, and ability in flexible problem solving 4.45.

A number of our respondents commented on the breadth of education, beyond that available at Harvey Mudd College, made possible by our sister Claremont Colleges.

Fifty supervisors of HMC graduates were also sampled; twenty-three replied, again including some who responded at length. The employers included technical corporations, insurance companies, and academic institutions. The mean rating given by supervisors in preparation for graduate school, in comparison with coworkers from other institutions, was 4.05; in preparation for employment, 4.31. In nine other categories the mean ratings ranged from 4.0 to 4.6; the 4.6 rating was on awareness of environmental impact of technology.

As of 1976, Harvey Mudd College had survived, established a good reputation, and had graduates contributing to the community at large. Having had the good fortune to remain in close touch with the college from 1976 to 1993, I am convinced that much more progress has been made since 1976. We have added many more graduates in whom the college can take real satisfaction.

There Is Much To Do

H.G. Wells wrote, "Human history becomes more and more a race between education and catastrophe."[4] I agree, if by education we mean developing the ability to use the knowledge mankind has accumulated. Learning to use tools for hunting and gathering, learning to cultivate plants and domesticate animals, and learning to use sources of power other than muscles were all major milestones in human history. Each increased our control over our environment. Each made it possible for this earth to support more people. Each bettered the lives of many of them. For ten thousand years, as this knowledge has been learned and tested, it has been passed down from generation to generation.

4. H.G. Wells, *The Outline of History*, Chapter XL, The Macmillan Co., 1921

In this last millennium, learning and the discovery of new knowledge have required an increasing fraction of the lives of people. We have dealt with the "knowledge industry"—which has grown much more rapidly than the population—by increasing the years of formal education, and by making each person responsible for a smaller fraction of the total: that is, by specialization. We commit an increasing fraction of our labor force to research and development. From these strategies have come amazing gains in life expectancy, food production, transportation, communication, and much else. My grandfather, who was born in 1849, entered a world population of one billion. There were two billion on the earth when I was born in 1915. Currently that figure is close to six billion, nearly all of whom are more aware of each other—more accessible to each other— than were the populations of 1849 and 1915.

Clearly mankind is in the midst of a major transformation in our thinking and in our ways of life. The outcome, we hope, will be a world in which we can live within our renewable resources on a reasonably undamaged planet, without irreversible harm to ourselves and our progeny. To realize this hope will take major changes in human behavior, comparable to those required to move from hunting to agriculture. We will need all the help we can secure from technology present and to come. The next two or three generations may well determine whether we successfully make the transition. Three generations—one century—is a moment in the span of our history.

The educational systems of our nations face new and important challenges. We know the schools and colleges of the United States have a great deal to do. Harvey Mudd College has defined for itself a very small fraction of the total task, but that fraction advances the wise managment of technology, which, I am convinced, is an essential part of any successful transition. Our particular mission seems to me even more important than President Eisenhower saw it to be in 1956. His overriding concern was necessarily the Cold War; all of us are now concerned about the world of the year 2000 and beyond. As of 1976, where this history ends, Harvey Mudd College had made a good beginning on its portion of the task.

Commencement processional

APPENDIX

FACULTY
1966-1976

(Faculty and staff records prior to 1966 are incomplete, and hence this listing covers those at Harvey Mudd College for the stated period only. Date of first appointment follows the name. If still on the HMC faculty in 1976, no terminal date is given. Career data are as of 1976 HMC records.)

CHEMISTRY

Barr, Terry L. 1971-72. Assistant Professor of Chemistry. B.S., University of Virginia; M.S., University of South Carolina; Ph.D., University of Oregon. Research Chemist, Union Oil Company; Post-doctoral Research Associate, University of Washington; Research Chemist, Shell Development Co.

Beckman, Tad A. 1961—. Assistant Professor of Chemistry. Associate Professor and Lecturer in Philosophy, 1967. Associate Professor of Philosophy, 1970; Professor, 1976. B.A., Northwestern University; Ph.D., University of California; Post-doctoral Research Fellow, Molecular Spectroscopy Laboratory, University of Minnesota; NSF Science Faculty Fellow, London School of Economics.

Beug, Michael W. 1971-72. Assistant Professor Chemistry. B.S., Harvey Mudd College; Ph.D., University of Washington.

Blake, Daniel M. 1969-70. Visiting Assistant Professor of Chemistry. B.S., Colorado State University; Ph.D., Washington State University.

Bowen, Ronald E. 1965-66. Research Corporation Post-doctoral Fellow in Chemistry. B.A., M.A., DePauw University; Ph.D., candidate, Kansas State University.

Byrd, James E. 1973-74. Assistant Professor of Chemistry. B.S., Roosevelt University; Ph.D., University of Chicago.

Campbell, J. Arthur. 1957—. Professor of Chemistry and Chairman of the Dept. of Chemistry, 1963-74. Seeley W. Mudd Professor of Chemistry, 1969. Dean of Faculty, 1974-75. A.B., Oberlin College; M.S., Purdue University; Ph.D., University of California. Research Scientist, Manhattan Project, University of California; Professor, Oberlin College; Fund for the Advancement of Education Fellow, Cambridge University; Program Director for Institutes, National Science Foundation; Director, Chemical Education Materials Study; Guggenheim Fellow, Kyoto University, Cambridge University; NSF Faculty Fellow, Harvard University; Visiting Professor: The Chinese University of Hong Kong; University of California, Berkeley; Ohio State University; Michigan State University.

Filseth, Stephen V. 1962-71. Assistant Professor of Chemistry. Associate Professor, 1967. B.S., Stanford University; Ph.D., University of Wisconsin.

Flood, Michael T. 1974-76. Assistant Professor of Chemistry. B.S., College of the Holy Cross; M.A., Ph.D., Columbia University; National Academy of Sciences Overseas Research Fellow, Brazil; Post-doctoral Fellow, Stanford University.

Garwood, Donald C. 1970-71. Assistant Professor of Chemistry. B.A., Kalamazoo College; Ph.D., California Institute of Technology. Senior Scientist and Department Manager, Aeronuatic Division of Philco Ford; Visiting Scholar and NIH Special Research Fellow, University of California, Los Angeles.

Harmon, Ann B. 1963-69. Research Associate in Chemistry. B.S., University of Washington.

Harmon, Kenneth M. 1958-69. Associate Professor of Chemistry. B.A., San Jose State College; Ph.D., University of Washington.

Kok, Gregory L. 1974—. Assistant Professor of Chemistry. B.S., Calvin College; Ph.D., University of Michigan. Teaching Fellow, University of Michigan; Post-doctoral Research, University of Michigan.

Kubota, Mitsuru. 1959—. Assistant Professor of Chemistry. Associate Professor, 1966. Full Professor, 1971. B.A., University of Hawaii; M.S., Ph.D., University of Illinois. Research Fellow, Visiting Assistant Professor, University of Illinois; NSF

Science Faculty Fellow, University of North Carolina; Fulbright Advanced Research Fellow, University of Sussex, England; National Institute of Health Special Fellow, California Institute of Technology.

Martinson, Per. 1969-70. Visiting Assistant Professor of Chemistry. M.S., Ph.D., University of Goteborg, Sweden.

McKay, Bruce M. 1969-71. Assistant Professor of Chemistry. B.S., Canisius College; National Science Foundation; Member, Board of Science and Technology at Buffalo; NASA Fellow.

Myhre, Philip C. 1960—. Assistant Professor of Chemistry. Associate Professor, 1966. Full Professor, 1971. Chairman of the Department of Chemistry, 1974-76. B.A., Pacific Lutheran College; Ph.D., University of Washington. Chemist, Stauffer Chemical Co.; National Science Foundation Post-doctoral Fellow, Nobel Institute of Chemistry (Stockholm); Visiting Associate, California Institute of Technology; Guest Professor, Swiss Federal Institute of Technology.

Palino, Gerard F. 1969-70. Visiting Assistant Professor of Chemistry. B.S., San Jose State College; M.S., Ph.D., Iowa State University; Post-doctoral Research Associate, University of California, Irvine.

Scroggins, William T. 1974—. Assistant Professor of Chemistry. B.S., University of California, Los Angeles; M.S., Ph.D., University of California, Riverside.

Sly, William G. 1958—. Associate Professor of Chemistry. Full Professor, 1966. Chairman of the Department of Chemistry, 1976-77. B.S., San Diego State College; Ph.D., California Institute of Technology. Post-doctoral Fellow, Research Associate, Massachusetts Institute of Technology; Visiting Assistant Professor, University of California, Berkeley; NSF Senior Post-doctoral Fellow, Swiss Federal Institute of Technology, Zurich; Visiting Professor, Oregon State University.

Stevens, Kenneth D. 1967-69. Assistant Professor of Chemistry. B.S., Harvey Mudd College; Ph.D., University of Washington.

Van Eikeren, Paul. 1972—. Assistant Professor of Chemistry. B.A., Columbia College; Ph.D Massachusetts Institute of Technology. Dreyfus Instructor in Chemistry, M.I.T.; Member of the Faculty of the Experimental Study Group, M.I.T.

Van Hecke, Gerald. 1970—. Assistant Professor of Chemistry. B.S., Harvey Mudd College; M.A., Ph.D Princeton University. Chemist, Shell Development Company.

Vaughan, Ronald J. 1971—. Assistant Professor of Chemistry. B.S., Duke University; Ph.D., Harvard University. Post-doctoral research, Harvard University.

Wegner, Patrick A. 1968-69. Assistant Professor of Chemistry. B.A., Northwestern University; Ph.D., University of California, Riverside. Research Chemist, E.I. duPont De Nemours & Co.

Whiteker, Roy A. 1957-74. Assoc. Prof. of Chemistry. Full Professor, 1967. Chairman of the Department of Chemistry, 1970-71. B.S., M.S., University of California, Los Angeles; Ph.D., California Institute of Technology. Assistant Professor of Chemistry, Massachusetts Institute of Technology; National Science Foundation Faculty Fellow, Royal Institute of Technology, Stockholm, Sweden; Associate Director, Fellowship Office, National Science Council.

ENGINEERING

Alford, Jack L. 1959—. Professor of Engineering. Director of Engineering Clinic, 1965. James Howard Kindleberger Professor of Engineering, 1966. Chairman of the Department of Engineering, 1969-1972, 1974-77. B.S., M.S., Ph.D., California Institute of Technology. Post-doctoral Research Fellow, California Institute of Technology. Engineering Officer, U.S. Navy; Research Engineer, Northrup Aircraft Co.; Supervisory Engineer, U.S. Naval Ordnance Test Station; Assistant to the Technical Director, Technicolor Corp.; Engineering Specialist, Jet Propulsion Laboratory; Registered Professional Engineer, California.

Charette, Andre. 1973. Visiting Professor of Engineering. On leave from University of Quebec at Chicoutimi.

Degani, Amin. 1973-75. Assistant Professor of Engineering. B.E. Poona Engineering College, India; M.S., Carnegie Institute of Technology; Ph.D., Carnegie-Mellon University.

Drellishak, Kenneth S. 1970-71. Adjunct Professor of Engineering. B.S., University of Detroit; M.S., Ph.D., Northwestern University. Aerospace engineer, NASA; Staff Scientist and Chief Scientist, Electro-Optical Systems.

Fischler, Alfred S. 1971-72. IBM Adjunct Professor of Engineering. B.S., University of California, Berkeley; M.S., Syracuse University. Research staff member, Staff Consultant, Project Engineer, Senior Engineer, IBM.

Fleck, Ray N. Union Oil Adjunct Professor of Engineering. B.A. University of California at Los Angeles; M.S., Ph.D., University of California at Berkeley, Ll.B., Southwestern University. Member, California and Federal Bars; Registered U.S. Patent Attorney; Chemical Engineer, Union Oil Company.

Francis, Benjamin. 1975—. Assistant Professor of Engineering. B.S., M.S., Stanford University; Ph.D., University of California, Berkeley. Technical manager, MicroMetals, Inc.; Research Associate, Lawrence Berkeley Laboratory.

Frankel, Jacob Porter. 1968-74. Professor of Engineering and Dean of Faculty. B.S., M.S., University of California, Berkeley; Ph.D., University of California, Los Angeles. Research Engineer, University of California; Lead Metallurgist, California Research and Development Corporation; Project Supervisor, Director of the Nucleonics Division, Systems Laboratories Corporation; Assistant Professor, University of California, Los Angeles; Associate Professor, Northwestern University; Associate Professor, Professor of Engineering, University of California, Los Angeles; Associate Dean and Professor of Engineering, Thayer School of Engineering, Dartmouth College.

Gilkeson, Murray Mack, Jr. 1961—. Associate Professor of Engineering. Full Professor 1964. Director of the Freshman Division of the Faculty, 1973-75. Director of the Intercollegiate Program in Public Policy Studies, 1973. B.E. University of Southern California; M.S., Kansas State University; M.S.E., Ph.D., University of Michigan. Associate Professor, Tulane University; Engineering consultant, Chief of Party, USAID Project RITA-Paraiba, Brazil; Visiting Professor, NSF Design Seminar Indian Institute of Technology (Delhi) India; Engineering Consultant, USAID, India; Visiting Professor, Centro de Ciências e Tecnologia (Campo Grande, Brazil.) Registered Professional Engineer, California.

Hwang, Yeong-wen. 1969-71. Associate Professor of Engineering. B.S., Taiwan National University; Ph.D., University of Oklahoma. Associate Professor, National Chiao Tung University, Taiwan; Director of Laboratories, Christian Chung Yung College, Taiwan.

Ingels, Don M. 1970-74. Assistant Professor of Engineering. B.S., M.S., University of Oklahoma; Ph.D., University of Houston. Production Engineer, Dow Chemical Company.

Kronenberg, Klaus. 1968-69. Lecturer.

Mack, Rex. 1969. Director of Engineering Clinic.

McClung, Donald H. 1971-72. IBM Adjunct Professor of Engineering. B.S., University of New Mexico; M.S., Stanford University. Associate Engineer, Development Engineer, IBM.

Mirsepassi, Taghi. 1967-68. Lecturer in Engineering. B.S., Tehran University; M.S., Columbia University; Ph.D., Columbia.

Molinder, John I. 1970—. Assistant Professor of Engineering. Associate Professor, 1972. B.S., University of Nebraska; M.S., Air Force Institution of Technology; Ph.D., California Institute of Technology. Project Officer, USAF; Senior Engineer, Jet Propulsion Laboratory. Registered Professional Engineer, California.

Monson, James E. 1961—. Assistant Professor of Engineering. Associate Professor, 1966. Full Professor, 1973. Harvey S. Mudd Fellow in Engineering, 1966—. B.S., M.S., Ph.D., Stanford University. Technical staff, Bell Telephone Laboratories, Hewlett-Packard Co.; Ford Foundation Resident in Engineering Practice, Western Electric Co.; Visiting Professor, Trinity College, Dublin; Fulbright Research Grantee, University Velko Vlahovich, Yugoslavia; Registered Professional Engineer, California.

Nahin, Paul J. 1971-73. Assistant Professor of Engineering. B.S., Stanford University; M.S., California Institute of Technology; Ph.D., University of California, Irvine. Digital Design Engineer, Beckman Instruments, Inc.; Member of Technical Staff, Hughes Aircraft Company, Ground Systems Group; Consultant, Beckman Instruments, Inc.; Senior Design Engineer, General Dynamics, Pomona Division.

Phillips, John Richard. 1966—. Assistant Professor of Engineering. Associate Professor, 1969. C.F. Braun Fellow in Engineering, 1969—. B.S., University of California, Berkeley; M.E., D.E. Yale University. Chemical Engineer, Stanford Research Institute; Staff Officer, U.S. Army CBR Combat Developments Agency; Research Engineer, Chevron Research Co.; Visiting Professor, University of Edinburgh, Scotland.

Remer, Donald S. 1975—. Oliver C. Field Associate Professor of Engineering. B.S., University of Michigan; M.S., Ph.D. California Institute of Technology; Economic Analyst, Senior Project and Process Engineer, Exxon Chemical Co.; Registered Professional Engineer, California.

Rosenthal, Daniel. 1969-72. Senior Professor. Senior Professor Emeritus, 1972. B.S., M.S., Ph.D., University of Brussels, Belgium. Assistant Professor, University of Brussels; Research Associate, Assistant Professor, Massachusetts Institute of Technology; Professor, Head of Material Divisions, University of California, Los Angeles.

Ruskin, Arnold M. 1963-74. Assistant Professor of Engineering. Associate Professor, 1966. Lecturer in Engineering, 1973. Union Oil Company Fellow in Engineering, 1967-72. Assistant Director of The Freshman Division of the Faculty, 1971. Full Professor, 1972. B.S.E., M.S.E., Ph.D., University of Michigan. Registered Professional Engineer, California.

Selman, Johan C. 1972. Adjunct (Associate) Professor of Engineering. Electrotechnisch Ingeniur, Technical University, Delft. Director, Joint Project of Xerox Data Systems and Southwestern Regional Laboratory for Educational Research and Development.

Serdengecti, Sedat. 1961—. Assistant Professor of Engineering. Associate Professor 1965. Full Professor, 1971. B.S., Syracuse University; M.S., Ph.D California Institute of Technology. Research Engineer, Chevron Oil Field Research Co.

Seven, Michael John. 1965—. Lecturer in Psychology. Assistant Professor, 1966. Associate Professor, 1967. Associate Professor of Engineering and Psychology, 1970. Professor of Engineering and Psychology, 1974. B.S., University of Illinois; Ph.D., Claremont Graduate School. Aviation Psychology Laboratory, University of Illinois; Social Scientist, The RAND Corporation; Consulting Analyst, General Electric Computer Department; Senior Scientist, Hughes Aircraft Company, Ground Systems Group.

Sigman, Elliot. 1974—. Assistant Professor of Engineering. B.S., Wayne State University; M.S., Ph.D. University of Michigan. National Science Foundation Fellow; Technical Staff Member, Hughes Aircraft Co.

Stern, Helman I. 1969-70. Assistant Professor of Engineering. B.S., Drexel Institute; M.S., Ph.D., University of California, Berkeley. Engineer, RCA, Servonics, Inc., Vitro Laboratories, Hughes Aircraft Company; Research Assistant, Acting Instructor, University of California, Berkeley.

Tam, Wing Cheung. 1974—. Assistant Professor of Engineering. B.S., M.S., Ph.D., University of California, Los Angeles. Post-Graduate Research Engineer, University of California, Los Angeles. Assistant Professor, Wayne State University.

Wessels, Philip S. 1965-69. Visiting Professor of Engineering. B.A., (Physics) Whittier College; M.S., California State University, Fullerton. Consolidated Systems Corp.; Lockheed Electronics Corp.; Fairchild Camera and Instrument Corp.; Aerojet General Corp.

Williams, Harry E. 1960—. Assistant Professor of Engineering. Associate Professor, 1965. Full Professor, 1971. C.F. Braun Fellow in Engineering. B.M.E. University of Santa Clara; M.S., Ph.D., California Institute of Technology. Research Engineer, Manchester University, England, Jet Propulsion Laboratory, California Institute of Technology; Liaison Scientist, Office of Naval Research.

Wilson, Warren. 1959-68. Seeley W. Mudd Professor of Engineering, 1963. Chairman of Dept. of Engineering, 1959-68. Director of Engineering Clinic, 1967-68. C.E., Lehigh University; M.C.E., Cornell University; M.S., California Institute of Technology; Ph.D., University of Iowa. Professor of Engineering, University of Colorado, Pennsylvania State University; President, South Dakota School of Mines and Technology; Dean of Engineering, Pratt Institute. Registered Professional Engineer, California.

Woodson, Thomas T. 1969—. Robert C. Sabini Professor of Engineering. Chairman of the Department of Engineering, 1972-74. Director of the Engineering Clinic, 1972—. B.S.E.E., Purdue University; M.S.E.E., Ohio State University. Research Laboratory, Major Appliance Divisions, General Electric Co.; Manager of Engineering, Waste King Corporation; Senior Lecturer, University of California, Los Angeles; Industrial Development Officer, USAID, Brazil; Editorial Advisor, John Wiley & Sons; Design Engineering Consultant; Consultant, USAID, India; Team Leader, National Science Foundation Seminar, India.

Wright, John C. 1969. Visiting Professor of Engineering. B.Sc., London; Ph.D., London.

HUMANITIES

Allen, William B. 1972—. Assistant Professor of Government. B.A., Pepperdine College; M.A., Ph.D., Claremont Graduate School. Lecturer, Université de Rouen, France; Assistant Professor, School of Government and Public Administration, The American University.

Blackmore, John T. 1972—. Assistant Professor of History. B.A., University of New Mexico; Ph.D., University of California, Los Angeles. NSF Research Fellow. Preceptor, University of California, Santa Cruz; Assistant Professor, San Fernando State College.

Boone, Daniel N. 1967-69. Instructor in Philosophy. B.A., Claremont Men's College.

Crawford, George. 1976—. Ph.D. candidate, Claremont Graduate School.

Davenport, William H. 1957-73. Professor of English and Chairman of Humanities and Social Sciences, 1957-68. Willard W. Keith, Jr. Fellow in the Humanities, 1968. Professor Emeritus, 1973. B.A., Dartmouth College; M.A., Tufts College; Ph.D., Yale. Professor of English, Department Chairman, University of Southern California.

Dick, Lucia. 1970-71. Instructor of English.

French, Milton L. 1967-68. Visiting Associate Professor of German. B.S., New York University; M.A., Columbia University; Ph.D., New York University.

George, Ronald J. 1970—. Assistant Professor of Psychology. B.A., M.A., California State College at Long Beach; Ph.D., Claremont Graduate School. Chief, Product Evaluation, Hunt Wesson Foods; Technical Staff Member, Autonetics Division of North American Rockwell Corp.

Heim, Mark William. 1967-69. Instructor in English. B.A., San Francisco State College; M.A., Claremont Graduate School.

Jones, Robert A. 1970-72. Assistant Professor of Sociology. B.A., University of Redlands; Ph.D., University of Pennsylvania.

Levy, Leonard W. 1974-1990. Mellon Professor of History. (Joint appointment with Claremont Graduate School.) B.A., M.A., Ph.D., Columbia University; Instructor to Earl Warren Professor of American Constitutional History, Brandeis University; Dean, Faculty of Arts and Sciences; Dean, Graduate School of Arts and Sciences, Brandeis University; William W. Clary Professor of History, Claremont Graduate School; Pulitzer Prize in History; Guggenheim Fellow; Fellow, Center of Study of Liberty in America, Harvard University; American Bar Federation Legal Merit Fellow; National Endowment for the Humanities Senior Fellow.

Moore, John A. Jr. 1967-68. Instructor in History. B.A., M.A., University of Tulsa.

Niwata, Yoichi. 1968-70. Instructor in Economics. B.A., International Christian University, Tokyo.

Olson, Richard. 1976—. Professor of History. B.A., Harvey Mudd College; Ph.D., Harvard University. Instructor, Tufts University. Assistant Professor, Associate Professor, Chairman, History Board of Studies, University of California at Santa Cruz; National Endowment for the Humanities Fellow.

Osler, Margaret. 1970-74. Assistant Professor of History. B.A., Swarthmore College; M.A., Ph.D., Indiana University.

Pahl, Gary. 1974-76. Assistant Professor of Anthropology. B.A., California State University, San Jose; Ph.D., University of California, Los Angeles.

Rae, John B. 1959—. Professor of History. Chairman of the Department of Humanities and Social Sciences, 1968-73. Willard W. Keith, Jr. Fellow in the Humanities, 1969—. B.A., M.A., Ph.D., Brown University. Assistant to President, Brown University. Associate Professor of History, Massachusetts Institute of Technology. National Science Foundation Senior Post-doctoral Fellow, Manchester College, England. Member, NASA Historical Advisory Committee. Founding member and President, Society for the History of Technology.

Saltman, Benjamin. 1965-67. Instructor in Humanities. B.A., University of Pittsburgh, M.A., San Francisco State College; Ph.D. candidate, Claremont Graduate School.

Sanders, David S. 1959-70; 1973—. Associate Professor of English. Full Professor, 1969. Professor of English and Chairman of the Department of Humanities and Social Sciences, 1973- . B.A., M.A., Ph.D University of California, Los Angeles. Instructor, University of Maryland; Fulbright Lecturer, University of Salamanca, (Spain); Instructor of English and Chairman, Department of Humanities, Clarkson College of Technology, 1970-73.

Sellery, J'nan M. 1970—. Assistant Professor of Literature. B.A., M.A., Ph.D., University of California, Riverside. Associate Professor 1976. NDEA Fellow; Guest Lecturer, University of California at Riverside.

Seven, Michael John. 1965—. Lecturer in Psychology. Assistant Professor, 1966. Associate Professor, 1967. Associate Professor of Engineering and Psychology, 1970. Professor of Engineering and Psychology, 1974. B.S., University of Illinois; Ph.D., Claremont Graduate School. Aviation Psychology Laboratory, University of Illinois; Social Scientist, The RAND Corporation; Consulting Analyst, General Electric Computer Department; Senior Scientist, Hughes Aircraft Company, Ground Systems Group.

Smith, Thad Diemer. 1968-72. Instructor in Political Science. Lecturer, 1969. B.A., Pomona College; Doctoral Candidate, Claremont Graduate School.

Speckman, William H. 1968-70. Teaching Intern in English and Literature. Instructor in English and Literature, 1969. B.A., Western Michigan University; M.A., Claremont Graduate School.

Strombotne, James. 1968-70. Lecturer in Art. B.A., Pomona College; M.F.A. Claremont Graduate School. Instructor in Art, University of California, Los Angeles; Teacher of Art, University of California, Riverside.

Swartzbaugh, William L. 1968-71. Associate Professor of Psychology and Dean of Students. B.A., Dartmouth College; B.D. Yale Divinity School; Ph.D., Ohio State University. Director of Religious Activities, Assistant Professor, Denison University; Program Director, Ohio State University; Dean of Students, University of Pittsburgh; Associate Dean of the College, Amherst College.

Viator, James. 1976. Ph.D. candidate, Claremont Graduate School.

Wagner, Emilie E. 1957-67. Visiting Associate Professor of German. B.A., Smith College; M.A., Pennsylvania State College; Certificat de l'Institute de phonétique, Université de Paris; Docteur de L'Université-Mention Lettres, Toulouse.

Waldman, Theodore. 1963—. Associate Professor of Philosophy. Full Professor, 1970. B.A., M.A., Washington University (St. Louis); M.A., Ph.D., University of California. Predoctoral Instructor, University of Michigan; Assistant Professor, State University of Iowa; Associate Professor, Arizona State University; Visiting Associate Professor, University of California at Berkeley; Visiting Tutor, St. John's College, Santa Fe, New Mexico.

Wichman, Harvey. 1967-68. Instructor in Psychology. B.A., M.A., Long Beach State College.

Wickes, George C. 1957-71. Associate Professor of English. Full Professor, 1966. B.A., University of Toronto; M.A., Columbia; Ph.D., University of California, Berkeley. Executive Officer, U.S. Educational Foundation in Belgium; Instructor, Duke University; Fulbright Lecturer, Paris, France.

MATHEMATICS

Bellenot, Steven F. 1973-74. Lecturer in Mathematics. B.S., Harvey Mudd College; Ph.D. candidate, Claremont Graduate School.

Borrelli, Robert L. 1964—. Assistant Professor of Mathematics. Associate Professor, 1967. Full Professor, 1973. Chairman, Department of Mathematics, 1974—. B.S., M.S., Stanford University; Ph.D., University of California at Berkeley. Assistant Professor of Mathematics, U.S. Naval Post-graduate School; Senior Engineering Specialist, Philco Corporation; National Science Foundation Science Faculty Fellow, Massachusetts Institute of Technology.

Brainerd, Walter S. 1972-73. Assistant Professor of Mathematics. B.A., University of Colorado; M.A., University of Maryland; Ph.D., Purdue University.

Busenberg, Stavros Nicholas. 1968—. Assistant Professor of Mathematics. B.M.E.,, Cooper Union; M.S., Ph.D., Illinois Institute of Technology. Instructor, Loyola University; Post-doctoral Fellow, Science Center of North American Rockwell, Thousand Oaks, California.

Coleman, Courtney S. 1959—. Associate Professor of Mathematics. Full Professor, 1966. Chairman, Mathematics Department, 1967-68. B.A., University of California, Berkeley; M.A., Ph.D., Princeton. Instructor, Princeton University; Assistant Professor of Mathematics, Wesleyan University; Visiting Scientist, Research Institute for Advanced Study.

Dayton, Barry S. 1969-71. Instructor in Mathematics. Assistant Professor, 1970. B.A., Pomona College; M.A., University of Southern California.

Fickas, Ernest. 1968-72. Assistant Professor of Mathematics. B.A., M.A., Ph.D., University of California, Berkeley. Assistant Professor of Mathematics, University of Victoria, British Columbia.

Greever, John. 1961—. Assistant Professor of Mathematics. Associate Professor 1965. Full Professor, 1970. Chairman of the Department of Mathematics, 1972-74. Director, Undergraduate Summer Research Mathematics Program. B.S., University of Richmond; M.A.; Ph.D., University of Virginia. Assistant Professor of Mathematics, Florida State University; Visiting Professor, Research Institute for Mathematical Sciences, Kyoto University, Japan; Research Associate, Department of Biology, University of California at Riverside..

Henriksen, Melvin. 1969—. Professor of Mathematics and Chairman of the Department of Mathematics, 1969-72. B.S., City College, New York; M.S., Ph.D., University of Wisconsin. Assistant Professor, University of Wisconsin, University of Alabama; Assistant Professor, Associate Professor, Professor, Purdue University; Department Head, Case Institute of Technology; Visiting Professor, University of California at Berkeley; Visiting Professor, University of Manitoba.

Ingram, Robert Richard Jr. 1967-68. Instructor in Mathematics. B.A., Pomona College; M.A., University of California, Berkeley.

Ives, Robert T. 1958—. Assistant Professor of Mathematics. Associate Professor 1964. B.S., Haverford College; Ph.D., University of Washington. Instructor in Mathematics, University of Virginia.

James, Robert C. 1957-67. Professor of Mathematics and Chairman of the Department of Mathematics, 1957-67. B.A., University of California, Los Angeles; Ph.D., California Institute of Technology. Post-doctoral Fellow in Mathematics, Harvard University; Associate Professor of Mathematics, Haverford College; Visiting Scholar, Institute for Advanced Study, Princeton.

Krieger, Henry Alan. 1968—. Assistant Professor of Mathematics. Associate Professor, 1971. B.A., Rensselaer Polytechnic Institute; Ph.D., Brown University. Bateman Research Fellow, Assistant Professor, California Institute of Technology. Visiting Professor, Technion-Israel Institute of Technology.

Manes, Ernest G. 1967-68. Assistant Professor of Mathematics. B.S., Harvey Mudd College; Ph.D. candidate, Wesleyan University.

McCutcheon, Thomas R. 1973-74. Lecturer in Mathematics. B.S., Harvey Mudd College; Ph.D., University of California, Los Angeles.

Meyers, Ann Marie. 1968-69. Lecturer in Mathematics. B.A., Rosemont College; M.A., Ph.D., Georgetown University.

Orland, George H. 1967—. Visiting Associate Professor of Mathematics. Associate Professor, 1969. B.E.E., City College of New York; M.S., University of Chicago; Ph.D., University of California, Berkeley. Mathematician, Institute for Systems Research, Chicago; Assistant Professor, University of Illinois; Assistant Professor, Wesleyan University.

Palmquist, Paul. 1974-75. Assistant Professor of Mathematics. B.S., M.S., Ph.D., University of Chicago.

Pixley, Alden F. 1962—. Assistant Professor of Mathematics. Associate Professor, 1966. Full Professor, 1972. B.A., M.A., Ph.D., University of California, Berkeley. Technical Sales Coordinator, International Business Machines; teaching experience at Berkeley, College of Notre Dame (California) and San Francisco State University.

Projector, Murray. 1972—. Adjunct Professor of Mathematics. B.S., City College, New York; M.S., Columbia University. Professional consulting actuary.

Savage, Thomas. 1975-76. Instructor in Mathematics. B.S., Trinity College. M.S. candidate, Claremont Graduate School.

Stone, Betty Jane. 1967-68. Visiting Assistant Professor of Mathematics. B.A., Swarthmore College; Ph.D., Stanford University.

White, Alvin M. 1962—. Assistant Professor of Mathematics; Associate Professor, 1966. B.A., Columbia University. M.A. University of California, Los Angeles; Ph.D., Stanford University. Assistant Professor, University of Santa Clara; Member Mathematics Research Center, University of Wisconsin; Visiting Scholar, Stanford University; Visiting Associate Professor, Division for Study and Research in Education, Massachusetts Institute of Technology; Danforth Faculty Fellow.

PHYSICS

Beeman, David M., Jr. 1969—. Assistant Professor of Physics. Associate Professor, 1974. B.S., Stanford University; M.A., University of California, Los Angeles; Ph.D., University of California, Los Angeles. Research Associate, Theoretical Physics Division, Atomic Energy Research Establishment, Harwell, England.

Bell, Graydon D. 1957—. Associate Professor of Physics. Full Professor, 1965. Chairman of the Department of Physics, 1971—. B.S., University of Kentucky; M.S., Ph.D., California Institute of Technology. Instructor, University of Kentucky; Assistant Professor, Robert College (Istanbul); Physicist, National Bureau of Standards; NSF Faculty Fellow, National Research Council of Canada.

Brown, Ronald Franklin. 1968-74. Post-doctoral Teaching Fellow in Physics. Assistant Professor, 1969. B.A., M.A., University of California, Riverside. Research Assistant, University of California, Riverside. Staff member, U.S. Electronic Laboratory, San Diego.

Carter, Lucian. 1974-75. Assistant Professor of Physics. B.S., University of Texas; M.S., California Institute of Technology; Ph.D. candidate, California Insitute of Technology.

Cary, Arthur S. 1969-74. Assistant Professor of Physics. Associate Professor, 1971. B.A., M.A., Fisk University; M.A., Ph.D., University of California, Riverside. Associate Professor of Physics, Tennessee Agricultural and Industrial State University.

Cooper, George S. 1969-74. Instructor in Physics. Assistant Professor, 1971. A.B., San Diego State College; M.A., University of California, Riverside.

Domb, Ellen R. 1976—. Assistant Professor of Physics. B.S., Massachusetts Institute of Technology; M.A., University of Pennsylvania; Ph.D., Temple University; Research Associate, University of Nebraska. .

Focke, Alfred B. 1959-72. Professor of Physics and Chairman of the Department of Physics, 1963-1971. Senior Professor, 1971. Senior Professor Emeritus, 1972. B.S., Case Institute of Technology; Ph.D., California Institute of Technology. National Research Council Post-doctoral Fellow, Brown University; Assistant Professor of Physics, Yale University; Bureau of Ordnance, U.S. Navy (Meritorious Civilian Service Award) Director, Research Department, Navy Electronics Laboratory; Director, Marine Physical Laboratory, Scripps Institution of Oceanography; Technical Director, Pacific Missile Range; Chief Scientist, Office of Naval Research, London.

Goodman, John Mott. 1965-71. Instructor in Physics. Assistant Professor, 1967. B.S., Swarthmore College; Ph.D., Cornell University.

Helliwell, Thomas M. 1962—. Assistant Professor of Physics. Associate Professor, 1967. Full Professor, 1973. B.A., Pomona College; Ph.D., California Institute of Technology. Consultant, Jet Propulsion Laboratory; NSF Science Faculty Fellow, University of Maryland; Research Institute of Astronomy, Cambridge University, England.

Orloff, Kenneth. 1975-76. Visiting Assistant Professor of Physics. B.A., Harvey Mudd College. Ph.D., University of California at Santa Barbara. Research Engineer, NASA Ames Laboratory.

Peterson, Daniel C. 1974—. Assistant Professor of Physics. B.A., St. Olaf College; M.A., Ph.D., Harvard University. Danforth Fellow; NIH Post-doctoral Research Fellow, The Johns Hopkins University; Visiting Research Physicist, California College of Medicine, University of California at Irvine; Visiting Professor, University of California School of Medicine, San Francisco.

Platt, Joseph B. 1956—. Professor of Physics and President. B.A., University of Rochester; Ph.D., Cornell University. Instructor in Physics, University of Rochester. Staff Member, Radiation Laboratory, Massachusetts Institute of Technology. Assistant, Associate, Full Professor, University of Rochester. Chief, Physics and Mathematics Branch, Research Division, Atomic Energy Commission. Associate Chairman, Department of Physics, University of Rochester. Science Advisor, U.S. Delegation to UNESCO, Paris, 1960 and 1962; Chairman, United States Committee on Sino-American Science Cooperation, 1964; Trustee, Carnegie Foundation for the Advancement of Teaching.

Robertson, Bennet E. 1962-70. Assistant Professor of Physics. Visiting Associate Professor of Physics, 1968. Associate Professor of Physics, 1969. B.A., University of Oklahoma; Ph.D., Ohio State University. Air Force officer; Lecturer in Physics, Air Force Institute of Technology; Chairman, Department of Physics, United States Air Force Academy.

Rojanksy, Vladimir. 1965—. Visiting Professor of Physics. Senior Professor, 1969. Senior Professor Emeritus, 1972. B.S., Whitman College; M.S., University of Oregon; Ph.D., University of Minnesota. National Research Council Fellow, Assistant Professor, Washington University, St. Louis; Professor and Department Chairman, Union College; Senior Staff Member, TRW Space Technology Laboratories; awarded the President's Certificate of Merit.

Sandmann, William H. 1963—. Assistant Professor of Physics. Associate Professor, 1966. Full Professor, 1973. Assistant Dean of Faculty, 1969. B.A., Reed College; Ph.D., University of Utah. Instructor, University of Utah; Assistant Professor, Grinnell College; Visiting Scholar, University of Texas at Austin.

Smith, Peter L. 1972-73. Assistant Professor of Physics. B.S., University of British Columbia; Ph.D., California Institute of Technology.

Stoddard, Alonzo E. 1960—. Associate Professor of Physics. Full Professor, 1967. B.S., M.S., Ph.D., University of Michigan. Physicist, California Research and Development Co. and California Research Corp.; Physicist, U.S. Geological Survey.

Townsend, John S. 1975—. Assistant Professor of Physics. B.S., Duke University, M.A., Ph.D., The Johns Hopkins University. National Science Foundation Graduate Fellow; Research Associate, Linear Accelerator Center, Stanford University.

Tubbs, Eldred F. 1963—. Assistant Professor of Physics. Associate Professor, 1966. Full Professor, 1972. B.S., Carnegie Institute of Technology; Ph.D., The Johns Hopkins University. Senior Physicist, American Optical Co.; Advanced Research Physicist, General Telephone and Electronics Laboratories, Inc.; Visiting Research Associate, Harvard College Observatory.

Waggoner, Jack Holmes, Jr. 1961—. Assistant Professor of Physics. Associate Professor, 1965. B.S., Ph.D., Ohio State University. Assistant Professor, Ohio State University and University of California at Riverside; Visiting Associate in Physics, California Institute of Technology.

Webb, Carol. 1970-72. Assistant Professor of Astronomy. Instructor in Physics, 1971. B.A., Sarah Lawrence College; M.A.,

University of California, Berkeley; Ph.D., University of Texas. Research Assistant, Lick Observatory; Research Associate, University of Texas.

Wicher, Enos R. 1961—. Associate Professor of Physics. Full Professor, 1970. Director of the Freshman Division of the Faculty, 1970-72. B.S., St. Ambrose College; M.S., University of Iowa. Chairman, Department of Physics, Olivet College; Chairman, Department of Physics, University of Georgia; Chairman of Sciences, Mexico City College.

Wolf, Robert P. 1963—. Assistant Professor of Physics. Associate Professor, 1968. Full Professor, 1974. B.S., Ph.D., Massachusetts Institute of Technology. National Science Foundation Faculty Fellow, Clarendon Laboratory, Oxford University, England.

JOINT PROGRAMS

Arce, William B. 1958—. Associate Professor of Physical Education and Director of Athletics. Full Professor, 1964. B.A., M.A., Ed.D., Stanford University.

Critchell, Iris. 1962—. Lecturer in Aeronautics. B.A., University of Southern California; FAA Certified Flight Instructor.

Ducey, Lawrence (Ted). 1959-75. Assistant Professor of Physical Education. Associate Professor, 1965. Full Professor, 1971. B.A., San Diego State College.

Easley, Roy C. 1968-69. Instructor in Physical Education. B.A., California State College, Los Angeles.

Farnaday, Dezso G. 1964-74. Instructor in Physical Education. Lecturer, 1967. Assistant Professor, 1968. Associate Professor of Physical Education and Lecturer in Fine Arts. B.A., University of Southern California; M.A., Claremont Graduate School.

Grall, Thomas. 1974. Assistant Professor of Physical Education. B.S., Springfield College; M.Ed., Westfield State College.

Klinker, Walter. 1965-68. Instructor in Physical Education. B.S., M.A. candidate, University of Colorado.

Lilley, John M. 1966-72. Instructor in Music and Choral Director. Assistant Professor, 1968. B.M.E., B.M., M.M., Baylor University. Graduate study, University of Southern California.

Merandi, Michael. 1970—. Instructor in Physical Education. Assistant Professor, 1972. B.S., M.A., California State College in Los Angeles.

Reel, S.F. Vincent. 1958-73. Assistant Professor of Physical Education. B.A., Occidental College.

Stalwick, Donald W. 1965-68. Associate Professor of Physical Education. B.S., M.A. candidate, University of California, Los Angeles.

Swan, Jesse R. 1958-72. Associate Professor of Speech and Drama. B.A., University of California, Berkeley; M.A., University of Southern California.

Zinda, John D. 1968. Assistant Professor of Physical Education. Associate Professor, 1973. B.A., M.A. candidate, California State College, Los Angeles.

COMPUTER SCIENCE

Weingarten, Frederick W. 1969-73. Assistant Professor of Computer Science. Director of Computer Services for the Claremont Colleges and Assistant Professor of Computer Science, 1970-72. Director of the Institute for Educational Computing, 1972. B.S., California Institute of Technology.; M.S., Ph.D., Oregon State University. Staff Associate, Office of Computing Activities, National Science Foundation.

STAFF
1966–76

PRESIDENT'S OFFICE
President:	Joseph B. Platt	1966–76
Executive Secretary:	Phyllis Colclough	1966–67
	Phyllis M. Heesch	1967–73
	Doris Cederlind	1973–76
Secretary:	Herta Erdoes	1967–68
	Grace Watson	1968–72
	Virginia Blackwell	1972–76
	Judith M. Renegar	1966–69
Administrative Assistant:	Thomas Holland	1966–67
	Richard T. Roessler	1967–68
	Joseph A. Deegan	1968–69
	Daniel Sisson	1969–71
	Gary Knight	1971–72
	Arthur Lorenzini	1972–73
	Peter Schotten	1973–74
	Eleanor Johnston	1974–76
Clerk:	Marguerita Chavez	1966–68

DEAN OF THE COLLEGE
Dean of the College:	Eugene Hotchkiss III	1966–68
Secretary:	Hilda Larson	1966–68
Assistant to the Dean:	Bruce B. Roberts	1966–67
	Ralph Locklin	1967–68

DEAN OF FACULTY
Dean of Faculty:	Jacob B. Frankel	1968–74
	J. Arthur Campbell	1974–75
	Samuel Tanenbaum	1975–93
Administrative Assistant:	William A. Gibson	1974–75
	H. Aileen Ingram	1975–76
Secretary:	Herta Erdoes	1968–69
	Janet L. Coleman	1969–71
	Cledith A. Rue	1971–74
	Mary L. Benzon	1974–76

DEAN OF STUDENTS
Dean of Students:	William Swartzbaugh	1968–71
	William Gann	1971–76
Secretary:	Hilda C. Larson	1968–72
	Carmen Garcia	1972–74
	Marjorie Dokken	1974–76
Assistant to the Dean:	Timothy Askew	1974–75
	Philip Wittman	1975–76

PLACEMENT
Placement Officer:	Hilda C. Larson	1972–76

DEVELOPMENT

Vice President:	George I. McKelvey	1966-76
Assistant to the Vice President:	Dorothy C. Harris	1974-76
Director:	Nichol M. Sandoe	1970-74
Associate Director:	Michael J. Kearney	1966-69
	Thornton H. Hamlin	1969-70
	Dorothy Harris	1969-74
Assistant Director:	Richard A. Morton	1966-67
	William Cole	1966-67
	Jack W. Charleville	1966-72
	Thornton H. Hamlin	1967-69
	Thomas Holland	1967-68
	Dorothy Harris	1966-69
	Alden C. Simmons	1968-70
	Eric K. Wolff	1969-70
	Harvey G. Pawlick	1970-71
	Russell A. Medevic	1970-72
	Joe B. Holmes	1971-76
	Charles E. Kittleson	1972-76
	Leonard Crowley	1975-76
Estate Planning:	Thornton Hamlin, Jr.	1973-76
Research:	May H. Weiser	1966-76
	Virginia Blackwell	1966-70
Special Events:	Virginia Blackwell	1970-72
	Ruth Cox	1972-73
	Marjorie Case	1973-76
Secretaries:	Cheryl Coulter	1966-67
	Doris Cederlind	1966-69
	Sharon Baker	1966-67
	Betsy Young	1967-68
	Helen Hoffman	1967-76
	Patricia MacAlpine	1967-68
	Wilma Henderson	1967-76
	Helen Hoffman	1967-69
	Virginia Simmons	1967-69
	Dorothy Pidhayny	1972-73
	Iris Terry	1973-76
	Helen Pierce	1974-75
	Marian Sawyer	1975-76
	Beverly Bolnik	1975-76
Gift Recorder:	Shirley Butterick	1969-76
Alumni Secretary:	Helen Hoffman	1970-74
	Patricia Toth	1974-75
	Deborah Tapley	1975-76
MT/ST Operator:	Judith Dimit	1969-72
	Patricia George	1970-72
	Dona Crawford	1972-73
	Gwen Jackson	1972-73
	Karen Keeth	1973-74
	Diane Blair	1973-74
	Evelyn Slive	1974-76
	Cheryl Rittenhouse	1975-76
	Barbara Mason	1975-76

BUSINESS AFFAIRS

Director:	William C. Radley	1966–76
Secretary:	Edith M. Davies	1966–74
	Jean R. Schmitt	1974–75
	Marilea Irby	1975–76
Accounting:	Raymond F. Fay	1974–75
	Donna Ray	1975–76
Secretarial Services:	Marilea Irby	1974–75
	Betty Clutters	1975–76

ADMISSIONS

Dean:	Emery R. Walker	1966–76
Associate Dean:	Robert G. Rogers	1966–76
Assistant Dean:	David R. Goodsell	1966–68
	Leonard A. Dickey	1968–69
		1972–76
Director Financial Aid:	Leonard A. Dickey	1970–72
	Denman P. Gambill	1972–76
Financial Aid Secretary:	Carole Garcia	1969–73
	Evelyn Desjarlais	1973–76
Admission Assistant:	Margaret Leahy	1966–69
Admissions Secretary:	Alberta Parisi	1969–73
	Carol Nageotte	1973–76
	Augusta Colonna	1974–76
Office Manager:	Herta Erdoes	1969–76
Secretary:	Jean S. Cottrell	1966–67
	Iris Vig	1966–69
	Shirley Miller	1966–67
	Ellen Joos	1967–69
	Paula S. Merrell	1967–70
	Dorothy Testa	1967–70
	Lillian Needles	1969–73
	Augusta Colonna	1969–74
	Carroll Nageotte	1969–73
	Evelyn Desjarlais	1969–73
	Lillian Albanese	1973–76
	Barbara L. Webster	1974–76

JOSEPH B. PLATT CAMPUS CENTER

Director:	Frederick Chamberlain	1966–72
Secretary:	Dorothy Pidhayny	1966–72

BATES AERONAUTICS

Lecturer:	Iris C. Critchell	1966–76
Secretary:	S. Catherine Layne	1966–69
	Mary Ann Robinson	1973–76

CHEMISTRY

Chair:	J. Arthur Campbell	1966–70
		1972–74
	Roy A. Whiteker	1970–71
	Philip C. Myrhe	1974–76
	William G. Sly	1976–77
Secretary:	Marcia Myers	1966–76
Lab Assistant:	George A. Glonka	1966–69
	Charles L. Marafioti	1970–72
	Earl E. Thornton	1972–76

ENGINEERING

Chair:	Warren Wilson	1966–67
	Jack L. Alford	1968–71
		1974–77
	Thomas T. Woodson	1972–74
Secretary:	Norma B. Kruger	1966–69
	Virginia Simmons	1970–72
	Janice Pickering	1966–68
	Judith A. Dimit	1972–74
	Kathy Frederickson	1974–76
	Helen White	1967–68
Technician:	Edward W. Newton	1966–69
	Lee Matthues	1969–72
	John Torcivia	1972–76

ENGINEERING CLINIC

Director:	Warren Wilson	1967–68
	Rex Mack	1968–69
	Thomas T. Woodson	1972–76
Secretary:	Doris Cederlind	1972–73
	Donna Crowe	1973–74
	Judith A. Dimit	1974–76

FRESHMAN DIVISION

Director:	Enos Wicher	1970–72
	M. M. Gilkeson	1972–74
	Arnold Ruskin	1974–76
Secretary:	Barbara J. Graham	1974–76

HUMANITIES

Chair:	William H. Davenport	1966–68
	John B. Rae	1968–73
	David S. Sanders	1973–77
Secretary:	Margaret Thompson	1966–76

MATHEMATICS

Chair:	Robert C. James	1966–67
	Courtney Coleman	1967–68
	Melvin Henriksen	1969–72
	John Greever	1972–74
	Robert Borrelli	1974–77
Secretary:	Marion Snyder	1966–76

MATH CLINIC

Co-director:	Robert Borrelli	1976
Co-director:	Jerome Spanier	1976
Secretary:	Marion Snyder	1976
	Linda Hudson	1976

PHYSICS

Chair:	Alfred B. Focke	1966–71
	Graydon D. Bell	1971–77
Secretary:	Evelyn Lee	1966–69
	Helen F. White	1970–76
Research Assistant:	Furman W. Lytle	1966–67
Lab Assistant:	William H. Hoesen	1966–76

PUBLIC INFORMATION OFFICE

Director:	Zaner Faust	1966–74
	Arthur Rense	1974–76
News Assistant:	Marian Gabler	1966–76

GROUNDS

Superintendent of Campus:	Oskar Soolepp	1966–67
	Donald J. Powell	1967–69
	Ralph C. Kemmerer	1970–76
Maintenance Superintendent:	James Litzsinger	1970–76
Grounds Advisor:	William C. Hoops	1970–76
Senior Groundsman:	Josef Lorincz	1970–76
Senior Custodian:	Robert Lanza	1970–76

REGISTRAR'S OFFICE

Registrar:	Evelyn O. Town	1966–72
	Norma B. Kruger	1972–76
Secretary:	Theresa Timko	1966–67
	Barbara Atherton	1967–69
	Betty Lumpkin	1972–76

RESIDENCE HALLS

Supervisor:	Irene Levy	1966–69
	Ursula Stolle	1970–76
Head Custodian:	Charles Gregory	1966–69

INDEX

Accreditation Board for Engineering and Technology, 212, 230
Achievement Rewards for College (ARCS), 97-98, 169
Adamian, Paul, 126
Alexander, David, 13, 196, 200
Alford, Jack L., 13, 131, 132, 149, 180, 214, 240
Allen, William B., 13, 182, 242
Alumni Fundd, 96, 149, 159
American Chemical Society, 226, 229
American Society for Engineering Education, 22, 24, 121, 165, 211, 216
Antiwar Protest Movement, 196-201
Appleman, Jack, 13
Arce, William B., 133, 185-86, 246
Armstrong, Neil, 195
Arnold, David, 189
Ashenfelder, Robert C., 81
Associated Students of Harvey Mudd College (ASHMC), 11, 73, 194, 199, 200
Association of Independent California Colleges and Universities, 32
Astin, Alexander (Sandy), 14
Atherton, John, 13, 196
Atwood, J. Leland, 12, 35, 117, 120

Bacher, Robert F., 17, 62, 121
Baez, Albert V., 129
Baker, D. Kenneth, 193, 201
Baker, Vivian, 193
Ballard, Doris, 92, 98, 137
Ballhaus, William, 170
Barden, James, 97
Barden, Llewelyn, 97
Barkan, William, 175
Barnhart, David, 180
Barr, Terry L., 180, 239
Barrera, Joseph, 13

Bates Aeronautics Program, 135, 136, 139, 164, 173, 186
Bates Foundation, 136, 170, 171, 186
Bates, Isabel, 135, 136
Baxter Science Building, 40, 49
Beaven, Robert H., 56
Beckett, Garner A., 18, 28, 33, 42, 43, 51, 91, 124, 177, 192
Beckman Instruments, 170, 187
Beckman, Tad A., 13, 126, 127, 179, 182, 239
Beeman, David M., Jr., 244
Bell, Charles V., 132
Bell, Graydon D., 12, 62, 64-65, 127, 184, 224, 244
Bell, Horace, 150, 156
Bellenot, Steven, 183, 243
Belmont, Steven, 136
Belmont, Yolanda, 136
Benezet, Louis T., 13, 155, 172, 192
Benson, Edward M., Jr., 175
Benson, George C.S., 13, 15, 16, 18, 36, 37, 40, 65, 70, 84, 123, 134, 143, 192
Benson, Shirley, 175
Bergmann, Gunnar B., 174, 215
Bernard, Robert J., 17, 18, 28, 32, 33, 36, 42, 70, 105, 124, 192
Beug, Michael W., 180, 239
Black Students' Union, 202, 203, 204
Black Studies, 203, 204
Black Studies Center, 203, 204
Black, Stuart E., 76, 77, 80
Blackmore, John, 171, 242
Blackwell, Virginia, 139
Blaisdell, James A., 23, 28, 32, 36
Blake, Daniel M., 239
Blodgett, Andrew, 73
Boelter, Llewellyn, 214
Boone, Daniel N., 242
Booth, Franklin Otis, Jr., 174, 177

Booth, Franklin Otis, Sr., 177
Borrelli, Robert, 12, 183, 193, 243
Bowen, Howard R., 172, 192
Bowen, Ronald E., 127, 239
Bowerman, Paul, 61
Brainerd, Walter, 187, 188, 243
Braun and Company, 76, 89, 90, 175, 199
Braun, Henry A., 174
Braun, Theodore W., 89, 90, 91, 96, 122, 151, 175, 176
Breyer, Arthur, 127
Briggs, Mitchell, 75, 76
Briggs, Stuart, 64
Brooks, E. Howard, 13, 192
Brown, George W., 121, 171-72
Brown, Lea, 128
Brown, Ronald F., 174, 244
Brown, Thomas B., 127-28, 129
Bubión, Octávio, 13, 206
Burns, Gerald, 139
Burton, Paul H., 86
Busenberg, Stavros, 12, 183, 184, 243
Byrd, James E., 168, 239

CF Braun Engineering Co., 174
Cambodia, 195, 198
Campbell, Dorothy, 13, 60
Campbell, J. Arthur, 60, 62, 64, 65, 72, 80, 102, 106, 126, 127, 136, 138, 140, 165, 179, 190, 226, 228, 239
Capaceta, Consuela, 138
Carmichael, Leonard, 80
Carnegie Corporation, 32, 78, 87, 88, 106, 115, 125, 161, 213
Carter, Lucian, 185, 245
Carter, Victor M., 172
Cary, Arthur S., 185, 245
Case Foyer, 159
Case, Gerald R., 97, 151, 158
Cederlind, Doris, 189, 190

Center for the Study of Higher Education, 55, 78, 118
Chamberlain, Frederick, 139
Charette, Andre, 181, 240
Charleville, Jack, 95, 98, 139, 189
Chase, Betty, 139
CHEM Study, 13, 60, 139, 165, 226-28
Chemical Bond Approach (CBA), 226
Chicano Studies Center, 204, 205
Church, Thomas, 52
Churchill College, 142
Civil Rights Movement, 195
Claremont College
　property exchange, 41
Claremont Graduate School, 11, 13, 14, 16, 24, 107, 125, 126, 134, 155, 156, 168, 172, 181, 182, 183, 184, 217, 219, 232
　Washington Delegation, 199
Claremont McKenna College (Claremont Men's College), 26, 32-33, 218
　Washington Delegation, 199
Claremont Men's College, 15 ,16, 18, 24, 27, 29, 33, 36, 40, 41, 43, 46, 48, 53, 64, 65, 70, 73, 84, 101, 102, 104, 106, 121, 123, 129, 133, 136, 139, 140, 143, 144, 191
　fundraising, 149
　joint programs, 40, 125, 185, 218
　shared laboratories, 49
Claremont University Center (Claremont College), 13, 14, 16, 17, 24, 26, 28, 29, 31, 33, 40, 48, 49, 50, 70, 94, 101, 102, 105, 123, 124, 149, 153, 154, 172, 176, 191, 192, 193
Clark, E. Hubert, Jr., 172
Clary, Hugh, 36, 176, 177
Clary, Huldah, 36, 176
Clary, William W., 18, 26, 28, 32, 70, 123, 124, 176, 192
Coberly, Victoria (Mudd), 12, 37, 52, 207
Coberly, William B., Jr., 12, 51, 87, 91, 105, 112, 121, 153
Cockroft, Sir John, 142
Coiner, Richard, 15-16
Colclough, Phyllis, 139, 190
Cole, William, 189
Coleman, Courtney S., 12, 130, 183, 243
Collins Hall, 41, 53, 54, 140, 143
Committee on Future Colleges, 14, 24, 26, 31
Cook, Janet, 76, 77, 80
Cooke, Jenny, 125
Cooke, W. Henry, 125
Cooper, George, 185, 245
Cooper, Robert, 197
Council of Presidents, 196, 197, 203, 204
Crawford, George, 182, 242
Critchell, Howard, 135, 136, 186
Critchell, Iris, 13, 135, 136, 186, 246
Cummings, Frank, 206
Curtis, Mark, 196, 203, 204
Cyprus Mines Corporation, 25, 26, 29, 30

Davenport, James F., 87, 90, 91, 105, 106, 122, 152, 205
Davenport, William H., 12, 13, 61, 62, 64, 65, 73, 101, 125, 136, 138, 151, 165, 182, 183, 242
Davies, David, 80
Davies, Edith, 189
Davis, Angela, 205
Davis, Paul H., 65, 66, 84, 85, 86, 89, 94
Davis, Richard, 74
Dayton, Barry S., 183, 244
Degani, Amin, 181, 240
Dell 'Osso, Linda, 13
Dick, Lucia, 242
Domb, Ellen, 185, 245
Douglass, Gordon, 199
Drellishak, Kenneth S., 240
DuBridge, Lee A., 56, 63, 64, 80, 97, 98
Ducey, Lawrence, 133, 186, 246
Duque, Henry, 89, 91, 122, 124, 176

Easley, Roy C., 246
Edwards, M. Guy, 94, 184
Edwards, Ray Lee, 129
Eggers, Henry, 48
Eisenhower, Dwight D., 22, 84, 162, 238
Eldridge, William C., 175
Elsbree, Langdon, 125
Endemano, Steven, 185, 201
Engineering Clinic, 96, 113, 145, 148, 158, 159, 173, 174, 179, 181, 184, 213-19
Evans, Marshall K., 173, 177

Farnaday, Dezso G., 186, 246
Faust, Zaner, 92, 98, 137, 138, 189
Fickas, Ernest, 183, 244
Field, A.J., 173
Field, Oliver C., 123, 135, 151, 173
Field, Ruby, 123, 135
Filseth, Stephen V., 127, 179, 223, 239
Finch, Robert, 199, 200
Fischler, Alfred S., 181, 240
Fleck, Ray N., 240
Flint, Miles, 95
Flood, Michael T., 179, 239
Focke, Alfred B., 128, 165, 184, 245
Fogg, Philip S., 36, 122 ,151, 170-71
Ford Foundation, 88, 112, 147, 148, 149, 155, 165, 186
Ford, Gerald, 195
Founding Friends, 55, 88, 89, 91, 92, 96, 124, 149, 153, 158, 170, 171, 173, 176
Francis, Benjamin, 181, 240
Frank, Betty, 206
Frank, Ken, 206
Frankel, Jacob P., 190, 240
Free Speech Movement, 196
French, Milton L., 242
Freshman Division, 168, 219-221, 222
Friends of the Claremont Colleges, 150
Frisbie, F. Donald, 64

Fund for the Advancement of Education, 88, 106, 115, 210, 213

Gabler, Marian, 138, 189
Galileo Society, 96, 97, 149, 158, 159
Gann, William R., 13, 190
Gardner, John W., 88
Garrett Fund, 46, 47
Garrett, Leroy A., 18, 28, 30, 31, 37, 46, 47, 48, 53, 84, 85, 87, 90, 104, 105, 114, 122, 123
Garrett, Marian, 12, 30, 31, 37, 46, 47, 52, 122, 123, 157
Garrett, Ray M., Mr. and Mrs., 53
Garwood, Donald C., 239
Gary, John M., 130
Gaulding, Edith, 139
Gentile, Frances, 65
George, Ronald, 182, 242
Giersch, Carlotta Busch, 158, 159, 173
Gilkeson, Murray Mack, 13, 132, 165, 180, 181, 214, 241
Gillette, Dean, 219
Gillette, George, 137
Glonka, George, 139, 189
Goals of Engineering Education, The, 22
Goheen, Robert, 149
Goldstine, Herman H., 60-61
Gonser, Gerber, Tinker and Stuhr, 148
Gonzales, Pedro, 137
Gonzalez, Raymond, 139
Goodman, John, 184, 245
Goodsell, David, 139
Gose, George, 12, 91,. 92, 93, 99, 108, 109, 112, 118, 122, 149, 169, 176
Grall, Thomas, 186, 246
Grant, Richard A., 122, 148, 152, 154, 155
Green, Laurence A., 170, 176
Greever, John, 12, 130, 183, 184, 244
Gregory, Charles, 189
Grimm, Homer, 138
Grinter Report, 22, 131
Grinter, Linton E., 22, 23, 131
Gross, Mary (Mrs. Robert E.), 169
Group Plan, 16, 17, 21, 23, 28, 32, 36, 176
Gunther, C. Godfrey, 25

Haley, Edward, 199
Halferty, James, 178
Hammond, Bert, 203
Hansch, Corwin, 62
Harmon, Ann B., 239
Harmon, Kenneth M., 127, 168, 239
Harris, Dorothy, 92, 98, 137, 189
Hartley, John W., 189
Harvey Mudd College
　accreditation, 75-76, 212, 230
　admission of women, 68, 69
　attrition (Class of '62), 77-80
　dedication of first building, 43-44
　diversity, 165
　dormitories, 41-45

ethnic programs, 201-05
founding, 16, 21-24, 26-28
founding class, 69-75
futures program, 93-95
honor system, 73
honorary degrees, 177-78
initial facilities, 40-41
Master's program in Engineering, 168,
    181, 231-32
president's house, 46-48
property exchange, 38-40
tenure program, 110
Washington Delegation, 199
Harvey S. and Mildred E. Mudd
    Foundation, 53, 158
Harvey, Anne-Charlotte, 126
Harvey, Michael, 126
Hastings, Robert P., 12, 18, 37, 39, 85,
    104, 112, 150, 153, 200, 205
Haugeland, Chris, 142-43
Heesch, Phyllis, 190
Hegener, Joseph L., 91, 122
Heim, Mark William, 242
Heist Report, 55
Heist, Paul A., 55, 78, 79, 118
Heitschmidt, Earl, 42, 43, 52, 53, 153
Helliwell, Thomas M., 12, 129, 184, 245
Henriksen, Melvin, 12, 183, 244
Hickel, Walter, 199
Hill, Louis, 34
Hill, Raymond A., 12, 18, 28, 34, 38, 43,
    51, 59, 104, 108, 110, 120, 171, 178
Hill, Richard C., 189
Hixon Court, 160
Hixon Professorship, 171
Hixon, Adelaide, 12
Hixon, Alexander, 12, 158, 159, 171
Hoesen, William, 138, 189
Holland, Thomas, 138
Holmes, Michael, 139
Hopfield, John J., 121
Hopkins, Gail, 186
Hornby, Robert A., 91, 122
Hoskins, Katherine, 125
Hotchkis, Preston, 151, 169, 176, 205
Hotchkiss, Eugene, 10, 11, 13, 79, 98, 113,
    116, 126, 138, 139, 141, 143, 189
Hotchkiss, Sue, 98, 138
Hough, Gordon L., 174
Howell, David, 193
Hsu, Paul, 136, 137
Huerta, Delfina, 137
Huggans, Jannelle, 137
Human Resources Institute, 204
Hwang, Walter (Yeong-wen), 181, 241
Hyland, L.A., 122, 150, 151, 154, 159

Immaculate Heart College, 154, 155
Ingels, Donald M., 181, 241
Ingram, Robert Richard Jr., 244
Institute of Mining, Metallurgical, and
    Petroleum Engineers, 25, 26

Ives, Lori, 75, 130
Ives, Robert, 75, 130, 183, 197, 244

Jacobs Science Building, 50
Jacobs, Joseph J., 50, 174-75
Jacobs, Violet, 174-75
James H. Van Dyke and Associates, 153
James, Robert, 60, 61, 64, 65, 130, 183,
    197, 224, 244
Japan, 22
Johnson, James, 13, 199
Johnson, Lyndon Baines, 195
Johnston, Eleanor, 190-91
Joint Programs, 134, 185-86
Jones, Robert A., 242
Jonsson, Eric, 175
Jonsson, Kenneth A., 175
Joseph B. Platt Campus Center, 54-56
Joseph, James, 199
Julin, Kenneth F., 122, 151, 158

Kearney, Michael, 13, 98, 139, 189
Keatly, Mary Ann, 203
Keck, William M., 173
Keeney, Barnaby, 192
Kelly, Gerald G., 123, 200, 205
Kent State University, 195, 198
Kindelberger Professorship, 131, 149
Kindelberger, James Howard, 35
King, Martin Luther, Jr., 195, 202
Kingston Hall, 53, 56, 112, 114, 139, 150
Kingston, Virginia, 53, 150
Kittleson, Charles, 158
Klein, Herbert, 199
Klinker, Walter, 185, 246
KNBC television, 197-98
Knight, Goodwin, 31
Koerntgen, Catherine, 180
Kok, Gregory L., 179, 239
Kotecha, Mahesh, 206
Krieger, Henry, 183, 244
Kronenberg, Klaus, 241
Kruger, Norma, 139, 189
KTTV television, 80
Kubota, Mitsuru, 12, 122, 179, 180, 223,
    239
Kusche, Pat, 12
Kusche, Ray, 12

Larson, Hilda, 139
Lavender, David, 26, 98, 138
Lee, Charles W., 55, 56, 99, 122, 124, 151
Lee, Evelyn, 139, 189
Leppo, William, 72, 73
Levy, Irene, 189
Levy, Leonard W., 11, 182, 242
Lewis, Claire, 174
Lewis, Malcolm, 174, 181
Lewis, Patton, 174, 181
Liberal Arts Clinic, 218
Lilley, John M., 186, 246

Lindvall, Frederick C., 116, 121, 171, 175,
    193
Little, Edward F., 13, 64, 65, 98, 126, 136,
    137, 138, 139, 189
Little, Nancy, 98
Loeb, Peter A., 76, 77, 80
Loebbecke, Ernest J., 12, 91, 95,
    195, 98, 117, 122, 176
Long, Everett J., 175, 176
Lorincz, Josef, 138, 189
Lowe, Katharine (Mrs. George C.S.
    Benson), 136, 137
Luhring, John, 96
Lynch, W.A., 218
Lyon, Wilson, 196, 202, 203

Mack, Rex, 181, 241
Make No Mistake, 151
Malouf, Florence, 98
Man Made World, The, 218
Manes, Ernest G., 244
Marks Hall, 153, 156-57
Marks, David X., 123, 153, 157
Martinez, Venus, 139, 189
Martinson, Per, 180, 240
Mason, Richard, 92, 98, 137, 139
Master Plan for Higher Education, 22
Mathematics Clinic, 159, 184, 217
McClung, Donald H., 181, 241
McCutcheon, Thomas, 183, 244
McKay, Bruce M., 180, 240
McKelvey, George I., III, 11, 13, 66, 85,
    87, 92, 95, 98, 99, 102, 136, 158, 189,
    190
Medevic, Russell, 158
Merandi, Michael, 246
Merritt, John B., 175
Messier, Rudolph, 189
Meyer, Loretta, 65
Meyers, Ann Marie, 244
Mildred E. and Harvey S. Mudd
    Foundation, 94, 158
Miller Professorship, 172, 182
Miller, Clifford A., 11, 90, 106, 175, 199
Miller, Jack, 80
Miller, Louisa, 172
Miller, Robert P., Jr., 158, 172
Mirsepassi, Taghi, 241
Molinder, John, 13, 181, 241
Monson, James E., 13, 132, 165, 180, 181,
    186, 188, 241
Moore, John A. Jr., 242
Moore, Richard A., 80
Morrill Act of 1862, 21
Morrison, Graham, 180
Moynihan, Daniel Patrick, 159, 199, 200
Mudd, Harvey S., 16, 25, 26, 28, 88, 89,
    94, 100, 191, 209
    portrait, 26
Mudd, Henry T., 12, 18, 25, 26, 28, 29,
    37, 80, 88, 89, 91, 92, 95, 100, 103,

104, 105, 106, 109, 115, 118, 133, 150,
151, 158, 160, 170, 172, 193, 207
memorial, 29-30
Mudd, Mildred (Mrs. Harvey S. Mudd),
18, 26, 27, 28-29, 37, 42, 43, 44, 68,
70, 72, 73, 83, 84, 91, 94, 100, 120,
123, 169
Mudd, Seeley W., 26, 170
Mudd, Seeley W., II, 170, 205
Mudd, Stuart, 188
Mudd, Virginia, 170
Murray, John, 80
Myers, Marcia, 139, 189
Myers, W. Gifford, 151
Myhre, Janet, 219
Myhre, Philip C., 12, 13, 127, 179, 180,
223, 240

Nahin, Paul, 187, 188, 241
Nathan, Bruce, 90
National Institute of Health, 225
National Science Foundation, 60, 106,
115, 138, 173, 180, 183, 184, 194, 218,
224, 225, 226, 227
Newton, Edward, 189
Niwata, Yoichi., 242
Nixon, Richard M., 195, 199
Northrop Corporation, 19, 170, 232
Northrop University, 19

O'Brien, George J., 123
O'Brien, William, 72, 73
O'Melveny, Stuart, 87, 88, 91, 105, 122,
171, 177
Oates, James F., 149
Olson, Richard, 13, 80, 82, 182, 242
Orland, George, 183, 244
Orloff, Kenneth, 185, 245
Osler, Margaret, 182, 242

Page, James, 88
Pahl, Gary, 182, 242
Palino, Gerard F., 240
Palmquist, Paul, 183, 244
Parents' Fund, 159
Parker, Andrea, 136
Parsons, Ralph M., 156, 170, 176, 177,
178
Patkay, Pierre, 159
Pattison, Lee, 71
Pawlick, Harvey G., 158
Peck, Clair L., Jr., 12, 122, 154
Persons, Charles E., 92
Peters, Thomas B., 76, 77, 80
Peterson, Daniel C., 185, 245
Petroleum Research Foundation, 225
Petroleum Research Fund, 180, 224
Phillips, J. Richard, 13, 180, 218, 241
Pidhany, Dorothy, 139
Pitzer College, 13, 33, 36, 148, 176, 191,
196, 218
fundraising, 149

joint programs, 219
Washington Delegation, 199
Pitzer Hall, 27, 40, 53
Pitzer, Kenneth S., 9, 12, 18, 60, 81, 91,
105, 107, 109, 110, 121
Pitzer, Russell K., 26, 27, 40, 81, 121
Pixley, Alden F., 12, 131, 183, 186-87,
188, 203, 205, 225
Platt, Jean, 5, 9, 11, 14, 64, 93, 193, 198
Platt, Joseph B., 61, 62, 70, 72, 73, 85, 93,
189, 198, 245
as president of Claremont Graduate
School and University Center, 191-
93
biography, 9-11, 36
Platt, William B., 72, 73
Pomona College, 13, 16, 17, 18, 23, 24,
26, 31, 32, 41, 49, 62, 80, 100, 129,
134, 183, 185, 187, 196, 197, 200, 218
fundraising, 149
joint programs, 132-33
property exchange, 38
student unrest, 203
Washington Delegation, 199
Popkin, Richard H., 125-26
Post, Mary, 138, 189
President's Committee on Education
Beyond the High School, 22
Project Libra, 153, 154, 155, 156, 157,
158, 166, 172
Projector, Murray, 183, 244
Purves, William L., 189

Quest for Commonwealth, 164, 179, 221-
23
Quist, Mary, 137

Radford, Arthur, 89
Radley, Margaret, 139
Radley, William C., 189
Rae, John, 80, 125, 165, 182, 183, 193, 243
Raiguel, Norma, 139
RAND Corporation, 213, 234
Rankin, W. Robert, 13, 44, 70
Reckard, Edgar C. (Pete), 13, 202, 206
Reel, S.F. Vincent, 133, 186, 246
Remer, Donald S., 13, 181, 241
Research Corporation, 180, 224
Rhine, Jenny, 71, 73
Ridgeway, David, 13
Riemer, Hugo, 150, 151, 157, 159, 160,
168-69, 193, 205
Riggs, Henry, 11
Robertson, Bennet E., 129, 184, 245
Rockefeller Foundation, 202
Rogers, Robert G., 65, 136
Rojansky, Vladimir (Ro), 130, 184, 245
Roller, Duane, 63, 64, 65, 110, 127
Rosenthal, Daniel, 222, 241
Routly, Paul, 62
Ruskin, Arnold, 132, 180, 181, 218, 242
Russell, Donald J., 81

Sacks, Frank, 186
Saltman, Benjamin, 243
Sanders, David S., 12, 13, 125, 165, 182,
183, 205, 243
Sandmann, William H. (Sandy), 129, 184,
245
Sandoe, Nichol, 158
Savage, Thomas, 183, 244
Schaufelberger, William, 138, 189
Schuster, Jack, 14
Scripps College, 13, 16, 24, 32, 33, 51, 53,
69, 70, 71, 72, 74, 126, 141, 144, 191,
196, 204, 206
fundraising, 149
joint programs, 40, 125, 134, 185, 186,
219
property exchange, 38, 39, 40, 41, 42,
49, 150
shared laboratories, 48-49
student unrest, 203
Washington Delegation, 199
Scroggins, William T., 240
Seaborg, Glenn, 226, 227, 228
Seaver, Sallie, 199
Seeley W. Mudd Foundation, 44
Seeley, Robert, 130
Seelye, John D., 125
Sellery, J'nan, 13, 182, 243
Selman, Johan, 181, 241
Serdengecti, Sedat, 13, 132, 180-81, 186,
187, 188, 218, 219
Sesnon, William T., 150, 154, 176
Seven, Michael, 182, 241, 243
Shannon, Edfred L., Jr., 158, 172, 176
Sigman, Elliot, 181, 241
Sisson, Daniel, 191
Sloan Foundation, 161, 180, 213, 218
Sly, William G., 13, 126, 179, 180, 224,
240
Smith, Peter, 185, 245
Smith, Richard, 131
Smith, Thad Diemer, 243
Snyder, Marion, 139, 189
Soolepp, Oskar, 137, 189
Soviet Union (U.S.S.R.), 22, 90
Speckman, William H., 243
Sprague Fund, 147
Sprague Library, 153, 160
Sprague, Caryll Mudd, 18, 28, 30, 37, 118,
147-48
Sprague, Norman F., Jr., 12, 18, 28, 30,
37, 41, 42, 53, 87, 88, 118, 147-48
Sputnik, 73, 90, 97
Stalwick, Donald, 186, 246
Standish, Mildred, 186
Stern, Helman I., 241
Stevens, Kenneth D., 180, 240
Stoddard, Alonzo E. (Ted), 128, 184, 245
Stoddard, Marjorie, 128
Stone, Betty Jane, 244
Stone, Edward Durell, 42, 47, 52, 53, 153
Strombotne, James, 243

Stuart Mudd Professorship, 189
Student unrest, 162
Students for a Democratic Society (SDS), 196, 200
Swan, Jesse, 125, 186, 246
Swartzbaugh, Jean, 190
Swartzbaugh, William L., 190, 243

Tam, Wing, 181, 242
Tanenbaum, Samuel B., 11, 13, 190, 236
Tapp, June, 126
Taylor, Joan, 171
Taylor, Trude, 158, 171
The Claremont Colleges, 16, 17, 18, 21-22, 23, 24, 26, 28, 29, 31, 32, 33, 34, 36, 40, 44, 46, 48, 49, 60, 100, 101, 104, 106, 115, 118, 146, 150, 162, 182, 187, 190, 193, 194, 196, 198, 199, 200, 201, 202, 203, 204, 206, 217, 218
    constitution of, 192
    fundraising, 112, 147, 149, 152, 155, 156
    graduate degrees, 107, 192
Thomas, Alfred R., 18, 28, 30, 65, 68, 69, 84, 113
Thomas, Elise, 30
Thomas, Mr. and Mrs. Ray, 53
Thomas-Garrett Hall, 53, 56, 112, 114, 139
Thompson, John, 139, 189
Thompson, Margaret, 137, 139, 189
Thornton, Charles B., 122
Time magazine, 76, 90
Town, Evelyn, 137, 138, 139, 189
Townsend, John S., 185, 245
Truxal, John, 218
Tubbs, Eldred F., 129, 184, 245
Tussman College, 222
Tussman, Joseph, 222
Tuttle, Holmes, 55
Twaits, Ford J., 18, 28, 33-34, 42, 43, 44, 68, 123, 192
Tweter, Clifford, 122, 171

United Mexican-American Students, 202
Upward Bound, 13, 165, 206

Valentine, Edward R., 87, 88, 89, 91, 105, 124
Valstyn, Erich, 181
Van Eikeren, Paul, 179, 240
Van Hecke, Gerald R., 13, 75, 179, 223, 240
Vaughan, Ronald J., 179, 240
Viator, James, 182, 243
Vietnam, 62, 162, 195
Vietnam War, 195, 196, 197, 198, 201

Waggoner, Jack, 12, 129, 184, 245
Wagner, Emilie, 125, 243
Waldman, Theodore, 13, 126, 165, 182, 222, 243

Walker, Dorothy, 65
Walker, Emery R., Jr., 13, 64, 65, 76, 101, 107, 136, 189
Walker, Irving C., 39
Walton, Jean, 13
Walum, Herbert, 130
Ward, Robert, 128
Washington Delegation, 198, 199-200
Webb, Carol, 185, 245-46
Wegner, Patrick A., 240
Weingarten, Frederick, 187, 246
Weiser, May, 139
Wells, David, 186
Wells, H.G., 237
Wessels, Philip S., 242
Western Association of Schools and Colleges, 75, 77, 229, 230
Western New England College, 19
White, Alvin M., 12, 130, 183, 197, 244
White, Myra, 130
Whiteker, Roy A., 62, 64, 65, 72, 73, 126, 127, 179, 240
Wicher, Enos, 129, 184, 197, 220
Wickes, George C., 11, 13, 61, 62, 64, 65, 70, 72, 125, 182, 183, 197, 201, 205
Wig, Rudolph J., 18, 28, 31, 32, 34, 58, 67, 68, 100, 104, 107, 109, 110, 112, 171, 192, 207
Wilbur, Van Rensselaer G., 18, 28, 33, 109, 123, 192
Wiles, Frances, 138
Williams, Harry E., 13, 132, 181, 242
Wilson, Warren, 110, 111, 131, 181, 242
Witters, Robert D., 127, 180
Wolf, Robert P., 12, 184, 246
Woods, Steve, 193
Woodson, Thomas T., 13, 181, 215, 242
Wooldridge, Dean, 63-64, 112, 115, 122, 171
Wright, John C., 242

Zarem, A.M., 169, 176, 218
Zinda, John, 13, 186, 246